DARKEST HOUR

DARKEST HOUR

The True Story of
Lark Force at Rabaul
Australia's Worst Military Disaster of
World War II

Bruce Gamble

ZENITH PRESS

**For Rachel Gamble,
and Ian Gamble,
and all the Diggers**

First published in 2006 by Zenith Press, an imprint of MBI Publishing Company, Galtier Plaza, Suite 200, 380 Jackson Street, St. Paul, MN 55101-3885 USA

ISBN-13: 978-0-7603-2349-6
ISBN-10: 0-7603-2349-6

Designer: Jennifer Maass

Printed in the United States of America

On the cover:
Top: Rabaul under attack. *National Archives*
Bottom: 2/22nd Battalion on parade. *Carl Johnson*

On the back cover: Japanese landing near Vulcan, Rabaul, by Geoffrey Mainwaring. *Courtesy Australian War Memorial*

Back Flap: Author Photo. *Ron Corn*

CONTENTS

ACKNOWLEDGMENTS

I first learned about Rabaul almost forty years ago, at the age of eight, when I discovered my parents' large, heavy copy of *Life's Picture History of World War II*. I spent many hours looking at that book, which included a dramatic photograph of Rabaul and Simpson Harbor under attack by American carrier planes. I also remember hearing one of my relatives, Uncle Johnny, mention Rabaul—by far the toughest target he flew against as a navigator in B-17s of the Fifth Air Force.

Thirty-some years later, after my own military flying career was cut short by retirement for medical reasons, I wrote two books about U.S. Marine Corps pilots in the Southwest Pacific. Some of the men I interviewed had flown numerous missions over "Fortress Rabaul," and they still spoke of it with a touch of awe. I wondered what made it such an extraordinary place. The more I discovered, the more fascinated I became, particularly in the story of Lark Force, the garrison that first fortified Rabaul in 1941. Numerous memoirs and photographic reference works were available, but no one had yet done a comprehensive narration of the entire Lark Force story. Hopefully, this book will help fill the void.

I am grateful for the many individuals who have provided assistance over the years. Topping the list is Dr. Brian Wimborne, undoubtedly the most capable (and cheerful) researcher I've ever had the pleasure of working with. As my direct liaison with the Australian War Memorial and the

Australian National Library, he previewed and then obtained literally thousands of pages of military documents, personal collections, and vintage newspapers. I am also indebted to several other Australians who enthusiastically gave their support. Lindsay Cox and Carl Johnson generously provided photographs as well as permission to quote from their respective books. Peter Stone helped with questions and allowed me to quote from his huge reference work (see bibliography). Ted Harris, a walking encyclopedia of "Digger History," was especially helpful in answering my questions on the Australian Army; Barb Angell graciously allowed me to borrow material from her extensive research on the army and civilian nurses; maritime expert Peter Cundall spent many hours assisting me with the naval aspects of this book; and Ian Hodges granted permission to quote from his stirring presentation at the Australian War Memorial in 2002.

The list of Stateside individuals to acknowledge is even longer. I am privileged to know five Pacific War experts who helped with a multitude of details: Rick Dunn, Larry Hickey, Henry Sakaida, Osamu "Sam" Tagaya, and Mike Wenger. I would also like to thank individuals at several research facilities who provided assistance: Dennis Case and Sam Shearin at the Albert F. Simpson Historical Research Center in Montgomery, Alabama; Donna Hurley at the Nimitz Library in Annapolis, Maryland; Helen McDonald at the Nimitz Museum in Fredericksburg, Texas; Dan Miller at the USGS Cascades Volcano Observatory in Vancouver, Washington; and Barry Zerby at the National Archives and Records Administration in College Park, Maryland.

All of the experts and researchers were helpful, but the people who truly made this project rewarding were those who experienced firsthand the events described herein. I am extremely grateful for the interviews, correspondence, and other support given by Peter Figgis, Bill Harry, Lorna (Whyte) Johnson, Fred Kollmorgen, John Murphy, and Bruce Thurst.

Last, but certainly not least, a hearty thanks to Richard Kane of Zenith Press and copyeditor Tom Kailbourn for their guidance and expertise.

PROLOGUE

2200 HOURS (10:00 P.M.), JUNE 30, 1942

The moon was nearly full as it ascended over the South China Sea, providing excellent visibility for the lookouts and watch officers standing on the open bridge of a rust-stained American submarine. For the past five days and nights, the USS *Sturgeon* (SS-187) had quietly hunted the warm waters off Cape Bojeador, Luzon, where an old stone lighthouse, its beacon long out of operation, served as a reference point.

The crew was growing restless. Their last action had occurred well to the south on June 25, when they fired three torpedoes at a Japanese merchantman traveling in a convoy from Manila. An escorting warship had immediately turned toward the sub, and they dove deep to elude a total of twenty-one depth charges. The crew heard an explosion that might have been caused by one of the torpedoes, but without observing it directly, the commanding officer was unable to confirm that a hit had been scored.

Afterward, the *Sturgeon* moved north to hunt for enemy ships entering or exiting the Babuyan Channel, a natural chokepoint at the northern tip of Luzon, but no one had sighted anything larger than a sampan. To make matters worse, the three previous war patrols had been disappointing, with only one small ship confirmed sunk, and now their fourth patrol was half finished. In all, they had patrolled the normally busy sea lanes off the Philippines for three weeks, with only the one inconclusive engagement to show for it.

The boring routine was becoming hard to endure. For virtually every member of the crew (five officers and fifty enlisted men), the long hours of daylight were the worst. Each morning before dawn, the *Sturgeon* submerged to avoid detection, then spent the next fourteen to fifteen hours hunting quietly at periscope depth. The twin propellers were powered by four huge electric motors fed by banks of more than 250 lead-acid batteries, which generated a tremendous amount of heat. Outside the hull, the water temperature averaged 85 degrees Fahrenheit: too warm to ease the crew's discomfort. An air-conditioning system removed some of the greasy odor, cigarette smoke, and moisture from the atmosphere, but it couldn't replenish the oxygen that was being steadily depleted by fifty-five men. Furthermore, whenever the sub was rigged for silent running, the noisy air conditioner was shut off. The temperature inside the boat then rose to more than 100 degrees with 100 percent humidity, and the interior dripped with condensation. As the hours passed, it was sometimes necessary to spread carbon dioxide absorbent or release small amounts of oxygen from the emergency bottles stored in each compartment, but even with those measures it was common for the oxygen content to fall so low that a cigarette wouldn't burn.

Despite the mind-numbing routine, none of the crew could afford to relax their vigilance. They carried out their duties with the underlying knowledge that the next instant could bring unexpected disaster. A roving aircraft, a drifting mine, or an enemy warship could kill them all in the blink of an eye. Conditions were generally safer after dusk, when the boat could operate on the surface with less risk of detection. To the crew's great relief, the deck hatches were opened and the foul-smelling air inside the hull was purged by electric blowers. As soon as the hull was safely ventilated, two of the sub's quadruple diesel engines were brought on line to turn the propellers and recharge the batteries. Watch officers and lookouts manned the bridge, and the hunt continued nonstop.

Finally, at 2216 on this humid night, after scanning the empty sea for about three hours, the lookouts were rewarded. A lone ship, identified as a large cargo-liner, had just exited the Babuyan Channel and was headed west at high speed, without lights. Observing it through a pair of powerful binoculars, the sub's commanding officer shouted orders to start the other two engines and called for flank speed. With a surge of adrenalin, the crew jumped into action.

To set up a proper attack, the *Sturgeon* first had to get well ahead of the target, then turn and fire a spread of torpedoes at right angles to the ship's path. But the submarine, supposedly capable of twenty-one knots on the surface (faster than just about any merchantman of the period), could not pull ahead. Duly impressed with the enemy's speed, the skipper decided to hang on for a while. An hour and a half later, the Japanese ship suddenly cut its speed to twelve knots. The *Sturgeon* continued ahead at full speed for another hour and forty-five minutes, then slowed to a crawl and descended to periscope depth.

Now that the submarine was several miles ahead of the ship, the crew had ample time to plot the attack. Here at last was a superb opportunity to make up for earlier disappointments. The *Sturgeon's* overall accomplishments would be measured not only by the number of ships sunk but also by gross tonnage, and the destruction of the approaching liner, tentatively identified as the *Rio de Janeiro Maru* of about 10,000 tons, would more than double the sub's existing record. And yet, as eager as the crewmen were to sink this ship, they would have willingly let it pass . . . if only they had known what it was carrying.

Eight days out of Rabaul, New Britain, the ship was bound for Hainan, an island off the south coast of China, with more than a thousand Allied prisoners crammed into its holds. The vessel bore no special markings, for the Japanese refused to recognize the conventions followed by most of the nations involved in the war. Thus, to the skipper of the *Sturgeon*, the approaching ship was simply a big *maru*, a legitimate target. As it continued to draw closer, he periodically relayed periscope information to a young lieutenant manning the torpedo data computer (TDC) console. The officer dialed the updated information into the computer, which solved several geometric variables and provided the firing solution for each torpedo.

At 0225 on July 1, the first torpedo shot from its tube. Three more, each carrying a twenty-one-inch warhead packed with the equivalent of seven hundred pounds of TNT, followed at eight-second intervals. Traveling at a speed of forty-six knots, they would cover the four thousand yards to the target in slightly more than two and a half minutes. Time seemed to almost stand still, but the TDC officer was supremely confident. "One of those will get him," he said aloud.

Unfortunately for the souls locked inside the darkened ship, he was right.

CHAPTER ONE

DIGGERS

"They were a great band of boys."

—Lorna Whyte Johnson, Australian
Army Nursing Service

William Arthur Gullidge was in a quandary. Many of his countrymen had volunteered for military service after Australia declared war on Germany in September 1939, but for months he struggled mightily with the idea of joining the army. For one thing, he was a pacifist. Although he dearly loved his country, his heart also belonged to that conservative Christian denomination known as the Salvation Army, an organization that shunned warfare and violence.

By day Gullidge worked as a printer, but he was far better known throughout Australia for his superb band compositions. For several years running he had captured top prizes at Australian and international music competitions, and some people went so far as to compare him with Glenn Miller, the famed American big-band composer. Thirty years old, Gullidge had a lot to live for. He shared an idyllic life with his wife and young daughter in Coburn, a suburb of Melbourne, and also served as the bandleader of the Salvation Army's Melbourne Central Division and the Brunswick Citadel Band, which together fulfilled both his love of music and his strong faith.

As the war progressed and thousands of Australians went off to fight in the North African desert, Gullidge and his friends in the Salvation Army realized that conscription might come at any time. Disturbed by the prospect of fighting and killing, they engaged in lengthy discussions about their future. None wanted to serve as infantrymen. Gullidge, who had some knowledge of military history, thought they might be able to volunteer as musicians. In European armies, bandsmen traditionally served as stretcher bearers during battle, a duty that would circumvent the moral dilemma.

And, thanks to his renown, Gullidge had connections. One of his good friends was Major Harry R. Shugg, the officer in charge of recruitment for army bands and a top musician in his own right. Recognizing the obvious benefits of obtaining several excellent musicians for the army, Shugg arranged for Gullidge and his fellow bandsmen to volunteer together as soon as the next brigade was formed.

In mid-1940, recruitment opened for the 23rd Infantry Brigade, 8th Division, 2nd Australian Imperial Forces (AIF). On July 15, a gloomy winter's day along the southern coast of Australia, Gullidge and sixteen other Salvation Army musicians stepped forward to enlist en masse at the Victoria Street Drill Hall. Only one hopeful, a thirty-eight-year-old euphonium player with poor eyesight, was rejected. The rest, in accordance with Shugg's arrangement, were inducted as bandsmen and posted to the newly formed 2/22nd Infantry Battalion. All were sworn in as privates except Gullidge, who as bandmaster was given the rank of sergeant.

The new volunteers received a week's leave to spend with their families before reporting to Royal Park, Victoria, for medical examinations and formal induction. During those last days at home, many sat for portraits in their new uniforms. Gullidge looked confident and dashing in his distinctive slouch hat, worn at a carefree angle with the right brim curled down, the left side turned up, and the leather strap tucked firmly under his broad chin. The other bandsmen looked much the same in their portraits, the anticipation of grand adventure showing clearly in their faces. A handsomer group would be hard to imagine.

In late July, the bandsmen reported to the encampment of the 2/22nd (pronounced "second twenty-second") at Trawool, fifty miles north of Melbourne. Their new home was a neatly arranged cluster of white canvas tents and temporary shelters along the western fringe of the Australian Alps. There was a wild beauty to the rugged, open countryside, but the days were cold and damp from the frequent winter rains, and at night the recruits shivered in their tents because there weren't enough woolen blankets to go around. To make matters worse, the primitive shower build-ing, known as the "ablution block," lacked hot water.

THE 2/22ND INFANTRY BATTALION, LIKE MOST BATTALIONS IN THE 2ND AIF, consisted of approximately one thousand volunteers. What made it unique was that the vast majority of its members hailed from Melbourne or the southern regions of Victoria, the second most populous state in Australia. Assignments were generally based on abilities and past experience, with most of the men ending up in one of the battalion's rifle companies. Others reported to the Headquarters Company, the Mortar Platoon, Pioneer Platoon, Anti-Aircraft Light Machine Gun Platoon, Reinforcement Company, or Carrier Platoon. Only thirty-three individuals—just over 3 percent of the battalion—held rank as commissioned officers, including chaplains and medical personnel.

From its inception, the 2/22nd was commanded by Lieutenant Colonel Howard H. Carr, who had volunteered for the 2nd AIF at the age of forty-one. He joined the army only four days before the battalion was formed, having attained his rank as a "Saturday afternoon soldier" in the Citizen Military Forces (CMF), the Australian equivalent to the National Guard. His regular job had been with the Victoria Telephone Department, and it was rumored that his ambitious wife had more to do with his promotions in the CMF than any ability on his part. Carr was the spit-and-polish type who stomped loudly to attention and rendered salutes with a quivering snap. However, beneath the façade he had a benign personality, and was regarded as a considerate soul rather than hard-boiled.

Carr also happened to be an avid gambler. His affinity for poker led to a popular nickname for the new battalion. Standing before the assembled troops at the first official parade, he announced that he was calling the bat-talion "Little Hell." The card players among them could appreciate the humor: a poker hand containing three twos (as in 2/22) was the lowest pos-sible three of a kind. Often it was enough for a winning hand, but three deuces could also create a devilish dilemma, especially when the stakes were high.

The battalion's second in command, Major William W. Leggatt, was four years older than Carr and had considerably more military experience. A veteran of World War I, he had served with distinction in France, earning a Military Cross for combat valor. Born on Malekula Island in the New Hebrides in 1894, he became a lawyer following the "Great War" and built a successful practice in Mornington, Victoria.

Several other members of the battalion had also served during World War I. Warrant Officer-11 Henry E. "Mac" McLellan, born in London in 1900, had earned a commission in the 1st AIF but did not deploy overseas. Charles R. Benson, also a warrant officer, was born the same year and did serve with the British Expeditionary Force. But neither man had anything on Lance Corporal Bernard E. L. Cox, who was born in London in 1897 and fought in France with the 2nd Pioneers. In all, three warrant officers and thirteen enlisted men had served during World War I, and many others in the battalion had close relatives who were part of that unforgettable conflict. All across Australia, people spoke with solemn reverence of strange-sounding places like Gallipoli, the Somme, and Ypres.

EXCEPT FOR THEIR SLOUCH HATS, THE SOLDIERS OF THE AIF WORE BRITISH-style uniforms; they also carried British weapons and followed British Army manuals. But to say that the AIF was modeled after the British Army would be to grossly understate the relationship. "We *were* British," explained historian Ted Harris. "We followed them slavishly. We called England 'The Mother Country.' People talked of 'going home,' meaning the UK, even though they had been born in Australia. The British supplied many of our senior training officers, we purchased our arms from them, we sang their songs, we watched their movies, we ate their style of food, and we looked to them for fashion."

Statistics support Harris' statement. One out of every ten soldiers in the 2/22nd was a native of Great Britain, with more than sixty from London alone. And yet, for all their British heritage, the Australian soldiers reveled in their own special qualities. If the most visible difference was their slouch hat, the most intrinsic was their cheerful nickname for themselves: "Diggers." It had originated sometime during World War I, but historians still can't agree whether it sprang from the trench warfare that defined much of that conflict, or was born of the fact that many troops were former prospectors and farmers. What mattered most was that Aussie soldiers everywhere were proud to be known as Diggers. They cherished mateship as much as courage, if not more, which made them unique among the world's armies.

At Trawool, the men of the 2/22nd spent much of their day "square-bashing," their jargon for marching in formation around the muddy parade ground in the center of the encampment. Infantrymen first, they were taught how to handle, shoot, and care for their .303-caliber Lee-Enfield rifles. With each passing day, soldiering became more natural. In addition to marching and weapons drills, they had regular physical training, including long hikes to build stamina. When not involved in company-strength drills, individuals trained at specialties such as marksmanship, communications, or intelligence gathering. Sergeant Gullidge and the other bandsmen did double duty, performing martial and ceremonial music as well as learning first-aid techniques.

Gullidge requested additional training time to spend with the band, which by late August had grown beyond its original nucleus of "Salvos." Battalion-wide, new recruits arrived periodically and original members departed—usually because of training injuries or other fitness concerns—and the band was no exception. Only a few musicians had departed, but ten more arrived as replacements. Two of the new bandsmen were non-Salvationists, including Private James R. Thurst II, who had been born in the United States and was technically an American citizen.

The journey that brought him to Trawool was a convoluted one. Thurst's father, the elder James, was born in England and raised in a Catholic home for boys until the tender age of nine, when he emigrated to America with his brother Bill. When they got a bit older, the two began working their way across the country, eventually reaching the Pacific Northwest. James took on jobs that were increasingly hazardous, working on trains as a railroader, riding logjams as a lumberjack, and later sailing around the world aboard square-rigged ships. He settled down long enough to marry Florence Burroughs, a schoolteacher from Wisconsin, and she gave birth to three children: Kathleen, James II, and Mildred, all born in Washington.

Soon after "Millie" was born, James and Bill Thurst headed for Australia to seek new fortunes. James promised to send for his family as soon as he was settled, and in due time Florence received steamship tickets to Sydney. She felt obligated to use them, but later admitted that if James had simply sent her money instead of tickets, she would not have gone. As it was, she and the children boarded the MV *Tahiti* and sailed to Australia in 1914.

The Thursts raised their family on a farm near Skenes Creek, four miles from Apollo Bay on the south coast of Victoria. Music was their main entertainment. James had a fine singing voice, Florence played the violin, and young Jim inherited musical talent from both of them. "He could pick up an instrument," said his younger brother Bruce, born on the farm in 1916, "and within half an hour he could get a tune out of it. He could play anything at all."

But when Jim was nine, tragedy struck. His father, invited to perform in a concert at Apollo Bay, was driving Florence and little Bruce to town in the family gig when they saw a man struggling to lift a trunk onto the back of a horse. The man was inebriated, so James got down from the gig to help. First he boosted the drunk into the saddle, then bent down to pick up the trunk. The horse kicked out, hitting James squarely in the forehead. He died from a massive concussion without ever regaining consciousness.

Unable to keep the farm, Florence moved the family to Colac, an inland town along the Princes Highway. She took odd jobs as a cleaning woman, but her family was constantly on the threshold of poverty. Jim earned money as a gardener, and developed into a quiet, methodical man. As an adult he remained near his mother, dedicating his free time to music and the Methodist church. "James played the cornet," recalled Bruce. "He was the number one cornet player in the Colac Brass Band; he was a scoutmaster; he was an elder in the church; he was everything that he was supposed to be, everything I wasn't."

Florence and Jim had moved back to Skenes Creek by the time the war began. Although none of the American-born Thursts had ever changed their citizenship, James felt a strong obligation toward his adopted country and enlisted in the 2nd AIF on his twenty-eighth birthday. Private Thurst was assigned to the 2/22nd and arrived in late August at Trawool, where Gullidge accepted him as a cornet player. Thurst proved to be unique: the only Methodist in the band and the only Yank in the entire battalion.

AFTER LESS THAN TWO MONTHS IN THE CROWDED TENT CITY, ORDERS CAME for the 2/22nd to relocate to a new training base farther north, near the border of New South Wales. The news frustrated the battalion's tennis players, who had just put the finishing touches on a brand-new court. They would have to leave it to the next batch of trainees.

The battalion's sister unit from Victoria, the 2/21st, was ordered to move from Trawool at the same time. The whole evolution was carefully planned as a march, which would spare the army the expense of transporting some two thousand men over a distance of 150 miles. The army would also benefit from the publicity generated by showing off the troops along the route.

After breaking camp, the 2/22nd began the long march on September 24. At the town of Seymour the battalion swung onto the Melbourne-Sydney highway, and for the next ten days they marched through small towns with lyrical names like Euroa, Benalla, Glenrovan, and Wangaratta. At each town, the bandsmen offloaded their instruments from a truck and formed at the head of the line, then led a brassy parade down the main street. At night the battalion bivouacked in fairgrounds and pastures. The final bivouac came on a chilly, crystal-clear night outside the small town of Tarrawingee. Giant bonfires were lighted and the men spent several memorable hours singing their favorite songs under a brilliant canopy of stars.

The tenth day's march brought the battalion to Bonegilla, a hamlet on the western shores of Lake Hume in the foothills of the Australian Alps. Training resumed immediately in the newly constructed camp of corrugated huts. The troops skirmished, performed maneuvers, and sharpened their fighting skills six days a week, the weather turning increasingly hot as the Australian summer approached. Weeks blended into months, and the soldiers endured "an endless round of drills, weapons training, parades and inspections."

To prevent complacency, harsh punishments were meted out for infractions or substandard performance. Restriction to barracks was a common penalty, an example being three days' confinement for a dirty rifle. Fines were also levied. Being absent without leave (AWL) could cost up to £1, and in 1940 an unmarried private in the AIF earned only £7.5 per month, the equivalent of twenty-four U.S. dollars. Fortunately, the most common punishment was heavy physical training. Clarence F. Hicks, a thirty-six-year-old corporal from Ascot Vale, Victoria, lamented his mistakes in the last verse of his poem "Defaulters."

> I'm chasing the bugle in Bonegilla sun,
> It's boiling and scorching while I'm on the run.

My thoughts ever wonder, Oh why the hell
Do poor foolish Diggers go AWL?

During off-duty hours, soldiers could visit the "welfare huts" run by the Salvation Army and the YMCA. Books and magazines were always available, and the troops were sometimes treated to concerts and informal lectures. The simple pleasures of socializing often led to impromptu songfests. Individuals lucky enough to get a weekend pass usually hitchhiked into nearby towns. Jim Thurst occasionally visited his sister Kathleen, who lived a few miles away in Wodonga, but most men continued a little farther to Albury. A sizeable town just across the Murray River in New South Wales, it offered the usual diversions that soldiers seek when they can escape army life for a few hours.

Arthur Gullidge received what was probably the biggest break of all from the daily grind. At the request of Major Shugg, he was given three weeks' leave and returned home to compose new music for the Australian Army. So good were his arrangements for "Church, Ceremonial, and Other Occasions" that they remained in use throughout the army for the next thirty years. However, when Gullidge returned to Bonegilla, he found himself at odds with Captain John F. Ackeroyd, the battalion medical officer.

A somewhat pudgy doctor, Ackeroyd wanted the bandleader to spend less time with music and more learning first aid and stretcher bearing. Frustrated with the additional duties, Gullidge requested a transfer to R Company, which he received. There, his duties allowed him spare time to write a new arrangement of Australia's national anthem, "God Save the King" (better known to Americans as "My Country 'Tis of Thee"). His music continued to earn recognition. A reporter from the *Melbourne Sun* wrote, "The Salvationists who joined the AIF in a body to form this band have won praise on every hand for their splendid music. When the 2/22nd Band plays the national anthem, everybody is pleased with the beautiful arrangement of the grand melody. I wish this music could be in the hands of every bandleader in Australia."

BY EARLY 1941, HAVING TRAINED FOR SIX MONTHS, THE MEN OF THE 2/22ND were becoming restless. Bored with the repetitive marches and long nights on "bivvy," they itched to get into real combat. Many were convinced that the battalion would be sent to North Africa, and some even began to acclimatize themselves prematurely, referring to streambeds as "wadies" and using other lingo appropriate to desert warfare. Otherwise, their routine did not change; therefore dozens of frustrated soldiers transferred into other battalions under the assumption that they would get into combat quicker. Little did they know that the winds of war were blowing the battalion in a different direction.

Throughout the first year of World War II, it was natural for Australians to focus their attention on Europe and North Africa. Mother England had survived the Battle of Britain, but the news became increasingly grim as the 2nd AIF encountered heavy Axis opposition in the desert. Within a year of the 6th Division's arrival in Egypt, three more Australian divisions had been committed to the battle, and before long they were bled white under a prolonged siege at Tobruk.

The service chiefs of the Australian War Cabinet, located at Victoria Barracks, Melbourne, would have done well to watch their own backyard. For nearly a decade the small but aggressive empire of Japan had been seeking to dominate most of Asia. The Imperial Army began in 1931 with the occupation of Manchuria, and less than two years later the Japanese withdrew from the League of Nations. In addition, while denouncing the Washington Naval Treaty, the government in Tokyo ignored restrictions imposed by the League of Nations on military development and began to build a powerful navy and two independent air forces. The Japanese also fortified several bases among their mandated islands in the Pacific, the most impressive being Truk in the Carolines. Only a few hundred miles north of Australian territory, it became the Imperial Navy's largest base outside the home islands.

At the same time, due to the worldwide economic depression, Australia's own military forces were woefully ill-equipped and undermanned. Recruitment into the 2nd AIF totaled fewer than 20,000 men during the closing months of 1939, and the following year only 123,000 joined, mostly during the winter months of June through August. Due to the lack of resources, the War Cabinet seemed satisfied to merely discuss the *potential* of Japanese aggression. For that matter, few Australian citizens believed the empire represented a credible threat. Japan was not only tiny, it lay far to the north of the Commonwealth. To reach Australia, its forces would first have to tackle the Philippines, then Malaysia, and finally the Netherlands East Indies, and no one believed the "Japs" could get past the Philippines to begin with. Douglas MacArthur, the flamboyant American military advisor in Manila, assured politicians and strategists that his American-trained troops would slaughter any invaders on the beaches. Having given himself the title of Field Marshal, he suitably impressed Americans and Australians alike with his predictions, and no one had cause to doubt him. Similarly, Sir Winston Churchill declared that Singapore was impregnable, giving the Allied governments equal confidence in the strength of British garrisons in the region. Thus, Australians widely believed that the Japanese would be foolhardy to attempt a conquest of the Pacific. Even if they tried, there would be plenty of time for Great Britain and America to intervene.

The prevailing attitudes created a false sense of security. In October 1940, delegates from Great Britain, India, Australia, and New Zealand met at Singapore for the Far Eastern Defense Conference. Plans and resources were discussed, and Australia offered troops for the defense of Malaysia—a gesture that the British somewhat haughtily rejected. At the conclusion of the conference, the delegates reported that Singapore was significantly weaker than Churchill had boasted, particularly in terms of naval and air power. However, little was done to correct the deficiencies.

In Melbourne, the War Cabinet also had to consider the defense of Australia's own mandated islands. Twenty years earlier, the League of Nations had authorized civil administration of a sizeable territory captured from Germany at the beginning of World War I. Renamed the Mandated Territory of New Guinea, the region included the Papuan Peninsula of New Guinea, the Bismarck Archipelago, the Louisiade Archipelago, and dozens of smaller groups. In all, there were literally thousands of islands, many still uncharted. Innumerable native villages, coconut plantations, and mission stations dotted the habitable islands, resulting in an eclectic mix of Melanesians, Europeans, Asians, and expatriate Australians. Some of the biggest islands had well-established towns with bustling waterfronts, such as Port Moresby on the southern coast of New Guinea and Kavieng on New Ireland. The largest and most cosmopolitan was Rabaul on New Britain, the capital of the mandated territory for the past twenty years.

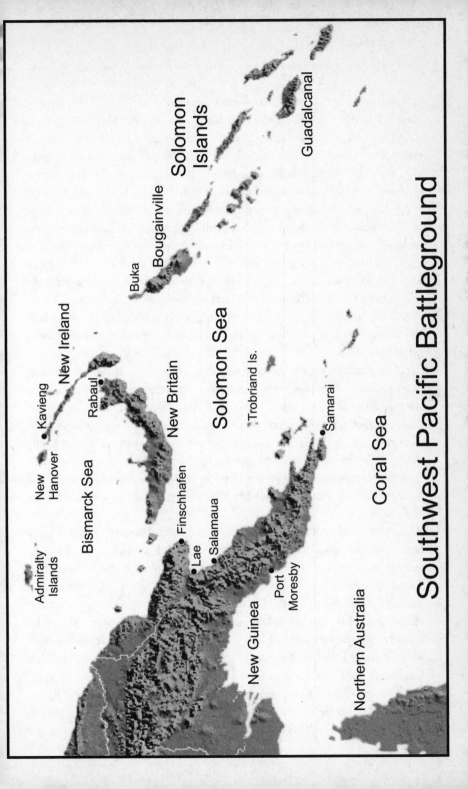

Southwest Pacific Battleground

Although the War Cabinet was responsible for defending the vast territory, it did virtually nothing to fortify the islands. The reasons were familiar throughout the Commonwealth: economic stagnation and lack of military resources. Not until November 1940 did the War Cabinet propose that warships of the Netherlands East Indies should *visit* Rabaul, hoping the gesture would encourage defense help from the Dutch. At the same time, the cabinet made a commitment to install two 6-inch coastal artillery guns for the defense of Simpson Harbor, Rabaul's superb anchorage. Months would pass, however, before the weapons were actually delivered. Finally, in early 1941, the AIF decided to send most of the 8th Division to augment the defenses at Singapore, minus the 23rd Brigade, which would garrison three islands north of the mainland: Ambon, Timor, and New Britain. The War Cabinet grandiosely referred to the islands as the "Malay Barrier," but each small landmass was separated by hundreds of miles of ocean.

The garrisons chosen to defend the islands received operational code names, though none sounded particularly inspiring. Sparrow Force, consisting of the 2/40th Infantry Battalion plus an antiaircraft battery and troops of the Netherlands East Indies, would be sent to Timor, east of Java. Gull Force, with the 2/21st Infantry Battalion as its nucleus, would fortify Ambon, two hundred miles farther to the north. The last but strategically most important assignment, the defense of Rabaul, went to the 2/22nd Infantry Battalion and its attached units, known collectively as Lark Force.

ALMOST TO A MAN, THE TROOPS OF THE 2/22ND WERE DISAPPOINTED BY THE news of their tropical assignment. Private Frederick W. Kollmorgen, having recently arrived from the 10th Training Depot, was especially frustrated. An infantryman, he had grown weary of waiting to get into action, and asked for a transfer to the 2/22nd after reading in a magazine that the band needed cornet players. A Salvationist and a tenor horn player to boot, he thought the transfer seemed like a good idea at the time. It wasn't until after he arrived that he discovered the 2/22nd was heading to Rabaul, not the Middle East.

The widespread disappointment soon evaporated with the receipt of some good news: the 23rd Brigade was going to Melbourne to participate in a grand parade. Delighted by the prospect of a day in the big city, the soldiers were measured for new tropical-weight uniforms. On the night of February 13, 1941, all three battalions donned their summer battle dress and boarded trains for the five-hour ride to Melbourne.

The first of five trainloads pulled into the city at dawn the next morning, and by 0800 nearly four thousand soldiers had assembled on Alexandra Avenue. Mobile canteens served hot stew and "pannikins" of tea, and the men washed in a nearby river before lining up three abreast for the parade, held to raise money for the Greek War Victims' Appeal fund. At precisely 1000 the marching orders echoed down the avenue: "Slope arms! By the left! Quick march!"

An estimated one hundred thousand citizens, many waving colorful flags, lined the streets of Melbourne to cheer for their boys from Victoria. The parade thrilled the entire city, according to one local reporter:

> Wheeling onto St. Kilda Road, the troops received a great cheer from the crowds on Princes Bridge. The column swung along Swanston Street past the Town Hall, where the Governor, Sir Winston Dugan, took the salute. Confetti and streamers and torn-up paper came spiraling down on the column from shop verandahs and office windows as the men marched smartly by. Keeping good order, knees and arms tanned almost to the deep brown of their boots, the men looked in capital physical condition.

At the front of the 2/22nd Battalion, the band played snappy new arrangements written by Sergeant Gullidge, including renditions from the soundtrack of the hit movie *The Wizard of Oz*, released just a year earlier. The lyrics of the theme song were remarkably appropriate: Australians had been calling their country "Oz" for years.

After the parade the 23rd Brigade returned to Bonegilla, where the routine seemed even harder to endure. However, the outlook for the 2/22nd improved when an advance party departed for Rabaul in late February to set up the battalion headquarters. The rest of the men received a few days of home leave prior to their anticipated deployment.

As there was no fighting yet in the Pacific, the soldiers tended to be optimistic during their brief visits, though they knew the value of a proper farewell before leaving home. Bandsman Herbert W. "Bert" Morgan, visiting his family in Fairfield Park, Victoria, spoke like a Salvationist in explaining that he was going to fight "for God and the King." On the morning of his departure he embraced his wife, daughter, and infant son, then hoisted his little daughter onto the mailbox by the front gate. Eleanor Morgan sat there, supported by her mother, and waved a small Australian flag while her father walked down the street and turned the corner with a final wave.

GRATEFUL FOR THEIR SHORT VISITS HOME, THE SOLDIERS TOLERATED A FEW more weeks of training back at Bonegilla. Once again the tennis players set out to build a court, but no sooner was it finished than orders arrived for half the battalion to embark to Rabaul. The selected troops traveled by train to Sydney on March 11 and boarded the steamship *Katoomba*, a grand old liner of more than 9,400 tons.

After departing Sydney, the liner stopped at Brisbane for a day, then steamed north along the coast, giving her passengers a dramatic view of the Great Barrier Reef before crossing the Coral Sea to the south coast of New Guinea. A three-day layover enabled the troops to explore Port Moresby, the hub of Australian activity on the Papuan Peninsula. The town boasted a large anchorage, a seaplane base, wharves, warehouses, commercial shops, churches, government offices, two hotels, a hospital, and an open-air theater. But three days were more than enough. The Victorians, unaccustomed to New Guinea's oppressive heat and humidity, were glad to be on their way to Rabaul.

The *Katoomba* steamed into Simpson Harbor on March 26 and docked at the Government Wharf. Representatives from the territorial government boarded the ship to give lectures about the local Tolai natives and the town's culture, after which the troops disembarked to a rousing reception from the townsfolk. Tanned businessmen wearing tropical suits of white cotton, ladies in colorful floral-print dresses, and pensioners from the Great War turned out in the hundreds to welcome the garrison.

Meanwhile, the remainder of the 2/22nd at Bonegilla chafed while awaiting their turn to deploy. Even a backwater town like Rabaul would be better than the isolated training base. Another month passed, however, before they finally received orders to entrain for Sydney. Unable to hide their enthusiasm, the soldiers chalked slogans on the sides of the train cars, turning them into rolling billboards. "HERE WE COME," stated one; "VICTORIA—2/22—LITTLE HELL," announced another; and someone even paid an indirect tribute to Gullidge and the battalion band: "WE ARE OFF TO SEE THE WIZARD."

Reaching Sydney on April 17, the second half of the garrison boarded another passenger ship that regularly plied the Pacific trade routes. A beloved member of the merchant fleet owned by the trading conglomerate Burns, Philp & Company (Australia's equivalent of Sears), the TSS *Zealandia* had served as a World War I troopship. Not only was she older than the *Katoomba*, but considerably smaller as well. Throngs of well-wishers observed the ship's departure, but there were not many relatives of the soldiers among the crowd. From Victoria, the journey to Sydney was simply too far and too expensive for most of the men's families to undertake. Jim Thurst's mother was said to be "too poor to cross the street," but his sister Kathleen did come to see the *Zealandia* depart. In the years that followed she reminisced about hearing "Now is the Hour," a touching New Zealand folk song played by the battalion band. Often called the "Maori Farewell Song," it was known by heart to most Australians:

> Now is the hour when we must say good-bye
> Soon you'll be sailing far across the sea
> While you're away, oh please remember me
> When you return, you'll find me waiting here

Steaming northward into the Solomon Sea, the *Zealandia* reached the coast of New Britain by April 24. Passengers at the portside rail could observe the island's dark, rugged mountains as the ship paralleled its 370-mile length. The next day the shoreline loomed even closer as the *Zealandia* entered St. George's Channel, a relatively narrow passage separating New Britain and New Ireland. Rounding Cape Gazelle, the liner turned west and steamed past the wharves and copra sheds of Kokopo (pronounced *Cocka*-po), a bustling little town on the north shore of the Gazelle Peninsula. The ship continued westward toward Rabaul, which was screened from view by several large volcanoes on a rugged promontory that curved from the north. Another point jutted from the south like an opposing thumb, and the *Zealandia* glided between the two points into horseshoe-shaped Blanche Bay. Six miles beyond, another volcano off the port rail marked the entrance to Simpson Harbor, at the north end of which stood Rabaul. At last the *Zealandia* coasted to a stop, her passengers unaware that they were floating inside a vast caldera.

Those who might have pondered their surroundings were soon distracted by a different sort of spectacle. The minute the ship dropped anchor she was surrounded by a boisterous parade of small craft. The arrival of any large ship was a festive event at Rabaul, but the liner's welcome this day was exceptionally keen. April 25th was ANZAC Day, a major holiday commemorating the debut of the Australia-New Zealand Army Corps at Gallipoli in 1915; therefore, the whole town was in a patriotic fervor when the ship steamed into the anchorage. Private Percy A. "Perce" Pearson, watching with his fellow soldiers from the *Zealandia's* main deck, was amazed by the flotilla of schooners, launches, and rowboats that maneuvered around the ship. He was especially impressed by the dozens of outrigger canoes, "paddled by natives and loaded with fruit for sale," which looked like a scene straight from an adventure movie.

After clearing inspection, the *Zealandia* proceeded to the main wharf. As the troops disembarked among throngs of noisy spectators and black-skinned stevedores, they were nearly overwhelmed by the humidity and the dockside din. The air was heavy with unfamiliar smells, and the soldiers sweated profusely as they formed ranks and marched up a tree-lined avenue toward their temporary camp. Along the way, they learned how the locals pronounced the name of their town. One of the marching newcomers playfully shouted, "Is this Ra-ball?"

To which an onlooker yelled, "No, it's Ra-*baal*."

As the soldiers would soon find out, there were many things they had yet to learn about their new home—some of which were less than desirable.

CHAPTER TWO

EVIL SPIRITS

"It was a very violent eruption."

—Dr. C. Daniel Miller, U.S.
Geological Survey

The troops of the 2/22nd were spellbound by their exotic surroundings, particularly the big volcanoes rising to the north and east. All around Rabaul, the landscape bore the scars of past eruptions, yet much of the evidence was covered by layers of thick vegetation. Few of the soldiers would have recognized the visual clues, and none had the background to fully appreciate the incredibly powerful forces that lay dormant beneath their feet.

Not even the scientists of the day knew much about the island's geological history. After a damaging eruption in 1937, the Australian Geological Society had posted Dr. Norman Fisher to Rabaul to monitor the area, but his simple observatory lacked the equipment to thoroughly study the caldera. Not until five decades later would an international team of vulcanologists visit Rabaul with an array of new technologies, including carbon-dating methods and other specialized measurements, with which they uncovered numerous clues about the caldera's spectacular development.

New Britain sits on a virtual powder keg, smack in the middle of one of the most seismically active zones on Earth. Just off the island's north-eastern tip, the boundaries of three tectonic plates converge beneath the seabed, their edges constantly grinding against each other with such enormous pressure that sufficient heat is generated to melt rock. The molten magma collects in fiery subterranean chambers, where intense gaseous pressures constantly force it upward, seeking weak spots in the surface. It is no coincidence, therefore, that several volcanoes exist on the northeastern end of the island. Some are ancient and extinct, others are regularly active, and all around them the ground is highly unstable.

Another geological phenomenon found near the volcanoes is a series of oval-shaped faults called "ring fractures," which measure several miles in diameter. Occasionally the fractures themselves erupt, not unlike a pot boiling over around the rim of its lid. If enough magma is ejected, the unsupported dome of the empty chamber is likely to collapse, causing a huge depression in the ground. Geologists call this a caldera, Spanish for caldron. Over the millennia, several such eruptions have either formed or modified the caldera at Rabaul, revealing the distinct outlines of two large, overlapping ring fractures.

The most recent of these caldera-forming eruptions occurred sometime around AD 600, though its exact date is a mystery. The eruption was cataclysmic—one of the most powerful since the time of Christ—and utterly devastated hundreds of square miles of New Britain and the surrounding islands. It likely began with a period of vigorous seismic activity which generated large quantities of magma beneath the existing ring fractures. Numerous tremors shook the island over a period of days or even weeks as pressurized gases weakened one of the old fault lines. The earthquakes grew in frequency and intensity until the conditions underground finally reached a critical state. At some point, the magma chamber not only boiled over, it blew apart.

The noise must have been stupefying. The ground literally ripped apart around the weakened ring fracture, from which a great ring of fire twenty miles in circumference burst forth. Pent-up gases exploded from below, hurling a thick column of rock, dust, and ash into the sky. The tiniest particles, boosted by heat and convection, soared an estimated one hundred thousand feet into the upper atmosphere. Larger rocks and glowing blobs of magma arced back to the surface, where they splattered against the ground or struck the sea with the sound of thunder.

The greatest devastation resulted from the terrible cloud itself. Most of the material hurtling skyward eventually lost momentum, then gravity took over and the outer portions of the dark, roiling column collapsed. Superheated to more than 1,800 degrees Fahrenheit, the material accelerated as it fell, and when it hit the ground it burst outward at more than one hundred miles an hour. Known as "pyroclastic flow," the incandescent cloud spread rapidly over the ancient volcanoes and raced downhill to the sea, boiling the water spontaneously as it blasted across the surface. Outlying islands were wiped clean in seconds. By the time the energy finally dissipated, the fiery cloud had killed every living thing on land and marine life near the ocean's surface for *thirty miles* in every direction.

Other destructive effects reached even farther. The prevailing winds carried heavy accumulations of ash fifty miles southwest of the volcano. Huts collapsed, crops were ruined, and the surviving islanders groped through blinding, polluted air. They too would be wiped out, doomed to eventual starvation unless they could quickly find a source of unaffected food.

Sometime after the eruption subsided, the unsupported roof over the empty magma chamber caved in. An oblong area approximately seven miles long and five miles wide collapsed suddenly, sliding downward for hundreds of feet. Additionally, the sea breached a portion of the southeastern rim and flooded most of the huge depression.

After the dust finally settled and the sea calmed, a large portion of the island resembled a bizarre moonscape. The pyroclastic flow had deposited grayish veneers of ash and pumice on the steep slopes of the old volcanoes, and low-lying areas around the caldera were buried under a hundred feet or more of the stuff. Based on vulcanologists' estimations, the eruption had disgorged ten cubic kilometers of magma and debris from the earth. (By comparison, the eruption of Mount Vesuvius in AD 79 displaced only three to four cubic kilometers, and the explosion of Mount St. Helens in 1980 displaced less than one cubic kilometer of material.)

Thanks to the tropical environment, the devastated landscape began to show signs of life within a surprisingly short time. Fast-growing kunai grasses and other vegetation thrived in the mineral-rich volcanic soil, and people eventually returned as well, most migrating from distant islands. They built new villages and resumed the familiar patterns of their ancestors, tending simple gardens, defending their homes, and practicing tribal rituals passed down from generation to generation. Stuck in the Stone Age, the primitive islanders did not develop a written language. Thus, they never created a permanent record of the disaster, and the great eruption gradually faded from memory with the passing of each generation. For almost a thousand years the island remained largely hidden from the outside world.

THE FIRST EUROPEANS TO APPROACH THE CRESCENT-SHAPED ISLAND WERE Portuguese and Spanish seafarers who explored the region in the early 1500s. By 1545 the Spanish had claimed New Guinea, the world's second-largest island, but most of the neighboring islands remained undiscovered for another 150 years. The underlying reason was fear: early explorers developed a strong aversion to malaria and cannibals, and rightfully so.

No one knew what caused malaria, only that if it didn't kill a man, it usually drove him to madness. That it entered the bloodstream by means of tiny female mosquitoes would not be discovered for centuries. In the meantime, treatment in the form of quinine was developed, but its source—the powdered bark of cinchona trees found only in the Andes mountains of South America—made it extremely hard to obtain. The early explorers didn't have it, and even much later the drug was often unavailable.

As for cannibals, the stories about shore parties being killed and eaten were frequently true. Cannibalistic tribes lived on many of the islands, as did fierce warrior clans which routinely attacked rival villages. After slaughtering the inhabitants, they made off with their victims' food and weapons— and often their heads. Believing firmly in sorcery and the supernatural, the smallish tribes held a common distrust of virtually all outsiders. Rival tribes were blamed for bringing evil spirits, considered the root of all unpleasant occurrences such as diseases, earthquakes, and volcanoes. It was not a moral issue, therefore, to kill a person or even an entire village if a threat was perceived. Indeed, knocking off rivals was one well-accepted method by which a tribe could assert its power, there being no better symbol of achievement than to put a collection of the enemies' heads on prominent display.

Finally, in 1700, English explorer William Dampier sailed completely around the crescent-shaped island and charted its coastline. Realizing that it was the largest island in a closely grouped archipelago, he christened it New Britain in honor of his homeland, then continued with the Anglican theme for the other important islands and waterways: New Ireland, New Hanover, the Duke of York Islands, and St. George's Bay.

However, even after Dampier contributed to the nautical charts, explorers avoided New Britain for the same reasons as before. Perhaps some captains took their ships into the flooded caldera, but they were satisfied to observe the volcanoes from a safe distance. Shore parties searching for water did not stray far from the beach, and for many years

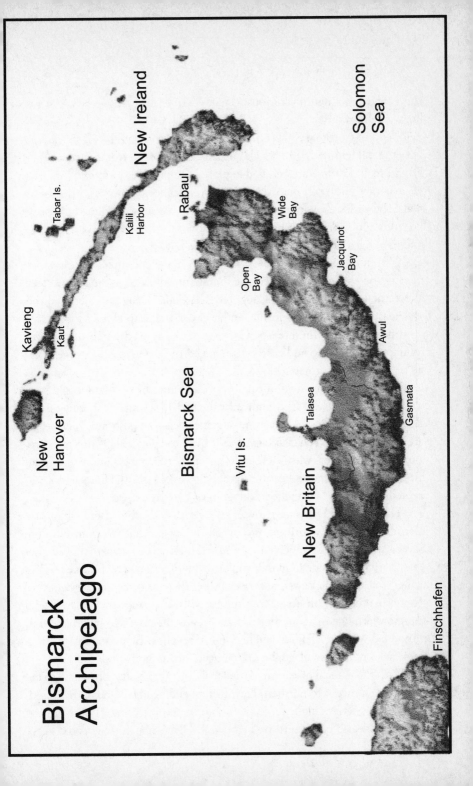

the island remained mysterious, a place where no man who valued his head should wander.

Captain Cortland Simpson of the Royal Navy sailed the HMS *Blanche* into the caldera in 1872 and claimed its "discovery." Ironically, another Englishman, Philip Carteret, had explored the protected waters a hundred years earlier and even named the biggest volcanoes; however, he did not name the various bays or natural harbors, and so Simpson claimed the privilege. In honor of himself he named the inner anchorage Simpson Harbor, and the large outer caldera became Blanche Bay.

Carteret's biggest contribution was to name the ancient volcanoes ringing the caldera. He named the dominant volcano, soaring 1,600 feet above the harbor, the North Daughter. The South Daughter anchored the southeastern tip of the peninsula, and between them stood the Mother, her twin peaks resembling breasts. Carteret also surveyed much of the surrounding archipelago and correctly changed the name of St. George's Bay to St. George's Channel.

Missionaries came next, for neither headhunters nor malaria could stop the inexorable spread of Christianity. By the mid-1800s, after first bringing the Gospel to Micronesia, European missionaries began to push into Melanesia, the "black islands." The cautious tribes proved to be incredibly diverse, confounding newcomers with thousands of different languages and rituals that included headhunting and cannibalism. Not surprisingly, the Europeans considered them to be "a wretched, barbarous race in the extreme."

The Reverend George Brown, a fervent Methodist, established the first mission on New Britain around 1875. Several natives from Fiji and Samoa, themselves converted to Christianity, served as catechists. The local natives responded favorably at first, but a village chief named Talili came to distrust the newcomers. Regarding them as sorcerers, he believed they were responsible for a frightening volcanic eruption in 1878. He therefore arranged the murder of four Fijian catechists, to which Brown responded with an Old Testament form of revenge. By personally leading an attack on Talili's village, he discouraged further uprisings.

With the gradual placation of the local Tolai (generally considered to be the people indigent to northern New Britain and nearby islands), the island was soon experiencing a surge of European settlers. Traders and sundry opportunists also began settling near the caldera, though none could keep pace with the missionaries. Numerous denominations built schools and churches all across the northern plateau, generating fierce competition between Catholics and Protestants to convert the natives. Despite some disputes, the customs of headhunting, cannibalism, and other taboo rituals gradually disappeared as the Tolai responded to the Christian message.

The missionaries failed, however, to gain much ground against the natives' belief in the supernatural. This was due mainly to the earthquakes, known by the Tolai as *gurias*, which frequently shook the island. Also, the Tolai believed that malevolent spirits called *kaia* inhabited the volcanoes. Although the Mother and the two Daughters were extinct, plenty of other vents and fumaroles were not. As early as 1791, English sea captain John Hunter had observed a vent next to the South Daughter erupting a large column of ash and smoke. Sixty years later, another eruption occurred along an odorous gully known as Sulphur Creek, which emptied into the eastern shore of Simpson Harbor near the old volcanoes.

There was nothing supernatural about these events. Magma still collected beneath the caldera, which alternately swelled and settled over the centuries. One result was the birth of Matupit Island, a bell-shaped landmass that rose like a blister from the harbor floor. Another geological phenomenon appeared literally overnight during the aforementioned eruption of 1878. Located near the western shore of Blanche Bay, the landmass featured a small crater that vented steam for several days. The locals named it Vulcan Island. Directly across Blanche Bay, a squat volcano called Tavurvur also erupted, killing vegetation for two miles downwind. It was the same volcano witnessed by Captain Hunter in 1791, and would continue to be a trouble spot. Other geological oddities included a tall outcropping of rocks nicknamed "The Beehives," which jutted from the middle of Simpson Harbor. Elsewhere, several small unnamed vents lined the banks of Sulphur Creek, which itself emitted strong-smelling gases. In all, the finger of land curving around Simpson Harbor was crowded with so many volcanoes, vents, and fumaroles that it became known as "Crater Peninsula."

COMPARED WITH THE ARRIVAL OF EUROPEANS AND EVEN THE DESTRUCTIVENESS of volcanic eruptions, nothing altered the landscape of New Britain like the humble coconut. In the mid-1800s, the German trading company Godeffroy und Sohn took an interest in processing coconut oil, fast becoming popular as a key ingredient in candles and soap. The industry expanded throughout the Pacific as demand for the oil grew, and evolved even faster after the Godeffroys made an important discovery: rather than shipping heavy caskets of smelly oil all the way to Europe, they chopped up the flesh of coconuts and dried it on racks in the sun. After drying, the pieces were bagged in burlap sacks and shipped to Germany, where presses extracted the oil. Thus was born the copra industry.

Within a few years the relatively flat terrain of New Britain's northern plateau supported dozens of huge plantations. When labor requirements began to exceed the population of able-bodied workers, natives from outlying islands were brought in and labor compounds sprang up. Various trading companies constructed a shipping center on Matupit Island, then expanded their businesses along the shore of Blanche Bay. Soon a network of roads connected the villages and plantations so that copra could be delivered directly to the wharves.

In 1884, imperial Germany claimed the archipelago as a protectorate and named it after the first chancellor, Otto Von Bismarck. A year later, after formally annexing a large portion of northeastern New Guinea, the empire chartered the privately held New Guinea Kompagnie (NGK) to administer the territory from company headquarters at Finschhafen. However, rampant malaria forced NGK to move to New Britain. The new headquarters was established at Kokopo, no doubt because of the town's proximity to Vunapope, a prosperous Roman Catholic mission led by a German bishop. As the regional headquarters for the Order of the Sacred Heart, Vunapope boasted a large, attractive campus of whitewashed buildings overlooking St. George's Channel.

Unfortunately for the Germans, Kokopo proved less than satisfactory as the headquarters for the Protectorate of German New Guinea. Its main drawback was the small harbor, which offered scant protection against the elements blowing in from St. George's Channel. In 1899 the administration reverted to government control, and within two years a governor was appointed.

Soon after Dr. Albert Hahl arrived to fill the position, he decided to move the headquarters to the north end of Simpson Harbor. The location offered superior protection but was choked with mangrove swamps, and heretofore had been considered unsuitable for development. Undeterred, Hahl obtained the necessary property in the name of the government, and with efficient German engineering the swamps were drained and cleared. The first wharf was built in 1904, several substantial buildings were erected within a year, and a narrow-gauge tram line was laid to move goods from warehouses to the waterfront. The ambitious engineers even cut a tunnel through the rim of the caldera, and a set of tracks went all the way to the village of Ratavul on the island's north coast.

By 1910 the capital was established in the new town, named Rabaul, meaning "place of mangroves." The well-designed community featured shade trees lining the main boulevards, sturdy wooden buildings in the commercial district, and attractive bungalows with landscaped gardens in the residential neighborhoods. Hahl lived in Government House, an impressive mansion on Namanula Hill next to a substantial hospital. Both of the buildings stood on piers to allow cool air to circulate underneath, and had deep verandahs to take advantage of the sea breezes and spectacular views. As Rabaul grew, it earned a reputation as one of the best shipping ports in the Southwest Pacific. Newcomers immigrated from Europe and Asia, bringing a sense of sophistication to the settlement until World War I interrupted in 1914.

With the onset of war, the British Admiralty appealed to Australia for help in capturing German installations throughout the Southwest Pacific. Responding quickly, a naval expeditionary force departed from Sydney on August 19. Escorted by six warships, two submarines, and three colliers, the ex-liner *Berrima* arrived in Simpson Harbor on September 11. Troops landed that afternoon to search for German wireless stations, and one party encountered resistance en route to Bita Paka, the site of a giant steel radio mast. Five of the expedition troops were killed in the fight, thus becoming Australia's first casualties of the war. That evening the expeditionary force captured the radio station, and the following day Rabaul was occupied without a fight. In less than a week, the Germans surrendered the entire protectorate.

For the duration of the war, the Australian army interned most of the German citizens in the territory and maintained martial law. The army also continued martial control for three years after the war until 1921, when the League of Nations authorized civil administration by the Commonwealth. The former protectorate was renamed the Mandated Territory of New Guinea, and Rabaul continued to serve as capital.

In some ways the new territory was a liability for the Australian government. Much of the land was wild and remote, and therefore received
little attention from politicians who were more interested in domestic
issues. Even after large gold deposits were discovered in the mountains of
the Papuan Peninsula, Canberra was disinclined to provide financial assistance for the territory. As for the Melanesian natives, the government's
record of dealing with its own aboriginals did not bode well for an effective
administration, especially considering the Melanesians' history of tribal
warfare, headhunting, and deep suspicion of outsiders.

With surprising efficiency, however, the Commonwealth gained the
support of many tribes and villages. This was achieved in large part by
training some of the tribesmen as constables and police-boys. The Tolai
and other Melanesians held great stock in "big men" who wielded local
power; thus, it was an honor to receive a government assignment, however small, especially when the position included a military cap or some
other token piece of uniform. Australian patrol officers trained the
natives and acted as regional administrators, mediating disputes and
other matters as necessary. The system worked well and resulted in a generally peaceful coexistence.

Also, the government had a clever method for rehabilitating former
German plantations and other businesses: Australians either purchased
them at a fraction of their value or commandeered them outright. During
the 1930s, the government even published advertisements seeking army
officers to take over plantations that had been "abandoned" by their
German owners. One of the many who responded was Richard K. P.
Moore, an ex-lieutenant from the Light Horse who had earned a Military
Cross in World War I. He submitted an application in the mandated territory and was simply given an entire plantation called Tatavana.

Meanwhile, mining companies were eager to develop the New Guinea
goldfields, and several large trading companies saw great potential in further developing Rabaul. Burns, Philp & Company and W. R. Carpenter
and Company constructed wharves, warehouses, and copra sheds all
around Simpson Harbor. They also opened department stores and
employed numerous citizens. The Asian neighborhood, naturally called
Chinatown, supported several swank establishments including the Chin
Hing Hotel on Yara Avenue and the Ah Chee Hotel across the street.

Rabaul, it was said, never lacked for a watering hole. During the 1920s a young vagabond from Tasmania named Errol Flynn was well known among the pubs and hotels, which he frequented between jobs in the goldfields.

The town's citizenry benefited directly from the cosmopolitan development. Rabaul boasted a movie theater, the Regent, which showed British and American films several days a week. Other public venues included a library, a book club, social clubs, druggists, a printing office, taxi stands, pool halls, gas stations for motorists, and an ice-making and cold-storage plant. Among the sporting facilities were a large concrete swimming pool (filled with seawater), a cricket field, a baseball diamond, and even a golf course, the latter built on a low volcanic plain at the edge of Crater Peninsula. Nearby, next to a coconut plantation named Lakunai, an airstrip served the weekly mail plane. On the eastern shore of Simpson Harbor, near the outlet of Sulphur Creek, a seaplane terminal and ramps were built for Queensland and Northern Territory Aerial Services (QANTAS), the oldest airline in the English-speaking world. Lastly, the Rapindik Native Hospital and a housing compound for Melanesian laborers stood near the airdrome. In the same general vicinity was the town dump, known by locals as "The Malay Hole."

That the native facilities were miles from town but close to the dump was no accident. Australia's white population was no different than their American counterparts when it came to racial discrimination and bigotry. Throughout the mandated territories, the Melanesians were commonly referred to as "coons" and "fuzzy-wuzzies," while the Pidgin English word for a European man was "masta." Some insisted that *master* was merely an honorific, but the whites generally projected an air of colonial superiority over the Melanesians and treated them like children. Virtually all of the European households employed natives for domestic chores but paid them minimal compensation.

By the late 1930s the population of Rabaul township had grown to approximately eight hundred Europeans, a thousand Asians, and three thousand natives. All were capably governed by Brigadier General Walter McNicoll (later knighted), a decorated combat veteran of World War I. His proudest achievement was leading the 6th Infantry Battalion ashore at Gallipoli, where he was twice wounded. As a postwar politician he steered the mandated territories through the depression with a tight but effective fiscal policy. Under his administration, Rabaul was said to be "euphorically comfortable in its established routine."

Underground, however, conditions were less than ideal. In choosing to develop Rabaul inside the rim of a caldera, Albert Hahl had evidently overlooked the island's geological history. Perhaps he was simply ignorant of the volcanic past, else he might not have built the town where it stood. The Tolai, on the other hand, were fearful of the *kaia* that supposedly dwelled within the volcanoes. White missionaries worked hard to dismiss such superstitions, but the natives' beliefs were eventually validated.

Strange things began to happen on the afternoon of May 28, 1937. First, a strong *guria* shook Rabaul for half a minute. It caused no damage, but the water in Blanche Bay withdrew and then surged back in a minor tsunami, stranding numerous fish on Vulcan Island. The following morning, residents of Rabaul felt another intense earthquake, then another, until eventually the whole town was rattled. Between tremors the residents felt a weird sensation, as if the ground itself was vibrating under their feet. At about four o'clock, Vulcan gave another heave, and a portion of foul-smelling reef rose up around the little island. Moments later, the vent on the islet opened up with a mighty roar.

Compared with the epic event that had occurred some 1,400 years earlier, the 1937 eruption on Vulcan Island was small, disgorging perhaps half of a cubic kilometer of material. Yet the results were devastating. Several natives who had paddled to Vulcan to gather the stranded fish were vaporized, a large sailboat crossing the bay from Matupit Island disappeared, and two Tolai villages were completely buried under volcanic debris.

As the eruption continued to build, heavy ash piled up on the landscape. Brilliant flashes of lightning split the air, sparked by static electricity within the cloud, and thunder added its din to the roar of the volcano. Mud and seawater, sucked into the already saturated cloud by powerful convection, fell to the ground in torrents of dirty rain.

Rabaul's residents, having dropped whatever they were doing to watch the spectacle, suddenly realized they were in the path of the ash fall. Thousands tried to flee by the only roads leading north out of the caldera—one over Namanula Hill, the other through Tunnel Hill—but both routes were soon jammed with refugees. Day turned to night as the thick gray cloud overtook them, the heavy flakes of ash accumulating on the heads and shoulders of panic-stricken citizens. Lightning and thunder added to the hellish experience, which lasted throughout the day and all that night.

Sunday morning revealed that Vulcan was no longer flat, nor was it even an island any longer. Overnight, it had been transformed into a conical mountain more than seven hundred feet high. On the surrounding plateau, everything within three miles had been destroyed. The Rabaul Dairy was gone, its entire herd of milk cows killed. In the two native villages near Vulcan, an estimated five hundred islanders lay buried for eternity under thirty feet of ash and pumice. Ironically, they had gathered to conduct secret Tolai ceremonies, much to the dismay of local missionaries. Casualties were light in Rabaul proper, where a Chinese woman was killed and a crewman from the American freighter *Golden Bear* was reported missing. Presumably he fell overboard, but his body was never recovered.

By Sunday afternoon most of the displaced citizens had gathered along the eastern shore of Crater Peninsula near the village of Nordup. Brigadier General McNicoll, who had been on New Guinea when the eruption occurred, flew in and began organizing emergency relief. A small fleet of steamships and sailboats gathered to transport the refugees south to Vunapope, which was adequately equipped to provide shelter until Rabaul could be cleaned up. During the afternoon, Tavurvur suddenly erupted with a blast of steam and heavy smoke. The flaming debris was frightening in appearance, but the eruption soon subsided, the only casualty being a man who had been seen hiking in the vicinity of the crater.

Two weeks later, the people of Rabaul returned to an eerie ghost town. The once-lovely streets lay in ruins. Trees had snapped under the weight of several inches of wet ash, cars lay buried as though by a gray blizzard, and outbuildings and sheds had collapsed. A thick sludge of pumice choked most of the harbor's surface. Ships were aground, scattered at odd angles on the beaches. Some roads had been buried by rockslides, while others were sliced by huge ravines. Most of the substantial buildings in town had suffered only minor damage thanks to their steeply pitched roofs; nevertheless the task of cleaning up was a long and frustrating affair.

Long before the job was finished, Rabaul was deemed unsuitable for continued service as the territorial capital. Three towns on New Guinea were considered as alternates. Salamaua prospered as the air-freight center for the goldfields, and Lae, twenty miles to the north, had a good airdrome.* The third choice was Wau, the administrative center for the goldfields high in the Bulolo Valley. The administration could not reach an agreement, however, and discussions dragged on until 1939, when the decision to shift the capital to Lae was finalized. Before Brigadier General McNicoll could complete the move, however, he fell seriously ill with malaria. Major Harold H. Page, the deputy administrator, assumed McNicoll's duties and remained happily in Rabaul.

Fifty years old at the time, Page had been awarded a Military Cross and a Distinguished Service Order during World War I, and was a popular figure around town. His older brother was even better known. One of the first Australians to own a car, Sir Earle Page had founded the Country Party, served as deputy prime minister under two governments, and even sat as prime minister for twenty days after Joseph Lyons died in the spring of 1939. The political connections were beneficial to Harold Page, who was still the acting administrator when the 2/22nd Battalion arrived in 1941.

By then, Rabaul had returned to its former splendor as a garden town. Hibiscus, frangipani, bougainvillea, and a dozen other varieties of flowers flourished among hedges and shrubs, and the overhanging branches of giant casuarinas and mangos shaded the main boulevards. "It was a beautiful place, so tropical," recalled Lorna Johnson, one of six army nurses who arrived aboard the *Zealandia* on ANZAC Day. "The flowers were beautiful, the birds were wonderful, and after you got used to the heat it was really quite nice."

Known then by her maiden name of Whyte, Lorna had been raised in the "back blocks" of New South Wales and was perhaps better accustomed to the heat than some of the other new arrivals. Private Albert R. "Bluey" Fry of Sydney, a drummer in the battalion band, described Rabaul as "terribly hot." Arthur Gullidge, in a letter to his wife Mavis, declared, "I don't think I have perspired so much in all my life."

The temperature was only half of the equation. Much of the discomfort everyone felt was caused by the high humidity. The monsoon season began in December and lasted six months, during which the humidity hovered at 90 percent or more and the prevailing winds often brought heavy rainstorms out of the northwest. One night, after the troops set up a temporary camp at the foot of the Mother, a downpour dumped eight inches of

---

* On July 2, 1937, only five weeks after the eruptions at Rabaul, aviation pioneer Amelia Earhart and navigator Fred Noonan took off from Lae and were subsequently lost.

rain in two hours. "I was sleeping in a tent then," wrote Private Thomas E. Hartley, a machine-gunner from Airey's Inlet, Victoria, "and my bed was floating about the tent."

Unfortunately for the battalion, the camp was down inside the caldera, where the humidity was much higher than on the breezy plateau. The soldiers hired "wash boys" to do their laundry, but between washings the clothing remained damp, creating conditions for all sorts of fungi and bacteria to develop. Men who failed to dry their feet and change socks on a regular basis found themselves afflicted with *tinea pedis*, commonly known as athlete's foot. Even with aggressive treatment, the jungle variety sometimes took a month or longer to eradicate.

Several other tropical maladies threatened the troops, and Captain Ackeroyd would have been overwhelmed with cases were it not for the personnel of the 2/10 Field Ambulance, a detachment of which arrived aboard the *Zealandia*. Major Edward C. "Ted" Palmer, the officer in charge of the detachment, became the senior medical officer in Lark Force by virtue of rank. He and Captain S. E. J. "Sandy" Robertson, another capable doctor, were supported by the six army nurses and twenty orderlies.

The medics treated numerous head colds and even a few cases of pneumonia during the garrison's first six weeks at Rabaul. Passing them off as "related to the period of adjustment to the climate," Palmer was not unduly worried. What concerned him more was malaria and its notorious cousin, dengue fever, both of which could be lethal. Neither showed an alarming level of initial incidence, but the potential for outbreaks was constantly high. Another serious threat was tropical ulcers, which could develop from almost any small cut or scratch into a festering ulcer in less than twenty-four hours. If left untreated, the patient ran the risk of serious infection or even blood poisoning. Using the ounce-of-prevention method, the medical staff made certain that hygiene and anti-malaria medication received top priority. Everyone took daily showers to ward off fungi, and each afternoon on the parade ground, the sergeants walked the ranks to ensure that "every man took his dose of liquid quinine, unceremoniously administered by spoon into an open mouth."

Thanks to the medics, the garrison adjusted to the climate without undue hardship, but the same could not be said of the six nurses. Referred to as "sisters" in the Australian Army Nursing Service, they wore ridiculous World War I–period uniforms: long dresses of gray cotton, a red cape, a white veil, thick brown stockings, and heavy shoes. The women greatly envied the nurses at the civilian hospital, who wore sensible short-sleeved frocks, so the senior army nurse decided to make some changes. Kathleen I. A. "Kay" Parker, a former matron of nurses at Ingleburn army camp in New South Wales, was free spirited and strikingly tall. "Right," she told the others, "this is fair enough; we're going to leave these awful cotton stockings off." Delighted, the nurses also decided to get rid of the red capes and shorten the sleeves on their dresses.

Unfortunately, the wrong people observed their cavalier behavior. "We went to work down in the tents along the shore," remembered Johnson, "and none of the boys took any notice. Well, they probably thought we looked a bit better. But one of the plantation owners was a First World War nurse, and her great friend was Matron [Hilda] Keary, the senior matron in Sydney. She wrote to Matron Keary and told her what we had done. The matron wrote back to us and said that if we didn't sew the sleeves back on and put the stockings back on, we were going to be discharged from the army when we returned to Australia."

The nurses also encountered difficulties with Major Palmer, who had been directed to establish a sixty-bed hospital. He tried to avoid the assignment, for he and Robertson saw themselves as battlefield surgeons. They preferred to do their doctoring in the field, where the ambulance men had earned glory during the last war, and feared that a hospital would anchor them to routine duties. To show their displeasure, they refused to let the nurses work alongside them.

Lieutenant Colonel Carr eventually had to intervene. "The colonel came to see us and was a bit horrified that we'd been treated like that," Johnson recalled. "He insisted that Major Palmer take us into the hospital. The boys wanted us down at the hospital, the orderlies and all the sick boys wanted us down there, but the major was objecting to us because he didn't want a hospital." Palmer conceded under direct orders from Carr, and the tent hospital was built near the beach adjacent to the encampment.

Within a matter of weeks, however, the very existence of the hospital and Lark Force's tent encampment were threatened by renewed volcanic activity inside the caldera. It was Tavurvur again. The ugly-looking volcano, known by locals as "Matupi," had awoken after four years of dormancy. On June 6, several earthquakes jolted Rabaul immediately after reveille. The air inside the caldera seemed to vibrate, then suddenly the volcano burst into eruption. Soldiers gaped at the sight of hot rocks and ash jetting from the cone, and Rabaul's civilians, expecting the worst, began an orderly progression out of town. They returned a short time later, having concluded that the volcano posed no immediate threat.

It was true: the emissions were little more than a nuisance, despite the fact that Tavurvur continued to spew thick clouds of noxious vapor with a sound like "a train going over a big overhead bridge." Some nights it rumbled so loudly that the entire camp was awakened, often to the accompaniment of earthquakes. "To stand," noted Private Pearson in his diary, "was to rock like a drunken man." Everyone grew weary of the stench of sulfur and the corrosive effects of the ash fallout, which rotted the fabric of tents and uniforms and caused pitting in metal surfaces. Weapons had to be constantly stripped and cleaned, and any scratches that appeared on the garrison's vehicles had to be painted over before corrosion would set in. The civilian vehicles in town, built of lighter gauge steel and less fastidiously cared for, developed gaping holes.

The eruption forced Lieutenant Colonel Carr to move the garrison to a more suitable location on the northwest side of Malaguna Road. Dubbed Malaguna Camp, the new facility featured wood-frame huts sheathed with compressed asbestos siding. The troops weren't aware of the dangers posed by asbestos; what mattered was that they were no longer exposed to the volcanic fallout.

The nurses benefited the most. The territorial capital finally shifted over to Lae, leaving Government House vacant, and the garrison converted it into a hospital. Wearing their heavy uniforms, the nurses were grateful to work up on the hill, where the sea breezes felt heavenly compared to the stifling humidity inside the caldera.

Meanwhile, Tavurvur continued to erupt intermittently for months. As additional components of Lark Force arrived by ship, the volcano greeted them with fireworks, almost as if the *kaia* were providing their own special welcome.

CHAPTER THREE

HOSTAGES TO FORTUNE

"[Make] the enemy fight for this line . . ."

—Herbert Evatt, Australia Minister
for External Affairs

To the military planners in Australia, the long string of islands comprising the Mandated Territory of New Guinea and the British-protected Solomons represented a sort of fence. Some in the War Cabinet even referred to it as the "Northern Barrier," though the islands weren't fortified until 1941. Lionel Wigmore, an esteemed Australian historian, more accurately described them as "a slender chain of forward observation posts."

In the fall of 1939, an officer of the Royal Australian Navy (RAN) set out to link the islands with a communications and intelligence network. Over a period of months, Lieutenant Commander Eric A. Feldt traveled "by ship, motor boat, canoe, bicycle, airplane, and boot" from New Guinea all the way to the New Hebrides, single-handedly enrolling dozens of plantation owners, traders, and assorted civilians into a loosely organized group known as the "coastwatchers." All of them would perform a crucial role the coming war, many at the cost of their lives.

Simultaneously, detachments of a small militia organization, the New Guinea Volunteer Rifles (NGVR), were established among the major islands. Representing the mandated territory's only infantry force prior to 1941, the NGVR was authorized the day after Australia declared war on Germany, and many of the region's able-bodied men were volunteers. Lieutenant Colonel John Walstab, the supervisor of police on New Britain, trained a unit of approximately eighty men who formed a rifle company, a machine gun squad, and a small headquarters unit.

The arrival of Lark Force in 1941 was a significant boost to the local military strength, and later that summer a commando unit garrisoned New Ireland. The 1st Independent Company, led by Major James Edmonds-Wilson, represented the extent of the War Cabinet's effort to defend the other islands of the mandated territory, but even that small force was sub-divided. Approximately 150 of the commandos fortified the main harbor town of Kavieng and a nearby airfield; the rest defended several remote airstrips scattered among the Solomons and New Hebrides islands.

Additional components of Lark Force were delivered by the *Zealandia*, which returned to Rabaul with a detachment of Royal Australian Artillery to install a pair of 6-inch coastal defense guns. A company of Royal Australian Engineers was also aboard, along with a detachment of communications specialists. Together, the three groups added two hundred officers and men to the garrison.

The engineers' first responsibility was to construct access roads and emplacements for the coastal guns. Praed Point provided the most commanding view of St. George's Channel and the approaches to Blanche Bay, but the steep topography of Crater Peninsula prevented the guns from being placed side by side in the conventional manner. Instead, they were stacked one above the other despite "expert and most urgent advice" to the contrary from several old soldiers. A number of veterans went out to Praed Point and criticized the engineers, but stacking the guns was the only practical solution that allowed both guns a wide firing arc. The bigger problem was the fact that there were only two vintage weapons to begin with.

Likewise, Rabaul's air defense was limited, the only weapons being a pair of 3-inch guns manned by militiamen. Captain David M. Selby, a slender, aristocratic-looking attorney from New South Wales, led the fifty-four members of the battery ashore from the liner *Neptuna* on August 16. They moved into several huts at Malaguna Camp, then set up their mobile guns near the beach and commenced an almost laughable training program. Permission to fire the weapons was denied because one of the weapons had a crack in its breechblock. In order to prevent further damage, the crews had to satisfy themselves with merely tracking the weekly mail plane. They pretended to shoot it down twice every Saturday—once during its approach to Lakunai airdrome and again when the plane departed. The rest of the week, one of the young gunners (invariably the fellow with the most accumulated demerits) supplied the target by running back and forth while holding a model plane aloft on a length of bamboo. Naturally he was the butt of many jokes, and the militiamen as a group endured endless wisecracks from their AIF campmates.

The final component of Lark Force, the 17th Antitank Battery, was delivered to Rabaul by the *Zealandia* on September 29. Commanded by Captain Gwynne Matheson, the battery of eight 2-pounder guns was served by six officers and 104 men. Unfortunately, like the other components of Lark Force, the weapons had serious limitations. The only ammunition shipped with the guns was solid-steel shot—good for target practice but almost useless in battle—and there were only twenty rounds per gun.

With the arrival of the antitank battery, Lark Force was complete. In addition to the 2/22nd Infantry Battalion, the hodgepodge of support units brought the garrison's total to approximately fourteen hundred men—and six nurses.

THE MILITARY WORKDAY AT RABAUL NORMALLY CONCLUDED WITH AN afternoon parade at 1600. Passes were usually available for those who wanted to leave camp, and if a bloke was lucky, he might get to accompany one of the nurses to a film at the Regent. Fraternization was frowned upon, but not everyone abided by the guidelines. "The nurses were not supposed to go out with the troops; we were only supposed to mix with the officers," recalled Lorna Johnson. "But that never troubled Kay [Parker]. If she saw somebody that she liked, and he came up and asked her to the pictures, it didn't matter if he was a private—she would go."

Rabaul offered several attractions besides the theater. Troops who had never traveled far from home marveled at the shops in Chinatown, exotic beyond anything they had ever seen. In the center of the neighborhood was the "Bung," a colorful, noisy market crowded with dark-skinned "marys" in Mother Hubbard blouses and bare-chested Tolai men wearing colorful sarongs around their hips. Rows of stalls were piled high with pineapples, coconuts, shellfish, betel nut, papaya, sugar cane, or fresh fish. Dogs scurried underfoot, and it was not unusual to see a domesticated fowl perched atop a mound of vegetables. Visiting the market for the first time, Private Pearson was enthralled by an old native woman who watched her stall while "sitting placidly by, smoking a filthy old pipe with the stem broken off near the bowl." Pearson also admired the strength of the native women. They worked harder than the men, and he observed one Tolai woman who walked eleven miles while carrying a load of heavy wares "plus a picaninny on her hip."

Sometimes the natives' appearance and customs shocked the Australian soldiers. A great many of the adult Tolai had open sores on their legs and feet, and more than a few suffered from grotesque ailments such as elephantiasis or gout. Men and women alike chewed betel nut, the intoxicating juice of which stained their lips and teeth a hideous red. Wherever they congregated, the dirt around them was splotched with red spittle.

SOLDIERS WHO LACKED EITHER THE FUNDS OR THE INCLINATION TO VISIT Rabaul made their own entertainment in Malaguna Camp. The canteen offered Castlemaine Beer and Fosters Export Ale for a shilling a bottle (about fifteen cents in 1941), and if the beer wasn't always cold, the men drank it anyway while playing two-up, their favorite coin game. Aussie soldiers had few equals when it came to gambling. They were known to wager on just about anything, from dice to cards to "which of two flies will rise first from the bar."

Even when they weren't gambling, the soldiers tried to outdo each other at every opportunity. Participation in sports was compulsory, with the battalion's various companies and Lark Force support units rotating between cricket, tennis, baseball, golf, and swimming. Saturday afternoons were set aside for boxing tournaments in camp or swim meets at Rabaul's modern concrete pool. The competition was fierce yet good natured, which added to the foundation of camaraderie that no amount of formal training could instill. One could not help but admire the soldiers' enthusiasm. "They were all outstanding young men, lots of them country boys, just bush boys," remembered Lorna Johnson. "All had a good sense of humor; all loved their glass of beer; all loved their fun. They would take on anything and anybody. They were a great band of boys."

She was correct in the sense that there were plenty of youngsters in the garrison—Private Andrew B. Bishop, a native of England, was only seventeen—but Johnson was looking through a prism of several decades in remembering them all as boys. Considering that the average life expectancy in 1941 was only about sixty-five years, numerous members of the garrison were actually past middle age. Older troops included Privates Thomas R. Connop and Wilfred J. Baker, both forty-one; Sydney McGregor, Lawrence Quinn, and Harry Bernstein, forty; and a host of others in their late thirties. Many in the ranks were significantly older than their officers. Private William Holmes, a thirty-nine-year-old native of Ireland, was batman for Lieutenant Alec R. Tolmer, twenty-seven, who led the 2/22nd's Pioneer Platoon. Other junior officers were even younger. Hatsell G. "Glenn" Garrard, a lieutenant in the Headquarters Company, was twenty-three but looked more like an adolescent cadet; Lieutenant Benjamin G. Dawson, one of the intelligence officers in the 2/22nd, was only twenty when he joined the battalion.

With such a wide span of ages and backgrounds represented among the members of Lark Force, there was no shortage of colorful characters. One of the most noteworthy was Private Norman D. Webster, thirty, an infantryman who had performed as a rough rider in traveling expeditions such as "Wild Australia" and "Thorpe McConville's Buckjump Show." Ever the entertainer, he was fond of storytelling and had a penchant for outlandish expressions. Another performer, although not a true professional, was Private A. Colin Dowse, a twenty-year-old farm boy from Victoria who "could thump out a honky-tonk tune while he bounced about on the piano stool."

A fair number of soldiers had two middle names and some had none at all; but in the unusual name category, few could compete with Private C. O. Harry. Raised on a farm north of Melbourne, he was accustomed to hard work and hard times, droughts and depressions. His grandfather, John Harry, a British seaman-apprentice, had jumped ship back in the 1850s when gold was discovered in New South Wales. He did not strike it rich but prospered all the same, obtaining acreage along the Murray River during the 1869 Land Act. Among John's four sons, Henry Harry had four sons of his own, and for some unknown reason he saddled the youngest with a lisp-inducing family name: Cuthbert Oswald. No one ever blamed the lad for choosing a common nickname. By the time C. O. enlisted at the age of twenty-three, he was known to everyone as "Bill," and no soldier was tougher.

Easily the most famous personality in the garrison was Sergeant Gullidge. He and the bandsmen became the pride not only of Lark Force but also of Rabaul, playing at all kinds of civic events in addition to their military duties. Boxing tournaments drew large crowds, and the band entertained them with marches and popular tunes between rounds. A favorite was the "Colonel Bogey March," to which the soldiers loudly sang their own bawdy lyrics. Gullidge was embarrassed but went along with the fun, making up for it on Sundays by singing in the Methodist church, one of Rabaul's most established Protestant houses of worship.

Soldiers who attended religious services in camp were alternately led by one of the garrison's two army chaplains. Captain Victor S. Turner of England was a Catholic padre, and Lieutenant John L. May of Tasmania represented the Protestants. Religious differences notwithstanding, the two men could hardly have been more dissimilar. At forty-seven, Turner was one of the oldest men in Lark Force, and as one officer put it, "only dire threats of punishment could secure anything like full attendance at Church Parade." May was more than twenty years younger than Turner, and his spontaneous, enthusiastic personality appealed widely to the troops.

Religion and faith were important to a great majority of contemporary Australians. A significant percentage of those living among the mandated islands were missionaries, making it inevitable that members of Lark Force would interact with some of them. During a detailed compass-and-chain survey of the Gazelle Peninsula, for example, a team from the intelligence section of the 2/22nd spent several days in the vicinity of Kalas, a Methodist mission school in the foothills of the Baining Mountains. Bill Harry befriended the Reverend and Mrs. John Poole, and the minister subsequently invited him on a "walkabout" to visit villages deep in the mountains. Harry was granted leave to go on the journey, and by the time they returned two weeks later, he knew more about the northern region of New Britain than anyone else in Lark Force.

Other soldiers gained some limited knowledge of the island during croc-hunting expeditions and hikes to explore the volcanoes, but such trips rarely went far from Rabaul. Furthermore, as the odorous discharge from Tavurvur continued to drift onto Malaguna Camp for weeks on end, most of the men lost their enthusiasm for tropical adventures. After the newness of their surroundings wore off, they grew weary of camp duties and garrison life in general, especially the bland army food. Consequently, the food service became the chief focus of their discontent.

The army diet of the day, like that in most Western cultures, was high in carbohydrates, protein, and sodium. A wartime study revealed that the per-capita consumption of beef in Australia was twice that of the United States, and Australians also ate more grains, twice the butter, and eleven times more mutton and lamb. The most common ration in the AIF was chopped-up meat, canned in gelatin to keep it moist. Known as "bully beef," it had been a staple of British and Commonwealth armies since before World War I. Other canned rations included "M and V" (meat and vegetables), the ubiquitous beans, and varieties of fruit. Somehow, an overabundance of tropical fruit salad had been shipped to Rabaul, forcing the cooks to serve it at virtually every meal. Before long, the soldiers loudly protested the seemingly endless supply. Some also complained that their tins of "Anzac biscuits" (cookies made of rolled oats) bore World War I labels.

A universal thread among armies is the observation that a bitching soldier is a happy soldier, which means that perceptions within Lark Force were normal. Similarly, a few of Rabaul's citizens began to grumble about the presence of so many soldiers, which put a strain on their once-quiet town. Accusations flew that Lark Force was poorly disciplined, and some veterans complained that soldiers who were nabbed for drunk and disorderly conduct in town were not being properly punished. Others protested the army canteen's underselling of its beer for half of what the same brands cost in Rabaul. If the old-timers tended to exaggerate the degree of rowdiness in the streets, they were partially correct in perceiving a problem within Lark Force.

It had not taken the men of the 2/22nd long to realize that Lieutenant Colonel Carr was unequal to the task of running a battalion-size force. Kindly but naïve, he was accustomed to being part of a larger organization where people with experience could lend help. At Rabaul he was on his own. Major Leggatt had received new orders to take over the 2/40th Battalion on Timor, and his departure left Carr unprepared for the responsibilities of leadership. Ultimately, Carr failed to gain the respect of his subordinates, who came to regard him as something of a joke. Behind his back they began to call him "the Bodger," slang for a bum coin, a loser.

The situation changed with the arrival of Colonel John J. "Joe" Scanlan, a decorated combat veteran. He arrived on October 8 and immediately took command of all ground forces in the New Guinea Area (NGA), while Carr stayed on as CO of the 2/22nd. Based on his combat record during multiple campaigns in World War I, including the receipt of a Legion of Honor, Scanlan certainly had the credentials for the job. Badly wounded at Gallipoli, he convalesced in Australia before returning to fight again in Europe, where he led a Tasmanian battalion through several campaigns and battles. After the war he made a failed attempt at farming along the Murray River, then accepted a position with the Tasmanian prison system. Reenlisting for another war, he arrived at Rabaul just prior to his fifty-first birthday.

Tasked with defending an enormous region, Scanlan had few resources to work with. At Rabaul alone, his priorities for Lark Force included not only the defense of the town but also the coastal guns at Praed Point, the seaplane base at Sulphur Creek, and *two* airdromes. In addition to the airdrome at Lakunai, there was a second airdrome eleven miles south of Rabaul named for a nearby Catholic mission, Vunakanau. Also known as "the Upper 'Drome," it sat on the plateau overlooking the caldera and served as a forward base for Royal Australian Air Force (RAAF) reconnaissance aircraft. In all, the line Lark Force had to defend extended from Praed Point all the way around the caldera to Raluana Point—a total of fifteen miles.

Initially, Scanlan made no changes to the fortified positions occupied by the 2/22nd battalion. Two rifle companies—A Company under Major William T. Owen and B Company under Captain Colin L. McInnes—were considered in reserve at Malaguna Camp. C Company, led by Captain Ernest S. "Pip" Appel, was deployed at Vunakanau; D Company, led by Captain Richard E. Travers, guarded a major intersection called Four Ways; and R Company, under Captain Frank E. "Eric" Shier, was entrenched at Praed Point.

It was virtually impossible for a single infantry battalion to defend a fifteen-mile-long line; therefore, the rifle companies were dispersed between a half-dozen strategic points. As for weapons, the infantrymen were armed with .303-caliber Lee-Enfield rifles (which predated World War I), supported by machine gun teams that used identical ammunition.

The automatic weapons included twenty-six Lewis light machine guns, twelve Vickers water-cooled medium machine guns, and two old Maxim machine guns commandeered from the native police. The Vickers and Maxim guns were cumbersome, requiring vehicles for all but the shortest moves. The same was true of the twelve 3-inch mortars, which utilized heavy base plates and tripods. If the mortars and machine guns had to be moved a significant distance, fully tracked Universal Carriers, also known as Bren Gun Carriers, were employed by the Carrier Platoon. However, the battalion was not considered a mobile force despite the possession of the tracked vehicles.

A WEEK AFTER SCANLAN'S ARRIVAL, LARK FORCE RECEIVED SOME GOOD news: the War Cabinet announced that the United States would provide additional fortifications around Simpson Harbor through the Lend-Lease program. The Americans would contribute six 7-inch coastal defense guns, eight 3-inch antiaircraft guns, and twelve heavy machine guns, all of which would represent a huge improvement over the current defenses. Oddly, the proposal failed to address the need for aircraft. Without planes, especially fighters, no amount of coastal weapons or antiaircraft guns would provide Rabaul with adequate air defense. Unfortunately, despite the fact that the Battle of Britain had proven the importance of aerial superiority, the Allies largely ignored the concept.

The Japanese, on the other hand, placed great emphasis on control of the skies. Reconnaissance planes of the Imperial Navy appeared over Rabaul as early as June 1941, as noted by Lieutenant Peter E. Figgis, the 2/22nd's senior intelligence officer. The first aircraft he sighted, a twin-engine Type 96 naval bomber, almost certainly came from Truk, seven hundred miles to the north. Since then, several other reconnaissance aircraft, including floatplanes from Japanese warships, had been observed overhead.

The sightings put Figgis in the spotlight. Born in England, he had soldiering in his blood. His father, a British mining engineer, was wounded while serving in France with the Royal Engineers and received a Military Cross for gallantry. After the war the family moved to Australia, where Peter earned a lieutenant's commission by drilling on weekends with the Melbourne University Rifles. Tall and tanned, he strongly resembled

British actor Alec Guinness. Sporting a clipped moustache that accentuated his mischievous grin, Figgis established a reputation as "a very capable fellow" and was transferred to Colonel Scanlan's NGA staff. November 16, which happened to be Figgis' twenty-sixth birthday, was highlighted by a spectacular blast from Tavurvur, the biggest eruption yet of the on-going disturbance. Figgis was unimpressed. He was tired of "the stink of bad eggs" and the corrosive effects of the ash, which caused chronic problems with the telephone lines and made his job of communicating between observation posts difficult.

AS THE YEAR 1941 DREW TO A CLOSE, FIGGIS WAS NOT THE ONLY ONE disenchanted with the situation facing Lark Force. Others knew instinctively that their position was weak, and they looked ahead to the promised Lend-Lease support from the United States. Some were no doubt pleased to hear General MacArthur claim publicly that the Japanese were overextended in China and would not attempt any aggression prior to the spring of 1942. When Sir Earle Page visited the Philippines in early October, McArthur told him that Japan was incapable of launching a Pacific war without a lengthy recuperative period. Page heard similar assessments in Washington, D.C. during the extended fact-finding trip, and later, his younger brother at Rabaul was among those who "collected the spray from this wave of optimism."

Despite such reassurances, Tokyo's militant actions had become a tangible threat, and by the first of December the Australians at Rabaul had good reason to be concerned. They were reasonably well informed, thanks to Amalgamated Wireless of Australasia (AWA), which had a station capable of pulling in broadcasts from around the world. In addition, the *Rabaul Times* provided timely articles about current events. On December 2, for example, the newspaper reported that the War Cabinet had conducted an emergency meeting the previous day in Melbourne and cancelled all military leave. It was portentous news, but Australians everywhere clung to the hope that the Japanese would be intimidated into pulling back from the brink—an illusion that was shattered when the Japanese blasted Pearl Harbor and several other Allied bases on December 8, Tokyo time. Even then, many people tried to rationalize what had happened, speculating that some "madness had overtaken Japan to challenge so great an enemy with so spectacular an insult."

Of course, the Japanese had done much more than hurl an insult, and there was little greatness apparent among the various Allied forces involved. Not only did the carrier planes of the Imperial Japanese Navy make a complete shambles of Pearl Harbor, but MacArthur had been caught flat-footed in the Philippines despite hours of advance warning. For all his boasting, he was principally to blame for the near-annihilation of the Far East Air Force (FEAF), America's largest overseas air component. Worst of all, at least from Lark Force's viewpoint, was the realization that the Lend-Lease fortifications promised by the United States had suddenly evaporated.

AT RABAUL, MOST AUSTRALIANS LEARNED ABOUT THE BOMBING OF PEARL Harbor from radio broadcasts. David Selby, the commander of the antiaircraft battery, first heard the news at breakfast on December 8. The mess hall conversation, he recalled, "was full of excited speculation about what was in store." Selby knew that numerous preparations still lay ahead—the guns had to be moved from the beach, for one thing—so immediately after breakfast he met with Colonel Scanlan for instructions.

Within hours, the two gun carriages had been towed up a narrow, serpentine road to Dr. Fisher's volcano observatory on the North Daughter. The long-barreled guns were unlimbered on the front lawn, and soon thereafter the geologist's residence was transformed into a fortified emplacement, every available space filled with piles of ammunition, supplies, and the personal effects of fifty-four officers and men. Fisher was aggravated at first, but in due time he accepted the necessary intrusion. Later he took up arms himself by signing on with the NGVR.

Soon after the battery was in place, the irrepressible Aussies nailed a sign bearing the name "Frisbee Ridge" to a coconut tree. It was a tribute to their popular commander, Captain Selby, who had followed a general recommendation that officers "ought to get a bit of hair on their faces." By cultivating a luxuriant moustache, he prompted the men to nickname him "Frisbee," a parody of the "mythical British Army officer type."

Manning their guns at 0430 every morning, the crews waited for the Japanese to come. From their lofty perch atop the North Daughter, Selby and his gunners never failed to be impressed by the spectacular colors that flared across the eastern horizon each morning, and almost every evening they enjoyed a similar extravaganza when the sun dipped low in the western sky. However, as the days passed with no action, the gun crews grew bored with the routine.

IN MELBOURNE, THE WAR CABINET SCRAMBLED TO RESPOND TO THE SUDDEN onset of war in the Pacific. Australian territory was not under immediate threat, but the Malay Peninsula had been invaded and units of the Imperial Japanese Army were rapidly advancing southward toward the 8th Division in Singapore. In response, the service chiefs made several critical decisions.

First, anticipating that the Japanese would attempt to occupy Ambon, Timor, and Rabaul, the brass decided that the current deployment of the 23rd Brigade would have to be enough: there would be no additional strengthening of the existing garrisons. Secondly, the War Cabinet decided not to place any large ships at risk in order to assist the isolated garrisons. And lastly, realizing that the occupation of the Bismarck Archipelago would be high on Tokyo's list of priorities, the cabinet was determined that Lark Force in particular should hold out for as long as possible.

The Minister for External Affairs, Herbert "Doc" Evatt, clarified the situation by sending a secret cablegram to President Roosevelt via the Australian ambassador. "In making this recommendation," he wrote, "we desire to emphasize the fact that the scale of attack which can be brought against Rabaul from bases in the Japanese mandated islands is beyond the capacity of the small garrison to meet successfully. Notwithstanding this, we consider it essential to maintain a forward air observation line as long as possible and to make the enemy fight for this line rather than abandon it at the first threat."

In other words, the government wanted to preserve the illusion that Australia was capable of defending itself, and was prepared to expend the garrison for that purpose. As a result, no contingency plans were made to rescue any soldiers who might survive the pending invasion. Lark Force was trapped on New Britain. There would be no relief, no miraculous Dunkirk.

Further evidence of Canberra's position regarding Lark Force appeared on December 12, a mere four days after Pearl Harbor. On behalf of Prime Minister Curtin, the War Cabinet transmitted another secret cable to Washington in which they acknowledged not only the likelihood of the garrison's defeat, but that there would be no rescue for survivors: "It would appear under present circumstances that the proposed plan [for American Lend-Lease support] will be greatly delayed or even impossible to fulfill . . . Under the foregoing circumstances, and as reinforcements and subsequent supply would be hazardous without United States cooperation, it is considered better to maintain Rabaul only as an advance air operational base, its present small garrison being regarded as hostages to fortune."

Hostages, no less! Weeks before the first shot was fired in the Bismarcks, Canberra essentially washed its hands of Lark Force on New Britain, the 1st Independent Company on New Ireland, and hundreds of civilians living in the region. Only a few days had passed since Pearl Harbor, yet the government was already willing to condemn the garrisons to whatever fate the Japanese had planned for them. The War Cabinet evidently wanted to appear resolute, but their actions in this case could hardly have looked more feeble.

The great irony was that the Japanese did not plan to invade Rabaul any sooner than the middle of January, more than a month away. The timing no longer mattered, however. Lark Force had already been given up for lost.

IN ALL FAIRNESS TO THE ECONOMICALLY STRAPPED COMMONWEALTH, THE War Cabinet did make two concessions on behalf of the Rabaul garrison. The first was the transfer of a Royal Australian Air Force composite squadron from its base in Queensland to Vunakanau airdrome. A trio of twin-engine Lockheed Hudsons from 24 Squadron landed on the grassy strip on December 7, and another arrived the following day. Next, ten CA-1 Wirraways landed at Vunakanau over a period of days, the last arriving on December 12. Employed as fighters by the RAAF, the two-seater CA-1s were actually duplicates of the North American AT-6 trainer, built in Australia under license by the Commonwealth Aircraft Corporation.

Commanded by Squadron Leader John M. Lerew, a veteran with eleven years of service in the RAAF, the pilots at Vunakanau were dismayed to find only a few structures in place. The most substantial was a piece of galvanized roofing on poles which served as both hangar and workshop. Flight Lieutenant Wilfred D. Brookes, the squadron's second in command, groused that "no facilities existed for operations, stores, medical section, armament, photographic, or parachute sections. Messing was provided by the army some distance from the aerodrome and left much to be desired."

In truth, just about everything at Rabaul fell short of expectations. The conditions that 24 Squadron experienced were simply consistent with the limitations which plagued Lark Force and almost every other Allied unit in the Pacific.

Canberra's second concession was a last-minute decision to evacuate the women and children from the mandated territory: European women and children, that is. Asians and Melanesians would have to fend for themselves. The evacuees were allowed one suitcase per person, and some families received only one or two days' notice to proceed to the nearest embarkation point. One passenger ship was dispatched to Port Moresby and two others were sent to Rabaul, where most of the European families outside New Guinea were instructed to gather.

Not all women were able to leave. The six civilian nurses at Namanula Hospital were considered essential public servants according to the local health director, who denied permission for them to evacuate. Harold Page, still the senior government authority at Rabaul, intervened and permitted the nurses to decide for themselves. One elderly nurse elected to sail for Australia, but the other five stayed, and the vacant position was actually filled by a retired nurse.

No such options existed for the six army nurses: they remained with the staff attached to the 2/10 Field Ambulance at the Government House hospital. Similarly, the nuns and female staff at Vunapope considered themselves duty-bound to remain at the mission, as did many women among the Protestant missions. Other strong-minded, independent women living among the islands—including several widowed plantation owners—ignored the evacuation notices and vowed to never give up their hard-earned properties. A few didn't have much choice. Alfred A. "Ted" Harvey, a former coastwatcher, chose to move his wife and eleven-year-old son to a camp hidden in the jungle near their plantation on the north coast of New Britain.

But for every holdout, hundreds of women and children did converge on Rabaul. By the afternoon of December 22, the Burns-Philp liners *Macdhui* and *Neptuna* were ready to embark passengers. The skies, dark with rain, reflected the somber mood throughout town as the evacuees filed aboard the two ships and found their assigned cabins. "There was a hushed atmosphere as the mothers and children gathered," remembered Diana Martell, then eleven years old. "Most of our fathers were still at work. When at last they came aboard, our parents were all talking earnestly, and there was the feeling that something really serious was happening. It was dark when I was called into our cabin to say goodbye to my father. I was not really distressed, as I could hardly imagine that I would never see him again."

Similar scenes were repeated in almost every stateroom. The bespectacled Rev. Laurie McArthur, the senior Methodist missionary in New Britain, said goodbye to his family; and John Poole, the missionary who had traveled the mountains with Bill Harry, bid farewell to Jean. The couple, married only two years earlier in the Rabaul Methodist church, had been happy at their mission at Kalas, and she was extremely reluctant to leave everything behind. But so it went, among hundreds of families aboard both ships.

That afternoon, a schooner sailed into the harbor carrying twenty rain-soaked women and children from Bougainville. The cabins aboard the two liners were already filled, so the newcomers were ushered into one of the *Macdhui's* salons just as darkness fell. The men were called ashore, and families said their last goodbyes, everyone trying to mask their concerns with lighthearted quips and other acts of bravado. The atmosphere that night seemed altogether foreboding, and for good reason. Within months, virtually every family present would be touched by the worst maritime disaster in Australian history.

In the days following the evacuation, the mood in Rabaul grew even more somber. The few Japanese families in the area were rounded up, but unlike their counterparts in America, only the men were interned. The Burns-Philp liner *Malaita* delivered them to Australia while the women and children tried to subsist on their own.

Many of the two-hundred-odd Australian civilians who remained on the Gazelle Peninsula stayed busy by digging slit trenches in their gardens. They also participated in air raid drills under the watchful eye of longtime territorial official Robert L. "Nobby" Clark, the chief warden. A civil engineer by trade, he organized the construction of a community air raid shelter just outside of town. The facility, located in a small valley dubbed "Refuge Gully," featured thatch-roofed huts named in jest after famous hotels. Arrangements were made to have various civic groups provide valet parking and serve afternoon tea, but the frivolous notions were abandoned after the women and children departed for Australia.

By late December, Rabaul seemed like a ghost town. The Christmas season—normally the start of the summer holidays for Australians—was gloomy. The only thing that held anyone's interest for long was the war news, especially the propaganda broadcasts from Tokyo. The army camp became a breeding ground for all sorts of wild rumors, including one that had the town's Chinese laborers making hundreds of grave markers, ostensibly for the men of Lark Force. Concerned about the effects such tales would have on morale, Captain Selby wrote detailed notes of the next radio broadcast, then typed out the particulars under the heading: "A.A. News Bulletin." The information sheet was passed around, and quickly gained such popularity that daily updates were distributed to all units.

Despite Selby's upbeat approach, an atmosphere of misgiving was kindled in Lark Force, primarily by Colonel Scanlan. On New Year's Day, 1942, he posted two ominous-sounding proclamations. "Every man will fight to the last," he wrote, followed by the boldly underlined announcement: "THERE SHALL BE NO WITHDRAWAL." Perhaps he had learned of the War Cabinet's position regarding the garrison, but if so, he kept the grim facts to himself. As a result, the abruptness of his declarations both puzzled and disturbed the garrison.

Scanlan's posturing may also have resulted from his perception that certain officers in Lark Force lacked fighting spirit. During a staff meeting, Captain Selby made the mistake of asking whether there was a contingency plan in the event that a withdrawal became necessary. Scanlan snorted, "That is a defeatist attitude, Selby!" In a different incident, the 2/22nd's supply officer recommended hiding some of the massive quantities of canned food—two years' worth had been stockpiled at Rabaul—in several strategically placed caches in the jungle. Scanlan's response was similar: he gruffly denied permission.

Nonetheless, members of the staff continued to quietly consider the alternatives to a pitched battle against the Japanese. The most logical idea was to pull back into the jungle and harass the enemy with guerilla-style warfare. Several men possessed considerable knowledge of the terrain, especially Private Harry, but when members of the NGA staff brought up the supply officer's suggestion again, Scanlan would not budge. "You will fight on the beaches," he told them brusquely. He may have intended to exhibit the sort of stalwart defiance that Winston Churchill showed before the Battle of Britain, but his attempt fell short. This was not England.

The colonel's stubbornness revealed a critical shortcoming: Scanlan was apparently still fighting the last war, at least in his mind. The weapons had not changed, and his own record for combat bravery was beyond question, but most of the conventions of that war were long outdated. Scanlan possessed other idiosyncrasies as well. A devout Roman Catholic, he sometimes went off to Vunapope for "retreats" that lasted days. At other times he just seemed out of touch, not only with the coming war but with his own troops.

To cope with his supercilious manner, Scanlan's subordinates held their tongues and hoped for the best. Few, if any, realized that they had already been cast off by their own government.

CHAPTER FOUR

PRELUDE TO AN INVASION

"We who are about to die salute you."

—Squadron Leader John Lerew,
RAAF 24 Squadron

Lark Force and 24 Squadron were terribly disadvantaged. Not only were they expected to defend an enormous region with inadequate weapons and equipment, they knew very little about the enemy they would have to face. Few people in the Western world did.

Only a few decades earlier, the island nation of Japan had been a feudal state, developmentally backward compared to the world's industrialized countries, and almost completely closed to foreigners. In a remarkably brief period, however, a central government radically overhauled the empire. By the conclusion of World War I, Japan had emerged as one of the five most powerful nations on Earth. Her people, believing they were linked by common mythical and spiritual origins going back almost 2,600 years, had never been defeated by outside invaders. Brimming with nationalistic fervor, the Japanese believed themselves superior in virtually every way to other races, especially those of the Eastern hemisphere.

The Japanese were determined to rule a much larger empire, but their own tiny islands lacked sufficient natural resources. Therefore, they created a program called the Greater East Asia Co-Prosperity Sphere, under the guise of which they intended to occupy territories rich in oil, rubber, and other resources important for continued industrialization. The expansion began in September 1931, thanks to a trumped-up clash with Chinese troops that Japan used to justify the occupation of Manchuria.

Almost ten years later, Japan "peacefully" entered French Indochina in the summer of 1941, after first sending a note to the Vichy regime demanding the right to occupy their country. Alarmed by the takeover, the American government responded by freezing all Japanese assets in the United States and placing an embargo on exports to the Japanese, particularly oil. Great Britain, the Philippines, and the Netherlands quickly followed suit by cutting off Japan's access to oil supplies in the Far East. The Tokyo leadership was infuriated. Many Japanese had hoped to avoid war against the coalition of countries in the Pacific, but as petroleum stockpiles dwindled to dangerously low levels—less than two years' worth for the empire's fleets and armies—the government and Imperial General Headquarters were pushed into a belligerent position from which there was no turning back.

Tokyo had already started preparing for war. Military planners completed their outline for the Southern Offensive, a massive, multi-pronged strike across the Pacific. On November 6, Imperial General Headquarters mobilized the Southern Army for the invasion of the Philippines, Malaya, and parts of Burma and Thailand; simultaneously the South Seas Detachment, an independent organization under the direct command of General Headquarters, was formed for operations against Guam and the Bismarck Archipelago.

The acquisition of strategic islands was a key element of the overall plan. Once fortified, the island bases would allow the military to secure a perimeter around the newly occupied territories, thereby forming an empire of truly hemispherical proportions. From the Kurile Islands, the line would extend southward to the Gilberts and the Marianas in the Central Pacific, then southwest through the Solomon Islands and the Bismarcks to New Guinea, and finally around Java and Sumatra to Burma—a total of more than twelve thousand miles. As a major component of that strategy, the South Seas Detachment had specific orders to capture Guam in cooperation with the 4th Fleet, after which the combined forces were to "occupy Rabaul at the earliest opportunity and establish air bases on New Britain."

Clearly, the Japanese considered Rabaul to be a vital objective of the Southern Offensive. Simpson Harbor would be developed into a major fleet headquarters, and there was ample flat terrain south of the caldera for the development of additional airfields. Rabaul was slated to become the hub of the Southeast Area, a stronghold from which new campaigns would be launched. As the center for both Imperial Army and Navy operations in the Southeast Area, it would eclipse even the great naval base at Truk.

When the Southern Offensive commenced on December 8, Tokyo time, the 5,500 troops of the South Seas Detachment were already en route to Guam, a small island in the Marianas defended by only 153 U.S. Marines and a few hundred Guamanian militiamen. Land-based Imperial Navy bombers from nearby Saipan began to pound the defenses that same day, and were joined by floatplanes from a tender attached to the 4th Fleet the next day. Consequently, when the invasion troops stormed ashore on December 10, the American garrison surrendered within minutes.

THE SOUTH SEAS DETACHMENT, RAISED THE PREVIOUS YEAR ON THE ISLAND of Shikoku, was led by fifty-one-year-old Major General Tomitaro Horii. A veteran of the war against China, he had fought in Shanghai ten years earlier and more recently commanded the 55th Infantry Group, from which his current forces were drawn. The main combat elements were the 1st, 2nd and 3rd Battalions of the 144th Infantry Regiment supported by the 3rd Company of the 55th Cavalry Regiment, a battalion of the 55th Mountain Artillery Regiment, and a company of the 55th Engineers. Ancillaries included a signals unit, a transportation company, a field hospital, a veterinarian unit (to care for the hundreds of horses used by the detachment), and a battalion of antiaircraft artillery.

The South Seas Detachment also included several hundred members of the Maizuru 2nd Special Naval Landing Force, presently involved in operations at hotly contested Wake. Often referred to as "marines," a misnomer, the SNLF excelled at amphibious assault tactics and specialized in beachhead defenses, including the rapid deployment of antiaircraft guns. After Wake fell on December 23, the naval infantry rejoined Horii's forces on Guam.

Back at full strength, the South Seas Detachment spent the rest of December preparing for the invasion of New Britain and New Ireland. On January 3, 1942, Horii and several other officers boarded a flying boat and flew 630 miles southeast to Truk for an important meeting with Vice Admiral Shigeyoshi Inoue, commander of the 4th Fleet. After their plane touched down in the lagoon, the army staff met with their navy counterparts in the wardroom of the light cruiser *Katori*, Inoue's flagship.

Such cooperation between the Imperial Army and Navy was unusual. Normally the two services shared a fierce rivalry, but they were under specific orders to work together. The directive from General Headquarters called for both services to "coordinately attack Rabaul" and specified that all defenders in the Bismarck Archipelago were to be "annihilated." Fond of using Roman letters, the Japanese gave the name R Operation to the invasion of the Bismarcks.

In the *Katori*'s wardroom, the assembled officers exchanged intelligence data, most of it obtained from aerial reconnaissance. The consensus was that Rabaul would be defended by a force of "about 500" soldiers, but allowed that a total of fifteen hundred Australian troops might be present. The Japanese were also aware of a "volunteer defense force," almost certainly a reference to the New Guinea Volunteer Rifles, which strongly indicates that some of their intelligence was provided by spies. It was true that many civilians at Rabaul still had unrestricted access to Australian positions, and members of Lark Force suspected Axis sympathizers of passing information to the enemy. But the Japanese did not interpret everything accurately. Rear Admiral Kiyohide Shima, commander of the warships that would escort the invasion fleet, received intelligence that the defenders might have as many as ten coastal gun emplacements on Crater Peninsula. Possibly because of this erroneous information, the assembled staff decided that the invasion should be made at night.

The next step was to discuss potential beachheads. The Japanese officers considered three landing sites: Kokopo, Talili Bay, and the Rabaul waterfront. They dismissed the first on the flimsy rationale that "the enemy will heavily guard the place as it was a landing point of the British army during the First World War." Likewise, they arbitrarily rejected Talili Bay on New Britain's north shore on the grounds "that the enemy must have set up some obstacles; that the enemy may quickly discover us because of lookout posts at Watom Island, and that well-grown coral reefs may hamper our landing." Compared with those arguments, some of the assembled officers deemed an assault deep inside Simpson Harbor "foolhardy," but it offered the most expedient means of capturing the two airfields. Therefore, the officers gave approval for a direct assault, albeit with a broadly worded escape clause: "The army plan will be adopted, but if the situation demands, the landing will be made at Kokopo instead."

Based on the approved invasion plan, the assault on Rabaul was going to be highly unorthodox. Few commanders would have considered making a large-scale amphibious landing into so deep a harbor, especially at night, but Horii and his staff put together a solid tactical plan. By landing in the darkest hour of the night with an overwhelming number of troops, they would use the element of surprise to smash through the Australian defenses.

ARRIVING BACK AT GUAM ON JANUARY 4, HORII RECEIVED ORDERS FROM Imperial General Headquarters to occupy Rabaul "as quickly as possible after around the middle of January." This was predicted to be the most appropriate time for a night invasion, as there would be little or no visible moonlight. The timetable also allowed for a period of preliminary bombing attacks to soften up the Australian defenses. For that purpose, two air groups from the Imperial Japanese Navy's 24th *Koku Sentai* (Air Flotilla) had already shifted about half their strength from the Marshall Islands to Truk. The experienced aircrews, undoubtedly eager to launch their first attack against the Australians, did not have long to wait.

ON THE MORNING OF THE FOURTH DAY OF 1942, A BRIGHT, CLEAR SUNDAY, a young plantation owner named Cornelius "Con" Page observed a formation of twin-engine bombers flying over his coconut groves. Recruited two years earlier into Lieutenant Commander Feldt's coastwatching service, Page was an adventurous Australian living on the tiny island of Tabar, just east of New Ireland. Warming up his big Amalgamated Wireless 3B radio, he sent word of the sighting to Port Moresby, which in turn relayed the information to Fortress Signals, the Lark Force communications unit on New Britain: Japanese bombers were headed directly toward Rabaul.

The air raid sirens began to wail shortly after 1100. Given ample warning, the antiaircraft gunners atop Frisbee Ridge waited almost thirty long minutes for the bombers to appear. Finally they droned into view, high above Watom Island off New Britain's north shore, a perfect V formation coming directly toward the battery. "It seemed impossible to believe that they were bent on destruction," remembered David Selby, "so serene and beautiful did they look." The youthful gunners were keyed up, talking and even laughing to hide their jitters. Someone asked Selby, "Can we really fire this time?"

"Too right we can," he said, "but for heaven's sake shut up. This is a war, not a Sunday school picnic."

As the planes came within range, the gun director shouted out elevation numbers and fuse settings to the crews, then yelled, "Fire!" Surprised at first by the ear-splitting noise and the heat reflected from those first shots, the gunners quickly settled down. They got off round after round from the two aging weapons, but even with the fuses set for maximum altitude, none of the shells reached the bombers' height. The only thing worth celebrating was the successful operation of the Number 2 gun's cracked breech; otherwise, the men watched helplessly as the formation flew over untouched and dropped their bombs in the vicinity of Lakunai airdrome.

According to Japanese records, a total of sixteen Navy Type 96 Land Attack Aircraft participated in the first strike against Rabaul. Known to the Allies as Mitsubishi G3Ms, the twin-engine bombers were part of the Chitose *Kokutai* (Naval Air Group) and possessed a combat radius the Australians could only dream of. The crews were highly trained, but in this case most of their bombs missed. Only three of the 60-kilo, high-fragmentation devices struck the runway, and another twenty killed fish in Simpson Harbor. Disastrously, the remaining seventeen bombs landed in the Rapindik Native Hospital and labor compound.

Designed for antipersonnel use, the so-called "daisy cutters" created terrible carnage when they exploded within the confined area. Fifteen natives were killed outright and fifteen others wounded, many with parts of limbs severed and other horrific injuries from the spinning shards of shrapnel. However, the loss of the natives did not greatly trouble Lark Force, and the contemporary accounts either glossed over the casualties or neglected to mention them at all. Major Palmer, the senior medical officer, stated in his report that the attack had not caused any casualties. Evidently, thirty dead or wounded natives didn't count.

THE JAPANESE STRUCK AGAIN AT DUSK. THIS TIME THE FORMATION consisted of Type 97 Flying Boats (Kawanishi H6Ks) from the Yokohama *Kokutai*. With their long parasol wings and slender fuselages tapering upward toward twin rudders, the four-engine planes resembled enormous dragonflies as they paraded overhead. The antiaircraft gunners counted eleven aircraft (Japanese records show nine), but none came within range of the battery. Aiming for Vunakanau airdrome, the flying boats dropped an estimated forty bombs, all of which missed by a wide margin in the rapidly fading twilight.

The next raid occurred on the morning of January 6. Several of the huge flying boats returned to hit Vunakanau again, and for some reason Con Page failed to provide an early warning. Serious damage resulted: A direction-finding station and a Wirraway were destroyed by direct hits, a Hudson was damaged, and the runway was pocked with craters. A single Wirraway attempted to intercept the formation and briefly managed to close within firing range, but the bombers took cover in some handy clouds and soon pulled away.

The following morning another formation of attackers flew over Page's plantation on Tabar. This time he radioed the alarm, having counted eighteen twin-engine bombers on a course for Rabaul at 1030. Two Wirraways immediately took off to intercept the formation, but once again the anemic fighters failed to make contact. At 1108 the Mitsubishis dropped their bombs on Vunakanau airdrome without opposition, demolishing a Hudson, a Wirraway, and some temporary buildings. Two more Hudsons parked near the runway suffered damage.

The Japanese ceased their raiding for the next several days, content to conduct high-altitude reconnaissance flights beyond the reach of the anti-aircraft guns. In the meantime, the RAAF organized a unique mission of its own. A specially prepared Mark IV Hudson of 6 Squadron flew from Kavieng to Truk on January 9 and returned with photographic evidence of a major buildup. (The daring flight, which exceeded 1,400 miles, was the longest combat mission yet undertaken by the RAAF.) The serviceable Wirraways at Rabaul were sent on daily scouting patrols, but their few attempts to intercept Japanese snoopers were negative.

The pre-invasion strikes resumed on January 16. Shortly past noon, a flight of nineteen Mitsubishi bombers destroyed a fuel dump, a bomb dump, and a store of flares at Vunakanau. Several hours later, a formation of five Kawanishi flying boats dropped fragmentation bombs on Lakunai, causing minor damage. Based on the systematic nature of the attacks, it was obvious that the Japanese were attempting to neutralize the airdromes while avoiding collateral damage to Rabaul. The Australians correctly interpreted this to mean that an invasion was pending. The only questions yet to be answered were the enemy's timetable and his current whereabouts.

Ironically, the War Cabinet had already received intelligence reports showing that not one but *two* enemy fleets were headed toward the Bismarck Archipelago. Inexplicably, that vital information was not forwarded to Rabaul, and the Commonwealth's indifference ultimately led to a chain reaction of unfortunate events.

ON JANUARY 14, THE NORWEGIAN-REGISTERED FREIGHTER *HERSTEIN* arrived from Port Moresby with a mixed cargo that included six Bren gun carriers, three thousand drums of aviation fuel, eighty Thompson submachine guns, and approximately two thousand aerial bombs. The wharves and warehouses were already full, so the bombs were stacked in the open alongside Malaguna Road. Lieutenant Hugh A. Mackenzie, the senior RAN officer at Rabaul, did not want the *Herstein* to be caught dockside by the next Japanese raid, so he cabled his superiors for permission to get the vessel underway as soon as the cargo was unloaded. The request was flatly denied. Instead, the government insisted that the freighter take on a full cargo of copra at the Burns, Philp & Company wharf, and loading began forthwith.

Harold Page tried to intervene on behalf of the Australian civilians, for whom there would be few other opportunities to evacuate. On January 15 he initiated a request to higher authorities for transportation aboard the *Herstein* for himself and the other men in town. Getting no response, he "continued to pester Canberra for instructions" until finally a terse reply came back several days later: "No one is to take the place of the copra on the *Herstein*." The response was yet another example of the Commonwealth's apathy, only in this case it directly affected hundreds of civilians. Lark Force had already been cast aside to fend for itself, and now Canberra ignored an opportunity to evacuate the non-combatants. Furthermore, the information that two enemy fleets were approaching Rabaul was still withheld. Perhaps the government rationalized that everyone was better off not knowing, the presumption being that a widespread panic might break out if the unvarnished truth were revealed.

R OPERATION HAD COMMENCED DAYS EARLIER. AT 1330 ON JANUARY 14, the South Seas Force Transport Fleet—nine ships carrying more than 5,300 men, hundreds of horses, and thousands of tons of vehicles and equipment—departed Apra Harbor, Guam. The troopships soon met an escorting fleet of warships that included three light cruisers, nine destroyers, and two large minelayers led by Rear Admiral Shima, commanding officer of the 19th Squadron. High above, reconnaissance planes out of Saipan scouted ahead for possible submarines.

Three days later, an even mightier fleet of warships departed Truk for a prearranged rendezvous with Horii's force near the equator. Fresh from their recent success at Pearl Harbor, four aircraft carriers of the 1st Air Fleet, commanded by pug-faced Vice Admiral Chuichi Nagumo, would be used to pummel the remaining defenses at Rabaul. Replenished in Japan, the *Akagi* and *Kaga* of the 1st Carrier Division carried a total of fifty-four Type 0 Carrier Fighters (Mitsubishi A6M2s, or Zeros), forty-five Type 99 Carrier Bombers (Aichi D3A1s), and fifty-four Type 97 Carrier Attack Aircraft (Nakajima B5N2s) which could be armed with either torpedoes or bombs. Similarly, the 5th Carrier Division (*Zuikaku* and *Shokaku*) added thirty fighters, fifty-four dive bombers, and fifty-four level bombers to the arsenal. Additionally, as if such an overwhelming strike force wasn't enough, Nagumo had the big guns of the battleships *Hiei* and *Kirishima* for fleet support. The capital ships were protected in turn by the heavy cruisers *Tone* and *Chikuma*, the light cruiser *Abukuma*, and nine destroyers. Lastly, Nagumo deployed two squadrons of submarines to patrol St. George's Channel and ambush any Allied ships that might happen along.

For the first few days out of Guam, the soldiers and sailors of Horii's invasion force enjoyed almost idyllic weather. The conditions changed drastically as they drew nearer the equator. "The heat began to increase all at once," wrote newspaper correspondent Toshio Miyake. "The decks seemed to be scorched and the cabins felt like steam baths. Sweat ran down our bodies like so many tiny waterfalls."

Miyake, who was likely aboard the army transport *Yokohama Maru* with Horii, was privileged if he was allotted some space in a cabin. The enlisted men were packed in the ship's stifling cargo holds by the hundreds. As far back as 1905, the Imperial Navy had introduced a method called the *tsubo* system for calculating the amount of personal space for soldiers aboard transports. The problem was that by 1941, the allowance had been cut to two-thirds of its original size, and the box-like holds were fitted with wooden 'tween decks to make use of wasted vertical space. Each soldier slept and stowed his gear on what amounted to a small platform, the total space adding up to only a few cubic yards.

Private Akiyoshi Hisaeda, from the Ehime Prefecture of Shikoku, kept a diary as he sailed to Rabaul aboard the transport *Venice Maru*. He described the conditions as "very cramped and uncomfortable," and noted that the temperature inside the ship reached 43 degrees Celsius (110 Fahrenheit). Life inside the other transports was equally awful. There was little fresh water, and the crude wooden *benjos* (latrines) were up on the main deck, which also happened to be where the meals were cooked. Down below, everyone was tormented by hordes of flies.

The Japanese soldiers were no strangers to terrible conditions or harsh environments. Their rigorous training system, based on the principle of instant obedience achieved through strict discipline, had prepared them well. From the moment they began training as recruits, they were immersed in a culture of degradation and abuse, a rude awakening for people who had spent their entire lives learning group harmony. Not only were recruits cursed and shamed in front of their peers, they were also beaten regularly. Sometimes they were hit on the buttocks with wooden sticks, other times they were slapped, usually with an open hand but occasionally with the sole from a hobnailed shoe. Many instructors were sadistic, barely more than thugs, and they had tremendous latitude to punish recruits with methods calculated to break down every vestige of individuality. Frequently the entire class or platoon received the same punishment: If one suffered, all suffered.

One of the cruelest penalties was meted out during evening meals. Picked at random, recruits were ordered to recite by memory from the *Gunjin Chokuyu*, "Emperor Meiji's Instructions to the Men of the Fighting Services." First issued in 1883, it exhorted warriors to carry out their duties with loyalty, propriety, valor, faithfulness, and simplicity. The wording was archaic, difficult to memorize, and if anyone made a mistake or forgot a passage, he was forbidden to eat. For recruits already bruised, exhausted, and ravenous from the day's training, the denial of food was excruciating. After six months or more of such extreme conditioning, the recruits emerged as well-disciplined soldiers, their "bodies and minds tempered hard as steel." The men of the South Seas Detachment were no different, and could tolerate anything that nature or the Imperial Army could throw at them.

WHEN THE INVASION FORCE REACHED THE EQUATOR AT 0500 ON JANUARY 20, the South Seas Detachment paused to commemorate a special event. In all of Japan's 2,600-year history, they were the first army force to cross the line. Miyake later described the scene aboard his vessel: "On the day we crossed the equator, all the men, fully armed and equipped, assembled on deck. 'At this time, when we are about to . . . advance into the southern hemisphere, we shall pay our respect toward the Imperial Palace,' said the commander toward his assembled subordinates. Solemnly, and with overflowing emotions, the men presented arms toward the north."

Without a doubt, the assembled troops also listened to motivational speeches designed to bolster their fighting spirit. One contemporary example, written by an Imperial Army lieutenant soon after the war began, drew upon the *samurai* ethics of ancient warriors:

> When we fight, we win. When we attack, we capture. The results of our recent glorious battles are acknowledged by all. . .
>
> The Imperial Family is the light, the life, the pride of Japan. In truth, Japan is Japan and the Japanese are Japanese because of the Imperial Family. From this consciousness the Japanese spirit is born. A loyalty is born, which utterly disregards the safety of the home and family—even one's own life—for the welfare of the Emperor and country. . .
>
> It is obvious that the road before us is not easy. We need strong determination to establish the New Order in Greater East Asia. Governors and governed must unite purposes and push ahead fearlessly with a single object in mind. Here I want to raise my voice and declare: "Carry out your duty with the Japanese spirit."
>
> The spirit of Bushido has been spoken of from olden

times in these words: "Among flowers, the cherry; among men, the warrior." With this spirit hold your ground without yielding a step, no matter what wounds you may receive, and thus make your end glorious by carrying out your duty calmly.

The soldiers were reminded constantly of the values extolled in the *Gunjin Chokuyu*, of which propriety was a keystone. "Inferiors should regard the orders of their superiors as issuing directly from Us," the instructions stated, which literally meant that verbal or written orders were to be construed as coming from the Emperor. This explains why the Japanese sometimes staged mindless banzai charges or committed suicide en masse without hesitation: they were merely complying with orders. In simple terms, it was relatively easy for a soldier to sacrifice himself at a superior's bidding. The alternative—refusing to die on the behalf of the Emperor—was the ultimate dishonor. Indeed, it would cause the soldier's family far more grief than his demise. The concept of surrender was so alien to the Japanese that they treated their own captives with absolute contempt. A man who willingly capitulated was as good as dead: something less than human.

IN ADDITION TO THE SPECIAL COMMEMORATION, THE SOLDIERS OF THE South Seas Detachment were treated to a naval spectacle on January 20. Nagumo's powerful carrier fleet arrived on schedule at the rendezvous point, and soon more than one hundred aircraft began taking off for a massive strike on Rabaul. In all, the attack force consisted of eighteen Nakajima bombers and nine Mitsubishi fighters from the *Akagi*, twenty-seven Nakajimas and nine fighters from the *Kaga*, and nineteen Aichi dive bombers each from the *Shokaku* and *Zuikaku*. Their leader was Commander Mitsuo Fuchida, renowned as the airborne commander at Pearl Harbor.

Adhering to Fuchida's strike plan, the aircraft gathered in three formations, the smallest numbering twenty planes, the largest more than fifty. Fuchida sent them off in three different directions, and at a prearranged time they turned inbound to attack Rabaul. Observing from one of the Nakajimas as the attack unfolded, Fuchida realized that his tactics were unnecessary. With such a massive force at his command, he "felt like a hunter sent to stalk a mouse with an elephant gun."

AT MIDDAY ON JANUARY 20, CON PAGE REPORTED THAT TWENTY AIRCRAFT had just passed over his plantation.* Despite the advance warning, the anti-aircraft crews at Rabaul were unprepared for the swiftness and ferocity of the Japanese attack. "The first indication of action," recalled Gunner David W. Bloomfield, "was our six remaining Wirraways wheeling and diving over Blanche Bay and not too far in front of our position. At first we thought that they were practicing maneuvers. Suddenly several aircraft swooped on them with amazing speed. It was like hawks attacking sparrows."

Two Wirraways were already patrolling the skies over Rabaul when Page's warning was received, and six more took off to intercept the attackers. However, one crash-landed at Lakunai due to engine failure, leaving only seven fighters to face the incoming raiders. But which way to turn first? The Wirraway pilots began to receive conflicting radio warnings in rapid succession. A formation of thirty-three planes was reported over Rabaul, having sneaked in undetected from the west, and another group of fifty enemy planes was spotted over the Duke of York Islands, just minutes away in the opposite direction. No wonder it looked as though the Wirraways were practicing maneuvers: the Australian pilots turned every which way as they tried to meet multiple threats.

The engagement was over in minutes. Three Wirraways were shot down in rapid succession, two others were forced down and crash-landed, one returned with repairable damage, and one landed safely with no battle damage. The Zeros had scored an entirely one-sided victory, killing six RAAF airmen and wounding five. Observers on the ground could scarcely believe what had happened. "We sat at our guns," remembered Bloomfield, "shocked by the massacre we had just witnessed."

After swatting aside the Wirraways, the Japanese bombed specific targets around Rabaul. At Vunakanau, the men of C Company had a difficult time compensating for the incredible speed of the carrier planes as they fought back with rifles and Lewis machine guns. The Japanese dropped dozens of bombs on or near the runway, of which at least twenty buried

---

* Page was awarded the rank of sub-lieutenant in the Royal Australian Naval Reserve in March 1942. Less than three months later he was captured by the Japanese and executed.

themselves in the soft ground without exploding. They penetrated to an average depth of fifteen feet, reported Captain Appel, whose troops spent hours digging up the duds. Miraculously, no one was hurt.

On the North Daughter, the antiaircraft battery opened fire with a continuous barrage the moment the enemy planes came into range. The crews finally succeeded in knocking down one plane, which crashed on the slopes of the Mother. An Australian tabloid later described the wreckage: "It was a bomber-fighter type, single engined. There were three dead Japs in it—stocky little fellows aged 24 or 25. Bombs were lying some little distance from the crashed plane." The pilot of the aircraft, a Nakajima Type 97 of the *Kaga*'s horizontal bombing unit, was Flight Petty Officer 1st Class Michinari Sugihara. A few weeks earlier, he and his two crewmen had participated in the attack on Pearl Harbor; now it was their destiny to become the first Japanese aviators killed at Rabaul.

Meanwhile, from their volcanic aerie atop Frisbee Ridge, the antiaircraft crews had a ringside view of an attack by several Type 99 dive bombers against the *Herstein*. The freighter was still loading copra at the Burns-Philp wharf when three aircraft swooped low and hit it squarely, starting several fires that quickly spread to the two thousand tons of oily cargo in her holds. Up in the superstructure, a defiant Norwegian sailor fought back with a mounted machine gun until forced by the flames to evacuate. Soon the intense fires enveloped most of the ship, which was set adrift when the mooring lines burned through. Eleven crewmen were killed and several others burned, some severely.

Other Aichi dive bombers concentrated on the *Westralia*, a once-elegant liner that had been out of service for years. Used as a floating coal bunker, the stationary hulk was an easy target and soon sank out of sight. Next the attackers swarmed over Lakunai airdrome, dropping bombs and machine-gunning the adjacent coconut groves to destroy encampments and supplies dispersed among the trees. The coastal guns at Praed Point received minor damage, after which a few planes tried to knock out the antiaircraft battery. Nothing but a precise hit on the razorback ridge would have destroyed the guns, but the crews held their collective breath anyway until the bombs tumbled down the slopes and exploded harmlessly.

Forty-five minutes after beginning the attack, the Japanese concluded it with a deliberate pageant. Zeros showboated with aerobatics and bombers wheeled overhead in formation, flaunting their power. Down below, plumes of smoke rose from the burning wharves and the red-hot hull of the *Herstein*, and clouds of dust swirled above both airdromes. Locally there had been few casualties aside from the Norwegian sailors, but the crewmen from the crash-landed Wirraways were hospitalized with an assortment of broken bones and bullet wounds.

At Vunakanau, Squadron Leader Lerew was doubly frustrated. Not only had the Japanese destroyed most of 24 Squadron, but his own superiors at Port Moresby were becoming antagonistic. Soon after the attack, a message from RAAF Operations and Signals ordered him to strike back at the enemy with "all available aircraft." Lerew had two Wirraways remaining, but one needed repairs and neither was fitted with universal bomb racks. The lone undamaged Hudson would have to do the job, a suicide mission against the powerful enemy fleet. A crew bravely manned the bomber and took off to find the Japanese ships, but they failed to find anything before darkness blanketed the ocean.

Glad to have the Hudson back, Lerew sent a message to Port Moresby stating that he intended to use the bomber to evacuate his wounded men. Headquarters had other ideas, and their next message instructed him to keep the squadron in a combat-ready status. Exasperated, Lerew turned to his intelligence officer, Flight Lieutenant Geoffrey R. Lempriere, for help in drafting a suitably sardonic response. The two men decided that a particular Latin phrase seemed appropriate, especially in light of their current situation. Lerew encrypted just three words: "MORITURI VOS SALUTAMUS." At Port Moresby, the staff was at first puzzled by the message, but eventually someone recognized it as the gladiators' legendary hail to Caesar: "We who are about to die salute you."

CHAPTER FIVE

CHAOS

"The whole operation was a shambles to begin with."

—Private O. C. "Bill" Harry,
2/22nd Battalion

In the shadows of the thick black smoke that towered above the burning wharves and crackling hulk of the *Herstein*, stunned townsfolk surveyed the bomb damage. Rabaul itself had been spared, apart from a few bombs that fell into a residential area on Crater Peninsula. Philip Coote, the supervisor for Burns-Philp operations in the territory, stumbled down Namanula Hill from his ruined home. Disheveled and weeping, on the verge of a nervous breakdown, he had survived by jumping into a slit trench moments before his fine new house was smashed by a direct hit. A large crater desecrated the lawn where his swimming pool and coral terrace had been.

Other leading residents, Harold Page among them, were likewise nervous, and with good reason. The size and intensity of the attack made it all too clear that the Japanese were bringing a large invasion force. The assault, when it came, was bound to be even worse than the air raid, and the presence of carrier planes meant the enemy fleet was somewhere nearby. The Australians could only guess. What they truly needed was information—the sort gleaned from aerial reconnaissance—but 24 Squadron was no longer in commission. The nearest operational unit was two hundred miles away in the Solomons, where 20 Squadron maintained an Advance Operating Base (AOB) with a few flying boats. A request went out for their assistance, and at dawn on January 21, a twin-engine

Catalina piloted by Flight Lieutenant Robert H. Thompson took off to search for the enemy fleet.

Several hours later the flying boat was abeam Kavieng when the copilot, Flight Lieutenant Paul M. Metzler, spotted "a number of gray logs nudging the surface of the ocean." Thompson radioed Port Moresby and reported four Japanese cruisers southwest of New Hanover. Before he could send additional information, bursts of antiaircraft fire chased the Catalina into a cloud. Minutes later, four Zeros attacked the flying boat from behind and shot it down. Thompson and Metzler maintained control just long enough to land the burning aircraft on the ocean, and they escaped the wreckage with three other crewmen. Metzler, convinced he could see the mountains of New Hanover in the distance, got the group swimming in that direction, but they made little progress. Two hours later the Japanese cruiser *Aoba* slid alongside the airmen. "Keep swimming," advised Thompson, "don't turn or look around, and for the love of God, don't wave at the bastards." Nevertheless the *Aoba*'s crew hauled the exhausted swimmers aboard, undoubtedly saving their lives. It was the Aussies' misfortune to become POWs so soon after the war began, but all five survived the next three and a half years of captivity in Japan and were repatriated.

WHILE THOMPSON AND HIS CREW WERE WINGING TOWARD THEIR FATEFUL encounter, Admiral Nagumo launched a carrier strike against the Australian defenses at Kavieng. The attack, conducted by fifty-two aircraft from the *Akagi* and *Kaga*, caused significant damage to the harbor facilities and disabled the 81-ton steel ketch *Induna Star*, the only seagoing transport available to the 1st Independent Company.

At the height of the raid, the *Star*'s crew attempted to get her underway from the main wharf. A half-dozen planes attacked, punching numerous holes in the hull and mortally wounding two soldiers manning a mounted Bren gun. In the wheelhouse, skipper Julius Lundin lost steering control, and the *Star* ran aground on a reef two miles south of the harbor. The survivors jumped overboard, then began swimming for a nearby island. All reached dry ground except a native crewman who was killed by a shark.

After the Japanese planes departed, the *Star* was refloated on the tide and taken back to Kavieng. With her leaky hull temporarily patched, she

was moved down the southern coast of New Ireland and hidden in a
remote cove.

AT RABAUL, FORTRESS SIGNALS RECEIVED WORD OF THE AIR ATTACK ON
Kavieng as well as the sighting of Japanese cruisers by Thompson's crew. As the
situation became clearer, Colonel Scanlan realized that enemy warships would
be close enough to shell Rabaul by nightfall. His first decision was to call
Lieutenant Colonel Carr into his command center for a private conference.
Explaining that he had no intention of waiting for Lark Force "to be massacred
by naval gunfire," he ordered the evacuation of Malaguna Camp. He also gave
Carr explicit instructions to tell the troops "that it was an exercise only."

Scanlan's first order made sense, but the second was highly irregular.
Carr never questioned it; instead he called his own staff together for a separate meeting and expounded on Scanlan's odd instruction. Lieutenant
Dawson later stated: "The CO told me that the Japanese fleet was on its
way to Rabaul, and that the commander of NGA had issued instructions
that no one apart from us was to be told that the enemy was about to
invade. Defensive positions were to be manned, but everyone was to be
informed that it was an exercise. The entire battalion, apart from those
who had been put in the picture, therefore went out under the impression
that they would return to camp within a few days."

Incredible as it seems, Scanlan fully intended to deceive his own men
by promulgating the story that they were leaving camp on an exercise. Was
he actually worried that they would abandon their posts if they learned the
truth—that a huge invasion fleet was coming and their own government
would neither reinforce nor evacuate them? If so, he had no faith in their
courage and did not trust their judgment. His rationale for the deliberate
deception remains an enigma.

Obeying the instructions passed down by the senior officers, the men
of Lark Force donned their dishpan helmets, tossed a few rations in their
haversacks, and picked up their rifles. Otherwise, believing they were
going out on an exercise and would return in a few days, they carried no
essentials for an extended stay in the jungle. Hundreds of troops not
already assigned to defensive positions—particularly A and B Companies
and the Headquarters Company—marched out of the encampment that
had been their home for nearly nine months.

Scanlan's order to evacuate Malaguna Camp was necessary. Other than a few slit trenches and primitive shelters, the facility had no defensive works and was completely exposed to aerial and naval bombardment. Before leaving the camp himself, Scanlan paused at the Fortress Signals switchboard, newly installed in an underground bunker. "I hope you will have time to use it," he said to the men on duty. Then, turning to Captain Keith H. M. Denny, the officer in charge of the signalers, he ordered the evacuation of all remaining personnel except essential radiomen.

Moving to the vicinity of Four Ways, an intersection atop the plateau along the road to Kokopo, Scanlan ordered new defensive positions for some of the rifle companies. He also cobbled together two new companies, forming Y Company with troops from the Pioneer Platoon, Protection Platoon, and quartermaster staff; and Z Company with headquarters personnel, vehicle drivers, and other nonessential troops. Because none had performed much infantry training during the past nine months, they would be used in combat only "as a last resource."

Most of the musicians from the band were scattered among the various companies as stretcher bearers. Sergeant Gullidge and two of the bandsmen were assigned to Fortress Signals, where their primary duty involved stringing telephone lines between the various defensive positions. However, Gullidge was subsequently hospitalized, his condition given as "seriously ill" due to an infected tropical ulcer. Two other musicians, Privates Austin B. Creed and Jack Stebbings, became dispatch riders because of their previous experience with motorcycles. Among the entire band, Private Kollmorgen was the only man with recent infantry training, and he was reassigned to a rifle company.

Elsewhere, Major Owen was ordered to take A Company to Lakunai airdrome and prepare it for demolition. Supervised by army engineers, the soldiers worked all day and well into the night to bury dozens of bombs in the airstrip. The explosives were then wired to a detonator, ready to blow huge craters in the runway and render it useless to the Japanese. Likewise, C Company rigged Vunakanau for destruction. Captain Appel and his troops had spent weeks digging machine-gun pits and erecting new living quarters, and now they made preparations to destroy their own handiwork. They buried nearly one hundred individual bombs, then bored several deep holes in the runway and filled them with tons of explosives. Working through the night and into the wee hours of January 22, they paused only long enough for 24 Squadron's lone remaining Hudson to take off at 0300 with a load of wounded men.

There would be no rest after their all-night effort. Just after daybreak, the troops at Vunakanau were startled when dozens of planes suddenly swooped down and attacked the airdrome with bombs, machine guns, and automatic cannon fire. Fifty planes had launched from the *Akagi* and *Kaga* for a repeat attack on Rabaul, and this time none of the coastwatchers detected their presence. The Australians retaliated with rifles and Lewis machine guns, but the Japanese dropped an estimated 180 bombs on the airdrome. Amazingly, for all the fragments and bullets flying about, only one member of C Company was wounded and a weapons pit was damaged.

Next, the attackers headed for the coastal gun emplacements on Crater Peninsula. They made a wide detour around Frisbee Ridge, much to the frustration of the antiaircraft gunners, who "stood and watched help-lessly as the destruction of Praed Point commenced." With deadly accuracy the Japanese dropped their bombs on the two big guns, and suddenly the conventional wisdom became clear. The upper gun, blown from its mount-ings, tumbled down the steep slopes and destroyed the lower emplacement. Eleven men were killed, some due to suffocation when a shelter collapsed. Major James R. P. Clark, the commander of the artillery detachment, suf-fered a severe case of shock after being buried in a slit trench for a brief time. Also wounded was Captain Herbert N. Silverman, the medical doctor assigned to the heavy battery.

After demolishing the coastal guns, the carrier planes dive-bombed and strafed anything that moved. Altogether, they remained over Rabaul for approximately forty-five minutes before heading back to their ships.

In the aftermath, conditions at Rabaul deteriorated rapidly. Word spread that the township itself was to be evacuated, prompting store man-agers to open their doors for residents to help themselves before a general exodus began. "Rabaul took on the appearance of a bustling business cen-ter," recalled Alice Bowman, one of the civilian nurses. "Grim faced men arrived in the few derelict vehicles that were still around. Customers wasted no time with friendly greetings and idle chatter as they dragged boxes, bags, and any available containers to be filled with the essentials for the uncertain days ahead."

If some of the civilians had lingering doubts about their future, the same could not be said of Lark Force. Any questions about the enemy's intentions vanished when lookouts on the North Daughter reported smoke on the northern horizon. Lieutenant Figgis, accompanied by the 2/22nd's Brigade Major (Chief of Staff), Captain Norman R. "Tusker" McLeod, rushed up to the antiaircraft battery and peered through the powerful gun telescopes. By mid-afternoon they could clearly distinguish several types of ships coming directly toward New Britain, including cruisers, destroyers, and troop transports. They counted approximately twenty-five vessels before a shroud of mist from an approaching storm obscured their view.

Figgis and McLeod reported their observations to Scanlan, who found himself facing the greatest dilemma of his career. The coastal guns had been destroyed, the airdromes were prepped for demolition, and there was little left for Lark Force to defend. The antiaircraft guns were still intact, but they were isolated from the rest of the force, and there wasn't time to bring them back down the mountain. Scanlan decided that they too would have to be destroyed, and sent McLeod to inform Captain Selby. After the job was done, Selby was to join B Company at Three Ways, an intersection on the Kokopo Ridge Road.

FOR ALL THE RIBBING THEY HAD ENDURED—OR POSSIBLY BECAUSE OF IT—THE antiaircraft gunners had developed enormous pride in their two old weapons. The task of destroying them proved heartrending, though the idea of the enemy getting them intact was even worse.

In response to Scanlan's orders, each gun was loaded with a round in the breech and another down the barrel. Next, the recoil dampers were disconnected, the ring-sight telescope was placed across the muzzle of the Number 2 gun, and lengths of wire were attached to the firing mechanisms. Two of the gunners ran the wires to a distant bunker, then connected the leads to a detonator and awaited Selby's signal. Unable to bring himself to give the order, he simply nodded. "The wires were pulled sharply, there was a great roar, then another, and flying pieces of metal whistled overhead," he remembered. "We emerged from our shelter and surveyed the damage. Both barrels had split up and opened out like a sliced radish for a couple of feet from the ends of the muzzles. At least they were useless, except as scrap iron, to the enemy."

Leaving thousands of rounds of ammunition behind, Selby and his men headed down the mountain aboard two dangerously overloaded trucks. The cargo beds were packed with various weapons, including a Vickers machine gun, an antitank rifle, cases of .303-caliber ammunition, and boxes of grenades.

While the gunners made their way around the caldera to Three Ways, other elements of Lark Force were also in motion. Scanlan rearranged his defenses like a nervous chess player, pulling some rifle companies away from the beaches to new positions astride key roads, ordering others to dig in at sites where the enemy might land.

As soon as the wrecked gun emplacements at Praed Point were cleared of the dead and wounded, Scanlan ordered R Company and the survivors of the Royal Australian Artillery detachment to evacuate Crater Peninsula. Captain Silverman checked himself out of the hospital and returned to Praed Point in his pajamas to help with the exodus. Most of the men walked around Simpson Harbor to Four Ways, where Scanlan had established his new headquarters near Noah's Mission, a small native church. R Company dug in alongside the intersection, while Captain Travers and D Company awaited orders to move forward toward Kokopo or reinforce Captain Appel at Vunakanau, whichever was necessary.

A Company, having completed the rigging of Lakunai airdrome, deployed to new positions inside the caldera just north of Mount Vulcan. Major Owen had his men dig in just behind the beach, which gave them a good field of fire across the harbor. Joining Owen's company was the local detachment of the New Guinea Volunteer Rifles, whose eighty-odd troops had been called to active duty two days earlier in a brief township ceremony. While some of the volunteers unrolled bales of barbed wire along the beach, others sighted in their single Vickers machine gun. Behind them, Major Matheson of the 17th Antitank Battery aligned his 2-pounder guns. Nearby, three mortar teams set up their weapons, setting the angle to drop their rounds just outside the wire. Finally, "Doc" Silverman erected a first aid station alongside the command post. Assisting him as medic was bandsman Bert Morgan, who had recently been promoted to corporal.

A few miles to the south, Captain McInnes directed B Company to dig in next to Three Ways. His orders were to prevent the Japanese from penetrating inland from Mount Vulcan while also blocking their attempts to approach up the Kokopo Ridge Road. Two Vickers machine guns were set up to flank both sides of the road, and the rifle platoons fortified their positions with coconut logs.

Finally, Scanlan ordered Captain Shier to take over the hastily formed Y Company and fortify Raluana Point, the only other defended beachhead besides Vulcan. The new company was supposed to be used only as a last resource, yet for some unfathomable reason Scanlan placed it on the exposed right flank of the Australian line. Not only was Y Company isolated from the next closest unit by seven miles of bad roads, but the phone line laid that night proved unreliable. The only positive element Shier could count on was the experience of his junior officers. Lieutenant Lennox "Len" Henry, for example, was one of the few professional soldiers in Lark Force. An excellent instructor, he had only a short time to prepare the "odds and sods" for combat.

WHILE THE VARIOUS RIFLE COMPANIES SHIFTED TO NEW POSITIONS, SCANLAN met with Squadron Leader Lerew to discuss the future of 24 Squadron. The pilot pointed out that his men had received virtually no field training; therefore, it made little sense for them to stay and "fight with the army as guerillas." Scanlan agreed. He regarded the airmen as "more nuisance than they were worth," and consented to an overland evacuation.

That afternoon, the personnel of 24 Squadron headed south in a convoy of eight trucks. Lerew's plan was to put some distance between his men and Rabaul while Sergeant Frederick G. Higgs, a radioman, raced ahead to find a working set. Locating the necessary equipment at Tol, a plantation on Wide Bay, Higgs encrypted a short message to Port Moresby: "Send flying-boats. [The men] will identify themselves with torch."

Meanwhile, the number of people in Lerew's caravan had grown significantly. Among them were Captain Denny and about twenty soldiers from Fortress Signals, none of whom had authorization to join the evacuation. After departing Malaguna Camp on Scanlan's orders, Denny had led his men to Bita Paka, the site of the old German wireless station, where they tried to get a field telephone in operation. The equipment broke down the next morning, so Denny took a few men to search for a replacement. During their absence, an unidentified RAAF officer passed through Bita Paka and informed the remaining soldiers that the Japanese had invaded.

The information was untrue, but there was no way for the signalers to con-firm it. Thus, when Denny returned empty-handed and learned of the alleged invasion, he made an arbitrary decision to join Lerew's group. Likewise, a few artillerymen and other stragglers from Praed Point had attached themselves to the exodus, as did several civilians. By evening of January 22, the number of evacuees had grown to more than 150 men.

EARLIER THAT AFTERNOON, WHILE CHECKING ON NEW DEFENSIVE POSITIONS along the Kokopo Ridge Road, Scanlan stopped at a new observation post manned by Lieutenant Dawson and several privates from the intel-ligence section. Located on a hilltop near Taliligap Mission, the observa-tion post provided a sweeping view of the plateau and Simpson Harbor, though the beaches at Vulcan and Raluana Point were below the line of sight. Scanlan admired the vantage point and decided to place his own command center there.

While waiting for his staff to arrive, Scanlan made an astonishing comment. "Well, it looks as though all we can do now is withdraw and attack the enemy's L of C," he said to Dawson, using the abbreviation for "lines of communication."

"That is a good idea," Dawson replied carefully, "but what food are we going to eat?" His sarcasm was evidently lost on Scanlan, who had suddenly found merit in the intelligence section's earlier recommenda-tions. He had snubbed them then, and now it came back to haunt him. There was little time to make changes, but Dawson knew of one last opportunity. A mound of canned food was stored at Vunakanau, and he immediately requested permission to have it moved to Malabunga Mission, the jump-off point into the Baining Mountains. Scanlan denied the request on the grounds that every vehicle was needed for moving troops.

However, as soon as the colonel was out of earshot, Dawson instructed some of his men to take the battalion's utility truck to Vunakanau and fill it with as much food as it could carry, then deliver it to Malabunga. Later, he learned that the rest of the stockpile at Vunakanau was deliberately ruined to prevent the Japanese from getting it. The food could have sustained the Australians in the jungle for months, and its loss would be sorely regretted.

LATER THAT AFTERNOON, AFTER THE ANTIAIRCRAFT GUNS WERE DESTROYED, several more deliberately set explosions shook Rabaul. First, the hundreds of pre-wired bombs imbedded in the runways at Vunakanau and Lakunai were detonated, rendering both airdromes temporarily unusable. At approximately 1600, a much heavier blast rocked the town as Royal Australian Engineers blew up the stockpile of bombs alongside Malaguna Road. Due to haste, misjudgment, or perhaps both, inadequate warnings were issued prior to the explosion. All two thousand bombs went off in a colossal blast that wrecked buildings and smashed windows for blocks around, and the delicate valves and vacuum tubes in the radio transmitter at the AWA office were shattered. Half a mile away, the switchboard at Malaguna Camp was likewise ruined. In the blink of an eye, all radio contact with the outside world was severed. Even worse, from a human standpoint, a few Tolai natives had been caught unawares in the blast zone and were killed by the concussion. In the confused aftermath, their bodies were left lying next to the road, some with their entrails exposed.

On Namanula Hill, the medical personnel at both hospitals had been busy treating injuries caused by the carrier strikes. The army hospital in Government House had no operating room, so the civilian facility was used for surgeries. Several Norwegians from the *Herstein* underwent treatment for burns, and there were numerous injuries among personnel from the collapsed coastal gun emplacements. Private Wilkie D. "Bill" Collins, a twenty-three-year-old driver in the 2/10 Field Ambulance, later described the operating theater as looking like "a slaughter house," with bloodstained dressings piled in a heap in one corner.

While the doctors and nurses treated injuries, Chaplain May moved among the wounded, offering words of comfort. Suddenly, in the midst of all the activity, the hospitals fell quiet. The remains of two RAAF men, sergeants Charles F. Bromley and Richard Walsh, were brought in on a truck. They had been shot down two days earlier and their corpses recovered from a Wirraway that crashed in the shallows off Praed Point. "The battered bodies were almost unrecognizable as the young men we had laughed and joked with a few days ago," remembered Alice Bowman. "One who looked no older than a schoolboy had been shot through the head. The other lay like a discarded puppet."

With so many wounded to care for, everyone was oblivious to events outside the hospital until the bomb dump exploded at 1600. Soon after, realizing that an invasion was imminent, the staff at both hospitals decided to evacuate their patients to a safer location. Vunapope agreed to make its spacious campus available, and a convoy of assorted trucks, ambulances, and private vehicles gathered to transport some eighty patients around the caldera.

The trip took twice the normal time. Trees had been dynamited across many of the roads, requiring the convoy to take a circuitous route. Adding to the difficulty, the storm that had shrouded the Japanese fleet earlier that afternoon arrived just before dark, and the journey was completed in a steady downpour. The convoy finally rolled into Vunapope late that night, and the patients were placed in a native hospital near the beach. Normally a restful site under swaying palms, the wooden building was a scene of anxious activity as the patients were moved onto rows of cots. When at last the transfer was complete, Lieutenant May and the exhausted medical personnel plodded off toward dormitories made available by the generous missionaries.

Elsewhere around the caldera, scattered elements of Lark Force waited in the darkness and heavy rain for the Japanese to come. Having arrived at Three Ways that afternoon per Scanlan's orders, Captain Selby and the antiaircraft gunners had just begun digging in when they received orders to reinforce Y Company at Raluana Point. The gunners, like most of the clerks and cooks that made up Y Company, lacked any sort of real infantry experience, but in compliance with orders they climbed back aboard their trucks for the slow, torturous ride around the caldera. Despite the heavy rain and pitch darkness, drivers were forbidden to use their headlights, so someone had to walk alongside the front bumper and shout directions. It was almost midnight by the time they reached Raluana Point and had a mug of soup, their only hot meal of the day.

In Rabaul, there was little for the civilians to do that night except seek shelter. One adventurous group set off in a schooner for Kokopo, but the rest climbed the hill to Refuge Gully, walking on roads made slick by the rain. Their progress was slow, the night seeming all the blacker because of drifting smoke from scattered fires and the sulfurous ash that billowed from Tavurvur. The mood at the shelter was grim, and not just because of the weather. The men gathered at Refuge Gully were extremely irritated, mainly over the indifferences shown by the Commonwealth. Many complained bitterly, while others held out hope for last-minute American intervention. "When the Yanks get here . . ." they said, as if to reassure themselves.

Conspicuously absent from the shelter was Harold Page, the corpulent administrator. Evidently he had given up in frustration after his repeated appeals for evacuation aboard the *Herstein* were refused. At noon that day, he and Harry Townsend, the treasurer of the mandated territory, started out on foot toward Kokopo. They told everyone they met along the road that there was nothing left in Rabaul. Their actions disgusted some citizens, but others chose to follow their example. Page and Townsend eventually joined up with Lerew's RAAF convoy, and others made their way south by whatever means of transportation they could find.

Ironically, in the middle of the afternoon the 330-ton steamer *Matafele* slipped quietly into Simpson Harbor. Upon learning of the pending invasion, the captain quickly prepared to get underway again. He had plenty of space for civilians, yet only a handful went aboard due to the fact that "consent [from Canberra] was not forthcoming." Dozens could have safely left the island, but far too many were accustomed to adhering to the whims of distant bureaucracy. Everyone, it seemed, forgot common sense. Later that afternoon, shrouded by the torrential rains, the *Matafele* sailed with her cabins mostly empty. A Japanese warship lurked near the entrance to Blanche Bay, but the *Matafele*'s captain steered the little steamer into a squall and escaped undetected.

FOR HOURS THAT NIGHT, JOHN LEREW AND HIS MIXED CONVOY OF RAAF personnel, soldiers, and civilians struggled southward along a rough and treacherous road. One truck missed a curve in the darkness and tumbled down a steep slope. No one was seriously hurt, but the remaining vehicles slowed to a crawl. The last segment of navigable roadway was little more than an overgrown track through the jungle, and it terminated at the Warangoi River. The men disabled the trucks and proceeded on foot to the riverbank, where they could see by flashlight that the muddy water was in full flood.

The only means of crossing the river was by native canoes, which had to be guided downstream and out to sea before they could be safely beached. With only two dugouts available, the process took hours. Afterward, the rabble continued on foot through the dripping jungle and forded another river before finally reaching a large, stylish plantation called Put Put in the middle of the night.

Allowing only a brief rest, Lerew split his group into two parties. He put Flight Lieutenant Brookes in charge of the civilians, Lark Force personnel, and married men, totaling about fifty individuals. Some were beyond middle age and struggled to keep up, so Brookes commandeered two small boats to take them the rest of the way to Tol plantation. He was appalled by the behavior he witnessed that night. "The action of certain civilians, including some senior civil servants, was disgraceful," he later reported. "Numerous cases occurred where [men] were deliberately dumped and left behind in order that a particular person could make his escape either a little more certain or faster."

Among those left behind were Harold Page and Harry Townsend, who decided to walk back to Rabaul with two other administration officials. Upon reaching the abandoned convoy at the Warangoi River on January 25, they made camp and waited for the Japanese to come and get them.

Meanwhile, Lerew and his party of RAAF personnel continued their journey on foot, covering another fifteen miles to Sum Sum plantation, just north of Adler Bay. They stopped to rest, and were driven under cover a few times when enemy scout planes flew over. Late that afternoon, the sound of aircraft engines sent the men scurrying under the trees once more, but someone recognized the distinctive note of Bristol Pegasus engines. The word spread quickly: there was an Empire flying boat nearby.

Actually, two of the huge four-engine seaplanes, formerly used by QANTAS for international passenger service, were searching for Lerew and his men. The radio message sent by Sergeant Higgs had been received at Port Moresby the previous day, and with no other information to go by, RAAF 20 Squadron sent aloft two Empires on a rescue attempt. However, upon learning of the imminent invasion of Rabaul, the crews elected to stop for the night at Samarai on the tip of the Papuan Peninsula. They took off again the next day, flew northward up the coast of New Britain, and were able to spot the flashlights being waved by the men at Sum Sum, just as Higgs' message had indicated.

Two of Lerew's men volunteered to take a boat to Tol and inform Brookes of the successful pickup, which left ninety-eight others to be ferried out to the Empires in small boats. The overloaded seaplanes failed to get airborne on their first attempts, and had to dump fuel before they were able to stagger aloft. They flew back to Samarai, where a flare path had been laid to guide them in for a hazardous night water landing. The evacuees received clean clothing and spent the night in a company store, then were airlifted the next day to Port Moresby.

Subsequently, a single Empire returned to New Britain on January 24 to pick up Brookes' party at Wide Bay. The first forty-nine men were ferried out in a dangerously overloaded boat while Captain Denny waited on the beach with a handful of his men. The nervous loadmaster refused to delay the takeoff, however, and Denny's small group was left behind. Gamely, they commandeered a boat and set off for the Trobriand Islands on January 27. From there, after several adventurous voyages in small boats, they reached Queensland on March 9.

Considering the lack of planning and the many variables involved, the successful evacuation of 24 Squadron was practically a miracle. Unfortunately, as word of the airlift trickled back to Rabaul by "jungle telegraph," hundreds of men in Lark Force were led to believe that the RAAF would return to Wide Bay and evacuate them, too. The rumors proved not only false, but resulted in an exceptionally cruel twist of fate.

CHAPTER SIX

VIGOROUS YOUTH FROM SHIKOKU

"The Japs simply walked ashore, and it was all over in one day."

—Lieutenant Peter Figgis, NGA
Headquarters Staff

From the bridge of his flagship *Okinoshima*, a 390-foot mine-laying cruiser, Rear Admiral Kiyohide Shima caught a brief glimpse of New Britain's volcanic mountains in the distance. The weather had been steadily deteriorating as the fleet approached the island on the afternoon of January 22, and soon a line of squalls obscured his view. The reduced visibility caused anxious moments. "As we gradually drew closer to the coastline," Shima wrote in his diary, "we were very much worried about being taken unawares by the enemy; and indeed, it was truly by the aid of the gods that we were not troubled by them."

The Japanese admiral had no real cause for concern. Although his ships were being observed through long-range telescopes, the Australians could do nothing to stop him. There were no aircraft or coastal guns left to oppose the invasion fleet, and it continued unmolested down St. George's Channel, zigzagging to kill time. By nightfall, the assembled ships were only three miles from Blanche Bay. Ahead of schedule, they held their position and waited for the signal from Major General Horii to commence landing operations.

Darkness and the poor weather favored the Japanese. The storm finally ended after midnight, leaving in its wake a low overcast that scudded over the anchorage, revealing occasional patches of starry sky. The night was moonless, perfectly suited for an invasion, and the Australians could see nothing of the fleet that had gathered offshore.

Aboard the transports, the soldiers of the South Seas Detachment were undoubtedly eager to begin the attack. They had endured nine days of unsanitary, overcrowded conditions, and assaulting the beachhead would be a relief. While they waited, they clipped their fingernails and toenails, then placed the clippings and a lock of hair into a tiny box that would be sent home for enshrinement if they were killed. They were not overly concerned about death; if anything, they were far more worried about the possibility of dishonoring their unit, their families, or their communities.

The much-anticipated invasion began with a methodical progression of orders. First, Horii signaled the transport captains at 2030 to prepare for landing operations. An hour later, he forwarded the message, "Prepare to infiltrate to the anchorage point," and the transports shifted to their pre-assigned launching positions. Some headed around the north shore of Crater Peninsula toward the village of Nordup, but most glided quietly into Blanche Bay.

Conditions inside the caldera were pitch black. Rabaul itself was dark except for the glow of a few fires that still burned from the morning's air attacks; and Mount Nakamisaki, the Japanese name for Tavurvur, spewed embers bright enough to serve as a "good landmark for reckoning directions in the darkness." Powdery ash drifted onto the decks of the ships, adding an eerie effect to the prevailing conditions. Also, an unidentified aircraft, possibly an RAAF Catalina out of Port Moresby, released parachute flares over the harbor periodically, and their bright colors reflected off the low-hanging clouds "with a weird beauty."

At 2235, Horii sent the long-awaited order: "Stop and weigh anchor. Begin the landing operation." At last, solders began clambering into dozens of Shohatsu and Daihatsu landing craft. The former, steel-hulled boats approximately forty feet long, had a capacity of about thirty troops. The more versatile Daihatsus could carry either seventy troops, twelve tons of cargo, or a medium tank.

The process of disembarking took about two hours and was completed without mishap—no small accomplishment considering the complexities of getting thousands of troops into their landing craft in pitch darkness. A strong tidal flow hindered operations and prompted the captain of at least one warship to risk turning on a searchlight to check his position.

The first group to hit the beach had the shortest distance to cover. The 1st Battalion of the 144th Infantry Regiment, commanded by Lieutenant Colonel Hatsuo Tsukamoto, landed near Praed Point at 0110 and quickly occupied Lakunai airdrome, accomplishing the first of General Horii's two main objectives. No Australians opposed the landing. Colonel Scanlan had withdrawn his forces from Crater Peninsula after the coastal guns were bombed and the runway at Lakunai was deliberately blown up. There was nothing else on the peninsula worth defending.

The Japanese were not aware of this, and one company fanned out with specific orders to capture all of the coastal gun emplacements. Faulty intelligence still estimated as many as ten batteries on the peninsula, and the 2nd Company had until 0400 to neutralize them. If they failed, Rear Admiral Shima would have to pull the invasion fleet beyond the effective range of the guns before sunrise. The 2nd Company found the two wrecked emplacements without difficulty but continued to search frantically for "the other eight batteries." The troops had plenty of motivation: if they did not signal their success by 0400 with a series of white star shells, the company commander was under orders to commit suicide.

IN CONTRAST TO THE BLOODLESS OCCUPATION OF CRATER PENINSULA, THE Japanese encountered resistance at their other landing sites. Three companies of the 3rd Battalion, led by Lieutenant Colonel Ishiro Kuwada, went ashore at two different positions along the rim of the caldera. They would accomplish their objective, the capture of Vunakanau airdrome, with a pincer movement. The plan called for the 8th Company to assault Raluana Point while the 7th and 9th Companies landed south of Mount Vulcan—but it didn't work out that way. In the darkness, the coxswains steering the 9th Company's landing craft strayed *north* of Vulcan, exactly where Major Owen's reinforced A Company and the NGVR were waiting for them.

Concealed behind coconut log fortifications, the Australians could clearly hear the rumble of diesel motors and the scrape of steel hulls on coral. John N. Jones, a twenty-three-year-old corporal from New South Wales, was patrolling the perimeter at 0225 when he saw the barge-like landing craft approaching the beach, their silhouettes faintly backlit by the fires burning in Rabaul. The first boatload displayed remarkably poor discipline. Some of the Japanese were talking, others laughing, and one

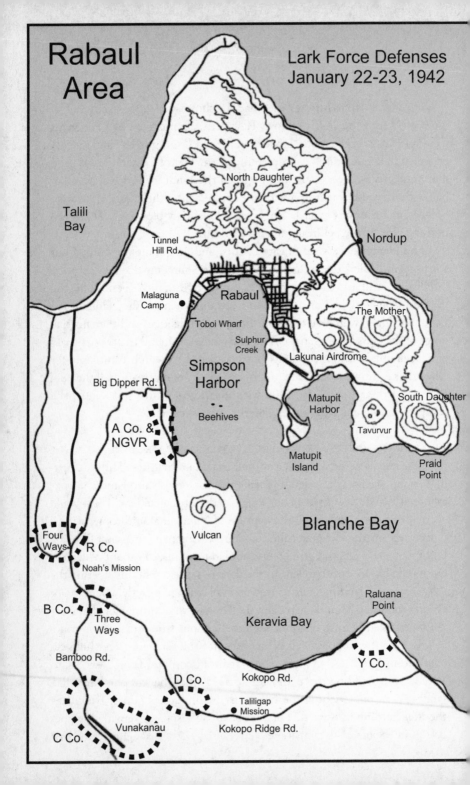

even shined a flashlight. Jones pointed a Very pistol skyward and pulled the trigger.

Seconds later, the flare cast a bright light over the beach, catching the Japanese troops by surprise. "We allowed most of them to get out of the boats," recalled Kenneth G. Hale, another corporal in A Company, "and then fired everything we had."

The Australians cut loose with a withering blast. The staccato chatter of machine guns and the popping of Lee-Enfield rifles blended into a solid roar. Some of the newly delivered Thompson submachine guns added their distinctive rattle, and Captain Matheson's antitank guns joined in with a nasty whip-*crack*. Lost among all the gunfire was the metallic thumping of mortar rounds leaving their tubes. Additional flares whooshed skyward, lighting up the beach just as the mortar shells began to land near the barbed wire. The Japanese, thrown into disarray by the explosions and concentrated firepower, twice attempted to rush the wire and twice were driven back.

The invaders withdrew into the darkness and moved laterally down the shore toward Mount Vulcan. Subsequently the Australians ceased firing, for they lacked the ammunition to blast away indiscriminately.

THROUGHOUT THE NIGHT, A SQUAD FROM D COMPANY HAD BEEN QUIETLY patrolling a little-used trail that led from Keravia Bay up to the plateau. An old ship's boiler lay rusting near the beach, hence the name of the overgrown path: Boiler Road. The previous evening, the seven men had shaken hands with the rest of their platoon and bid them farewell. "I didn't think we'd see them again," wrote Private Pearson in his diary, "[because] we were going out on rather a hopeless mission."

Led by Corporal Richard V. S. Hamill, the squad was all that potentially stood between the Japanese—if they chose to land anywhere along the wide stretch of Keravia Bay—and easy access to the plateau. The Australians had a Lewis machine gun and a Tommy gun in addition to their rifles, and a light truck filled with plenty of ammunition, but no radio or field telephone. "If the Japs came up that road we were to send up a red Very light and fight a retarding action until our company came down to reinforce us," added Pearson. It wasn't much of a plan.

In the middle of the night, a bright flare over Simpson Harbor encouraged Pearson. "We were also told that the Americans were coming to give us support, and when a Catalina dropped a parachute flare in the early hours of the morning, we thought it was a light to guide them in."

Only much later did the Australians realize that the expected help from the United States was a myth. In the meantime, the sound of gunfire and mortars reached the squad from the direction of Vulcan Crater, a few miles to the north. The moment of truth had arrived.

AT RALUANA POINT, CAPTAIN SELBY AND HIS TIRED MILITIAMEN WAITED tensely alongside Y Company. They had not reached the position until midnight, whereupon Captain Shiers directed them to place their single Vickers gun down on the beach. But only one small trench had been dug, and there were no wire defenses, so Selby detached five men armed with rifles to cover the machine gun, and moved the rest back to an old World War I emplacement behind the beach.

By this time, the Australians at Raluana Point were no longer deluded into believing they were on an exercise. Thanks to the faulty telephone service, Lieutenant Dawson had paid a personal visit during the night, and he'd informed Shelby and Shier about what they were up against. "I told them about the Jap task force and told them that it was no exercise," he later stated. "Thus I disobeyed the orders I had received from Scanlan."

At about 0230, a star shell burst high above St. George's Channel. There, gut-wrenchingly close to the shore, were the dark silhouettes of Japanese ships. Moments later the landing craft of Kuwada's 8th Company approached the beach.

As Gunner Bloomfield later remembered, the battle commenced with a haunting sound:

> An enemy bugler started to blow a call, which ended abruptly, followed by a short period of silence. Then all hell broke loose. Naval guns flashed, followed by shells bursting overhead and behind us. Star shells again lit the area and we could see landing craft approaching. They were going to land at Raluana.
>
> As they came within range our mortar crews went into action and as soon as the landing craft scraped on the sand and lowered their front platforms, the order "open

fire, open fire" was being shouted and every gun on Raluana opened up.

Bathed in the surreal glow of star shells, the Australians poured small-arms fire into the invaders, and the first wave got no farther than the beach before their advance faltered. Japanese soldiers could be heard moving about in the surf and exhorting their troops to prepare for another attack, but after a few bursts from the Vickers gun, the noises stopped.

The silence lasted only a few minutes before the Japanese charged again. Simultaneously, the 8th Company sent landing craft around the far side of Raluana Point, and a few boatloads of troops rushed the defenders from behind. The Australians lacked the personnel and weaponry to withstand encirclement, and soon expended their ammunition. Once that happened, their fortitude quickly faltered. Noncoms and officers could be heard shouting "fall back," and "the beach is lost!"

Selby had just started toward the beach when he heard "a crescendo of wild, savage yells." The sounds, which came from the Japanese as they charged uphill, further unnerved the Australians. Selby met a sergeant from Y Company coming in the opposite direction and was told: "Shier's orders are to retire to Three Ways. The beach is in enemy hands."

In military terms, "retire" usually implies an orderly withdrawal. But as the 8th Company swarmed ashore, the Australians were soon routed. They dashed recklessly through the undergrowth to their parked trucks, and one vehicle stalled, its clutch stripped by a frantic driver. The rest of the trucks, filled to overflowing, crawled up the steep incline to the plateau. Gaining the top, one driver proved overzealous in his bid to get away from the Japanese and failed to negotiate a sharp curve. The truck overturned, spilling men into the ditch. No one was seriously hurt, but the soldiers had to walk or hitchhike several miles to Three Ways, and some did not arrive until nearly dawn.

WHILE THE 2ND COMPANY, 1ST BATTALION SEARCHED IN VAIN FOR THE phantom gun batteries, more Japanese troops landed on the north shore of Crater Peninsula. The 2nd Battalion, led by Colonel Masao Kusunose, went ashore near the village of Nordup, but at less than full strength. Missing were the 4th Company and the 55th Mountain Artillery, both of which remained aboard the transport *China Maru*. The ship had become temporarily lost in the darkness, and Kusunose chose to proceed without it rather than upset the timetable. Not that it mattered. The troops that landed were never challenged as they advanced from Nordup up Namanula Hill. They occupied Government House at 0500, then moved down into the dark, empty streets of Rabaul.

INITIALLY, KUWADA'S 7TH COMPANY MET NO OPPOSITION WHEN IT LANDED south of Vulcan Crater, but the going was slow. Hemmed in by the steep sides of the caldera, the troops could not locate a road that had been marked in aerial photographs. Teams of sappers turned to the arduous job of felling trees to clear a path for the heavy vehicles that would be landing at daybreak.

To the 7th's right, the 9th Company began moving southward around the base of Mount Vulcan, having twice failed to penetrate the Australian defenses. Using deep ravines for cover, the Japanese concentrated most of their forces against the Australians' right flank. However, the rough terrain temporarily held the Japanese in check, and the assault broke down into firefights that gradually intensified.

The telephone line linking A Company to headquarters was severed, leaving Major Owen and his men isolated below the rim of the caldera. Their situation continued to deteriorate as more Japanese landed south of Vulcan, beyond the range of the mortars, and gathered in the ravines. They used signal flags to mark rallying points, and continually probed against the Australian defenses. Private Edward P. Saligari, a machine-gunner from Cavendish, Victoria, suppressed many of the enemy's signaling attempts and was credited with silencing a machine gun team. At times the fighting raged close to the Australian defenses. Five members of A Company were killed during the night, including Owen's batman, cut down by a Japanese soldier who broke through the lines.

With the communications cut, no reserves or supplies came down from the plateau, and the mortar crews began to run low on ammunition. Captain Dudley F. "Fred" Field and Private James N. Olney made two trips up the escarpment in the darkness and returned with enough rounds for the crews to extend their barrage. The teams shifted targets every time they sighted a rallying flag or signal flare, but by dawn their supply was exhausted. The mortar crews had fired some 300 shells, and still the Japanese poured onto the beaches.

CROUCHED IN HIS OBSERVATION POST ON THE PLATEAU ABOVE VULCAN Crater, Lieutenant Dawson was frustrated. Not only had he violated a direct order the previous night by informing Selby and Shier about the invasion fleet, he had spent the next several hours listening helplessly to the battle that raged below his position. He could not see what was happening down in the caldera, as he had lost contact with A Company and the other units at Vulcan soon after the fighting began.

When daybreak finally came, Dawson hiked to a primitive native church overlooking the anchorage. He was stunned by the vista of enemy ships spread out before him. In the foreground, four destroyers steamed smartly into Simpson Harbor in line abreast, and a cargo ship approached the Government Wharf. Landing craft swarmed everywhere, some bringing reinforcements to the nearby beaches, others heading across the harbor toward Crater Peninsula. Out in the roadstead of Blanche Bay and St. George's Channel, Dawson could see two aircraft carriers, a landing craft transporter, several more cruisers, troopships, and a host of support vessels. He counted thirty-one ships in all, and figured more were out there.

Near the little church, a rough track led down the steep side of the caldera toward Vulcan. Believing he could use the trail to guide Major Owen and his men up to the plateau, Dawson hastened back to headquarters to find help. After first giving Lieutenant Colonel Carr a quick situation report, he rounded up privates Leslie W. "Curly" Smith and Norris Kennedy, and they started off toward the church in a battalion car.

But as Dawson later explained, they did not get far.

> On turning the last curve before the mission we saw there in the middle of the road a full platoon of Japs and several natives. With them was one of the local German missionaries shaking hands with an officer who appeared to be the platoon commander. I had seen the German earlier in the morning and he impressed me as being very pleased about something. It was now clear. The impression I got was that these natives had led the Japs up the

track, because it was utterly impossible to find from the lower end. That was the reason I was going down to lead A Company out.

The Japs opened fire at a range of about 50 yards. The car stopped and I got out. The two men ran around in front of the car and I think they must have been killed. I went round the back of the car and made off, running back along the road until I got around the corner.

Smith, a thirty-year-old fisherman from the Victoria coast, was indeed shot dead. Kennedy, known by his friends as "Norrie," managed to escape into the jungle but was later found by the Japanese and taken prisoner.

Dawson, disoriented after running to safety, found a trustworthy Tolai native who agreed to guide him to the next road junction. As they approached the intersection, however, Dawson saw that some enemy soldiers had gotten there first. He ducked into the jungle and "broke bush" through the heavy undergrowth, struggling for hours while the sounds of battle intensified around him. At last he emerged onto the Kokopo road and met a platoon from D Company.

The Australians had been instructed to walk toward Malabunga Mission, so Dawson steered them down a track that led in the general direction. Near Vunakanau, a sudden burst of machine gun fire drove them back into the bushes, and they ran through fields of tall, razor-sharp kunai grass until Dawson called a halt. Stunned by the terrible turn of events, exhausted by the exertion of their retreat, they dropped to the ground and spent the rest of the day in hiding.

DOWN AT VULCAN, MEANWHILE, BILL OWEN HAD DECIDED IT WAS FUTILE TO continue resistance. With the coming of daybreak, he could see waves of enemy landing craft still approaching the beach, and Japanese troops hiding in the ravines were "doing a lot of yelling." Worse, artillery shells began to fall among his positions, some fired by warships in the harbor, others by pack howitzers in the streets of Rabaul. On the left, several landing craft began to disgorge more troops. Soon they would cut off the Australians' main escape route, a steep road called the Big Dipper, which led up to the plateau. Antitank guns fired almost point-blank into the landing craft, but the solid-steel practice rounds caused minimal damage.

Shortly before 0700, Owen ordered his men to withdraw to Four Ways and instructed them to make for Tobera plantation individually if the Japanese held the intersection. Leapfrogging one another, the platoons provided covering fire as they pulled back. The last moved out with "the Japs very close" behind them, and men clawed their way up the slopes, dumping weapons and equipment as they struggled through the thick vegetation. Enemy aircraft suddenly appeared overhead and strafed the retreating troops, who were almost too weary to hide by the time they reached the top of the escarpment.

Owen was among the last to leave. He started up the Big Dipper, then noticed that the truck assigned to the aid post was sitting idle, its driver missing. Taking over the vehicle, he started up the hill just as Doc Silverman climbed aboard. Shells were "bursting round the truck," recalled Captain Field, as the two officers drove up the road and left the beachhead to the Japanese.

ABOARD HIS FLAGSHIP, REAR ADMIRAL SHIMA WATCHED AS 0400 CAME and went. Seeing no flares to confirm the capture of the coastal guns, he reluctantly ordered all vessels to "retreat to special anchorage positions." Simultaneously, Major General Horii issued a signal for his troops to prepare for a second assault on Crater Peninsula. The orders had barely been communicated, however, when three white flares burst high above the South Daughter.

Shima ordered the fleet to hold its position. Later, it was determined that the company commander had been reluctant "to fire signal shots irresponsibly," and risked his own neck to make absolutely certain the two wrecked emplacements were the only ones on the peninsula.

Now that his ships were safe, Shima ordered several ships to proceed directly into Simpson Harbor. At approximately 0530, the *Okinoshima* and another large minelayer, the *Tsugaru*, steamed to the waterfront and offloaded 170 members of the Maizuru 2nd Special Naval Landing Force. Shortly thereafter, the *Tenyo Maru* delivered another 130 SNLF troops which had previously completed a sweep of nearby Credner Island. The naval infantry "mopped up the city," claimed an Imperial Navy summary, though the soldiers of the 2nd Battalion had actually gotten there first.

AFTER BOARDING A LANDING CRAFT FROM THE *YOKOHAMA MARU*, MAJOR General Horii went ashore on Matupi Island briefly to observe the overall situation. He ordered the 1st and 2nd Battalions to converge on Rabaul, then returned to the landing craft and headed toward Rabaul. During the ride across Simpson Harbor, he was inspired by the sight of 3rd Battalion troops as they landed "in the rain of shells which poured down from Vulcan." He disembarked at the waterfront and proceeded to Chinatown, where Tsukamoto and Kusunose briefed him on the invasion's progress. At about 0830 a message arrived from Kuwada: the 3rd Battalion was encountering resistance at Three Ways, and the capture of Vunakanau airdrome would be slightly delayed. In response, Horii directed Kusunose to shift his battalion toward the southern plateau to assist Kuwada.

The order was unnecessary. The Japanese already owned Rabaul and Lakunai airdrome, and the fleet was now moving into the safety of Simpson Harbor. Horii's troops had accomplished all this within a couple of hours; so quickly, in fact, that the sun was still rising above the islands east of the anchorage. Cliché or not, the sight must have greatly inspired the general and his staff. They needed only to mop up a few pockets of resistance and occupy Vunakanau in order to complete yet another lopsided victory.

Horii would not rest, however, until every Australian was killed or captured. He did not care which.

CHAPTER SEVEN

EVERY MAN FOR HIMSELF

*"The warrior's blood runs hot as the
Rising Sun flag advances."*

—From a victory song of the
South Seas Detachment

During the critical early hours of January 23, while Japanese troops stormed ashore at Vulcan Crater and Raluana Point, Colonel Scanlan was busy moving his headquarters. It was the second time in the past twelve hours that he had changed locations. The previous afternoon, after evacuating Lark Force from Malaguna Camp, he'd elected to set up his headquarters near the observation post established by Lieutenant Dawson. Then, at 0300, a mere thirty minutes after the Japanese began landing along the south rim of the caldera, Scanlan decided to withdraw his headquarters to high ground near Toma, a coconut plantation several miles to the rear.

To cover his withdrawal, Scanlan ordered D Company to occupy new positions between Taliligap Mission and Vunakanau airdrome on the Kokopo Ridge Road. He then asked Private Harry, the local terrain expert, to guide him and his staff to the new headquarters position on a hilltop known as Tomavatur. Familiar with a little-used footpath that was more direct than the main roads, Harry started off with Scanlan and the NGA staff at 0330. For the next few hours, the commander of Lark Force was out of touch with his garrison.

The timing of Scanlan's move was certainly poor, but there was no question that his former headquarters near the rim of the caldera was vulnerable. Furthermore, the new location at Tomavatur provided a good view of the harbor and St. George's Channel. Even better, a communications truck was hidden in a coconut grove at Toma, just a short distance down the Glade Road.

The truck was one of the last links between Lark Force and the outside world. The only other radio with the transmitting power to reach Port Moresby was in the hands of Lieutenant Mackenzie and his independent Royal Australian Navy detachment, which had begun moving the so-called "portable" set toward the Baining Mountains the previous afternoon. They hoped to operate the radio beyond the reach of Japanese patrols, but transporting the set was a monumental effort. The bulky AWA Model 3B included a separate transmitter, receiver, and loudspeaker, and was powered by large, automobile-type batteries. Gasoline was required for the engine-driven battery charger, which weighed seventy pounds. Altogether, the equipment was more than Mackenzie and his signalers could carry without a vehicle, and the passable roads ended a few miles beyond Malabunga Mission. Thus, they were compelled to wait until native porters could be obtained.

Guided by Private Harry, Scanlan and his staff reached Tomavatur at about 0600. Although they were miles from the nearest action, Scanlan drafted a message to Combined Defense Headquarters at Port Moresby that described "the deteriorating situation as well as it could be interpreted." He then gave the draft to Harry and sent him to find the radio truck.

At approximately the same hour, Lieutenant Figgis drafted a hasty warning to Port Moresby just before evacuating his forward observation post near Rabaul. He cranked up a field telephone and got through to Captain Appel, then asked for a dispatch rider to take his message to Toma. "To CDH, Port Moresby," he dictated: "One aircraft carrier anchored off Credner Island." That done, he sped off on a motorcycle to find Hugh Mackenzie and his precious radio. Appel sent the runner to the radio truck, but somehow Figgis' message became corrupted during encryption. When decoded at Port Moresby it read, "MOTOR LANDING CRAFT CARRIER OFF CREBUEN ISLAND." No one could make any sense of it.

By the time Bill Harry reached the radio truck, which had been moved far into the plantation to avoid enemy aircraft, he found it "hopelessly bogged" in the soft ground. Harry handed Scanlan's message to rifleman

David A. Laws of the NGVR, a radio expert who had spent the past several years maintaining equipment owned by Amalgamated Wireless. Laws accepted the draft with every intention of getting it out, but it was never transmitted. Harry surmised that another strafing attack must have knocked out the truck before Laws finished coding the message.

Dozens of Lark Force's vehicles were attacked by Imperial Navy planes that day. Pilots from the *Akagi* and *Kaga* took off well before dawn and enjoyed absolute control of the skies over Rabaul, with upwards of thirty Zeros and eighteen Type 99 dive bombers in the air at any given time. Their instructions were to provide "aerial protection for the ground units . . . and scout for information on the enemy's disposition," which allowed them plenty of flexibility to hit targets of opportunity. The first attacks started at 0430.

Aerial superiority was arguably the most important component of the invasion. Although the South Seas Detachment had the biggest role in the overall plan, the relatively few planes involved contributed significantly to the rapid collapse of Lark Force. Twin-float reconnaissance planes from the *Kiyokawa Maru*, a converted seaplane tender, cruised without fear over the Gazelle Peninsula and searched for targets. Whenever the observers spotted a likely position or vehicle, they called warplanes from the *Akagi* and *Kaga* in to attack. Zeros prowled in three-plane sections and shot up anything that moved. Dive bombers pounded key intersections and roadways with antipersonnel bombs.

The well-coordinated attacks also contributed to the breakdown of communications between Australian positions. Telephone lines had been strung haphazardly through the trees alongside the roadways, and whenever a vehicle swerved out of control or was knocked off the road, it often damaged a section of wire. Other lines were cut by shrapnel from the antipersonnel bombs, such that by early morning only B and C Companies still had an operating connection.

Among the outlying platoons and isolated patrols, almost total confusion prevailed. "Mac" McLellan, the London-born warrant officer, led a five-man squad from B Company to bury land mines in a secondary road, after which they were to await further instructions. Hours passed with no word, so the squad started back toward Three Ways. A burst of enemy machine-gun fire raked the road, sending the Australians into a ditch.

Private Webster, the rough-rider and bulldogging champ, later regaled his friends with a colorful account.

> I was flat in the side cut of the road. My head seemed low enough but I was not so sure of my arse, so I shifted my tin hat. My old mate "Gabby" Searle went through a patch of bamboo like a mad native with a bush knife. As for "Bombhead" Naylor, he was sprinting to get over the rise with the soles of his feet showing so often that I thought he was kneeling in prayer. Gee, I wish I'd seen those Japs come over those land mines; there would have been rice everywhere.*

Webster escaped from the ambush along with Privates Donald N. Searle and Peter J. "Joe" Kelleher, but McClellan and Private Milton R. Naylor were captured.

Other isolated units experienced similar difficulties. Corporal Hamill's patrol was still guarding Boiler Road when daybreak came, and they had not heard from D Company headquarters since the previous evening. At 0800, Hamill heard the sound of trucks getting underway in the vicinity of company headquarters and ordered his squad into their own truck. They started up the hill but were soon flagged down by Lieutenant Henry, who was unaware that they had been down on Boiler Road all that time. He warned them that Japanese troops were within a hundred yards of head-quarters, then sent them on their way. A few minutes later, while driving north on the Kokopo Ridge Road, they were flagged down again, this time by Major John C. Mollard. "He said we were overwhelmed," recalled Private Pearson, "and to go for our lives."

Mollard, who had become the second in command of the 2/22nd when Major Leggatt departed, was under orders to hold the Kokopo Ridge Road open as long as possible. Directing traffic that passed through Taliligap, he

---

* Webster's ethnic wisecrack was more accurate than he knew. Japanese sol-diers went into battle with "emergency rations" for five days, including 1/2 pound of hard candy, a package of hard tack, and a small sack of polished rice. Additionally, the landing orders of the South Seas Detachment required every soldier to carry a two-day supply of Field Ration B, which included more than a pound of rice.

urged Hamill's driver to get beyond Three Ways before the intersection was cut off. First, however, he held the truck briefly so that additional soldiers could jump aboard. Some squeezed onto the running boards while others clung fiercely to the canvas top, all of them willing to take their chances with the Zeros rather than be captured.

Speeding northwest, the truck safely reached Three Ways, and the driver turned inland on the Bamboo Road, which skirted around Vunakanau airdrome to Malabunga Junction. As the truck bounced over the rough road, the passengers saw several shot-up vehicles in the ditches. No one was very surprised, therefore, when several Zeros had "a go" at their truck. Somehow they made it unscathed to Malabunga Junction, then followed the Glade Road to Toma.

Others were not so fortunate. The well-coordinated strafing attacks caused mayhem on the roads between Vunakanau and the caldera. Australians trying to withdraw from advancing Japanese troops found themselves being strafed from above with machine guns and 20mm automatic cannons. Trucks became potential death traps. "Vehicles could not travel on the roads," Lieutenant Figgis reported, "and traffic between Vunakanau and the other companies was brought to a standstill."

Drivers tried to run the gauntlet anyway, and some paid the price. Private James A. Ascott of Burwick, Victoria was killed as he drove a truck down the Kokopo Ridge Road near Taliligap. Sitting beside him in the cab, Lance Corporal Herbert G. "Graham" Parsons was shot in the upper torso and staggered from the truck when it rolled to a stop. Of the three men riding in the cargo bed, two were killed immediately. The third man, Private Merton G. Carmichael, jumped out only to be fatally wounded seconds later. Parsons, the only survivor, wandered in the jungle for hours before finding a road that showed fresh tracks from a Bren gun carrier. Bleeding heavily, he followed the tracks until he linked up with a platoon from C Company.

AT TOMA, A SIZEABLE GROUP OF AUSTRALIANS BEGAN TO GATHER. HAVING successfully gotten past the Zeros, the troops were told to rest under cover while the officers conferred. At about midday, everyone climbed back aboard the trucks and drove without mishap to Malabunga Mission, where they found the food Lieutenant Dawson had sent down the day before. It was a godsend. While the ravenous troops tore open cans of bully beef and fruit, someone boiled a "billy" of water for tea.

Perce Pearson, though he had not eaten since the night before, was too keyed up to eat. He tried, but couldn't swallow solid food. The cure for his jangled nerves, he discovered, was to drink "about three pannikins of tea." It was not just a drink to the Australians. Like their English cousins, they considered tea an essential element of everyday life. Brewing it was almost as soothing as drinking it, and they steadfastly maintained the rituals even in the heat and humidity of a tropical island.

ALTHOUGH NUMEROUS SKIRMISHES OCCURRED ACROSS THE PLATEAU DURING the early hours of January 23, the Australians dug in at Three Ways had still not encountered any Japanese troops as of 0800. Carrier planes had been harassing them since daybreak, but the only soldiers to pass through the intersection were Aussies, mostly stragglers from Raluana Point. Captain Selby and his militiamen, for example, had arrived at dawn and dug in alongside B Company.

The erstwhile gunners were bone weary. In the past twenty-four hours they had endured an air attack, blown up their own guns, relocated to the opposite side of the caldera, been overrun at Raluana Point, and survived a hair-raising retreat in the darkness. No one had slept during that entire time, but after digging in at Three Ways they napped in spite of the enemy air activity.

The Zeros did not concern Selby, who later described their shooting as "wild and inaccurate." What did worry him were the Japanese troops that suddenly crested the rim of the caldera. "Over the ridge about 800 yards away, the enemy appeared like a swarm of black ants, threw themselves down and opened fire."

The Australian rifle platoons and two Vickers machine guns returned fire, but the Japanese poured onto the plateau and began to maneuver around the defenders' right flank. Captain McInnes could not afford to let them cut off the Bamboo Road, in which case B Company and the attached personnel would have no escape route. By 0830, the two Vickers guns were nearly surrounded. The crews pulled back under a barrage of counter-fire from nearby mortar teams, but soon thereafter McInnes' command post came under small-arms fire. In addition, carrier planes increased their attacks in support of the advancing Japanese troops. As Selby later put it, the "dive-bombing and machine-gunning from the air were becoming unpleasant."

At 0845 McInnes and Captain Appel conferred by telephone. Appel wanted to make certain that A Company, thought to be still withdrawing from Vulcan, made it safely through Three Ways. McInnes informed him that Owen and his men had already passed through the intersection, then added that he was about to withdraw his own company. Appel, realizing that R Company and the headquarters personnel at Noah's Mission would be trapped if the intersection were abandoned, urged McInnes to stay in position as long as possible.

A moment later, Major Mollard took the phone from McInnes and gave his own assessment. Having arrived at Three Ways mere minutes ahead of the Japanese, he considered the situation there hopeless. Mollard not only supported McInnes' plan to withdraw from the intersection, but ordered Appel to cover their withdrawal. Once they were safely away, Appel was to move C Company to Malabunga Junction south of Vunakanau, and the two companies would form "a fresh front."

Appel, a former pharmacist from St. Kilda, Victoria, thought the two companies should consolidate northeast of Vunakanau in an attempt to close the breach in the Australian defenses. Such a position, he argued, would give them a "good front with good depth" and force the Japanese "to come out into the kunai grass country." Mollard would have none of it, and repeated his original order: Appel was to cover B Company's withdrawal from Three Ways, then move C Company to Malabunga Junction.

It was the correct thing to do. Appel's desire to slug it out with the Japanese was commendable, but from his distant location at Vunakanau he lacked an accurate picture of the situation at Three Ways. Mollard, on the other hand, could clearly see that the Japanese were surrounding the intersection. Furthermore, even if Appel's recommendation had been accepted, it would not have changed the outcome. General Horii had already arrived in Chinatown and learned of the delay at Three Ways, whereupon he ordered an additional battalion to assist with the capture of Vunakanau. Soon, the Australians would be facing twice as many Japanese.

WHILE THE ENEMY ADVANCED ONTO THE PLATEAU, LIEUTENANT COLONEL Carr decided to follow Scanlan's example by moving his headquarters.

First, he conferred with Scanlan using one of the few field telephones still in operation. He then left Noah's Mission and moved the battalion headquarters to Malabunga Junction. Thus, Carr was preoccupied during critical periods of the invasion, much like Scanlan had been a few hours earlier. Unaware of many of the events unfolding around him, he relied on dispatch riders to send and receive messages. Later he attempted to rationalize the situation: "Owing to the difficult country, the long distances to HQ, and the fact that most of these were moving, very few messages and orders got through and it was then felt that the companies would have to fight practically independent actions."

Carr made it sound as though he initially possessed some control over the widely scattered elements of his battalion. To the contrary, the companies fought independently from the moment the Japanese landed, with little or no input from Carr.

OUT IN SIMPSON HARBOR, LIEUTENANT COLONEL TOSHIHARU SAKIGAWA waited his turn to disembark from the transport *Mito Maru*. The commanding officer of the 2nd Company, 55th Transportation Regiment, he was awed by the sights and sounds of battle. "The mountain air filled with smoke from the summit of the active volcano Nakamisaki weighed upon us," he noted. "The flotilla moved into Rabaul Bay, and from then, we understood the magnificence of the battlefield with the roaring noise of the [machine guns] and the sweeping fire of our planes as they flew in formation seeking out the enemy."

After the assault troops secured the landing areas, Sakigawa led several Daihatsu craft loaded with light reconnaissance vehicles to the beachhead south of Vulcan Crater. He investigated the surrounding terrain on foot, walking about fifty yards through the jungle before he found a road, then returned to the beach and supervised the unloading of the landing craft. He was concerned that the scout cars and motorcycles would bog down in the volcanic soil, but the crews offloaded the vehicles onto bamboo mats without difficulty. By mid-morning, Sakigawa's high-speed *butai* (squad) was ready to scout ahead.

Soon after the mechanized column started off toward Rabaul, incoming mortar rounds and gunfire forced the Japanese to take cover. They advanced on foot into a coconut grove and spotted a camouflaged truck, which they sprayed with bullets before cautiously approaching. The truck was empty, but the littered ground around it revealed useful information. "At intervals in the grass in this area," wrote Sakigawa, "large quantities of guns, MG bullets, rifle bullets, and shells had been left behind. In vehicles were abandoned clothes and utensils enough for about one *butai*. Traces of a hurried flight were clearly evident."

The amount of discarded equipment was indeed an indication that the Australians were pulling back under considerable duress. The Japanese needed only to increase the pressure slightly, and the withdrawal would turn into a rout.

CAPTAIN APPEL'S PLEA TO HOLD THREE WAYS OPEN HAD NOT FALLEN ON deaf ears. At 0900, Mollard personally risked the Zeros and went by car to Noah's Mission. He ordered R Company and the remaining personnel from the Headquarters Company to evacuate immediately, and vehicles of every description were rounded up for transportation, including a taxi from the Rabaul Carrying Company. Soldiers piled aboard regardless of rank and were sent off with instructions to get through Three Ways as quickly as possible. When they were safely away, Mollard rejoined McInnes and ordered him to withdraw his company.

The Australians pulled back from Three Ways in an orderly fashion, though not everyone had the luxury of a ride. "McInnes gave the order to retire by way of Malabunga Junction," remembered Captain Selby, "and most of the company moved off in whatever transport was available. The majority of my men went with them, but rounding up stragglers I found four of my men who had not succeeded in boarding any of the trucks. We set off on foot under heavy fire from the enemy who were now coming through in great numbers, but their shooting continued to be very wild and erratic."

Gunner Bloomfield, a member of Selby's small party, had no ammunition and felt "completely helpless with only an empty rifle and a bayonet" as he advanced cautiously along the Bamboo Road. The five men soon came across a mortar crew who cautioned them "not to stick around." It proved to be good advice. Moments later three Zeros roared over and strafed the mortar position. Selby's party dived into the bushes and waited for a few minutes, but heard no further sound from the direction of the shot-up mortar team.

Rattled by their close call, the antiaircraft men started off again toward Malabunga Junction. It was a harrowing journey, as Selby later described:

> I wondered what a good company commander would do in the circumstances—run, crawl or walk. Running seemed both pointless and provocative, and the silly thought crossed my mind that the surest way of being chased by a fierce dog is to run away from him.
>
> Crawling was too slow, so we walked at a brisk pace, only taking cover when diving planes roared down on us. Eventually a truck dashed by, then pulled up in answer to our hail and we climbed aboard. At frequent intervals planes would dive on us, their machine guns blazing, and we would leap off the truck and take cover at the roadside.

The truck, from the 17th Antitank Battery, also stopped a few times for the benefit of other stragglers. During the entire trip, two men rode out on the running boards and kept a constant lookout for enemy planes. They were able to provide ample warning before each strafing attack, which undoubtedly saved lives. One flight of Zeros made three separate strafing runs, according to Bloomfield, but for all their shooting they scored only a single bullet hole in the truck and caused no injuries.

AFTER THE AUSTRALIANS WITHDREW FROM FOUR WAYS AND THREE WAYS, truckloads of evacuating troops raced toward Toma with an increasing sense of urgency. Those that made it past the gauntlet of Zeros on the Bamboo Road just kept going when they reached Malabunga Junction, the drivers refusing to stop even though battalion officers tried to flag them down. Watching as the trucks sped past his headquarters, Lieutenant Colonel Carr heard the occupants shout various warnings and gathered the impression that the Japanese had broken through by the thousands.

The atmosphere of alarm and the disturbing rumors were more than he could handle. "Carr rushed off telling anyone he met that the Japs were coming close behind—when in fact they were busy settling things down in Rabaul," attested one officer. Carr's adjutant, Captain Ivan L. Smith, and the brigade major, Captain McLeod, both attempted to halt some of the speeding trucks, but Carr told them to let the vehicles go. He feared that a traffic jam would block the intersection and prevent everyone from escaping.

At Tomavatur, Colonel Scanlan could also see the stream of trucks that sped along the Glade Road toward Toma. Thus, when Carr phoned him to report on the rapidly deteriorating situation, he decided that it was "useless to prolong the action" and told Carr to withdraw the 2/22nd Battalion to the Keravat River. The order made no sense. Scanlan knew—or should have known—that Carr had no telephone communications with his scattered companies and could no longer direct their movements.

Carr suggested that the companies withdraw beyond one of three landmarks, whichever was closest: the Keravat River for soldiers in the northern area of the plateau, the Warangoi River for those in the south, and the Baining Mountains via Malabunga Mission for everyone in the middle. Agreeing to this, Scanlan voiced his opinion that it was now a case of "every man for himself."

In hindsight, Scanlan's comment was nothing short of astounding. Clearly he was frustrated by his inability to stop the Japanese. It is equally apparent that he never anticipated the profound effect his words would have on virtually every soul in Lark Force. For one thing, the unimaginative Carr interpreted Scanlan's phrase as an instruction. He passed it verbatim to the signalers "for transmission to all companies," and also sent dispatch riders to make certain the scattered companies were informed of the latest development.

One of the riders, Private Creed, found a number of stragglers at Noah's Mission. Not everyone had gotten the word about the withdrawal, and the new arrivals were milling about in confusion, as though waiting for someone to tell them what to do. Among them, Private Fred Kollmorgen was surprised to see his Salvation Army friend pull up near the old church on a motorcycle.

> Austin Creed rode up and said, "I have a direct order from the colonel in charge of the whole area: It is now a matter of every man for himself. Get out of this pickle if you can."
>
> If it had been anybody else, I would have thought that maybe he'd gotten things mixed up, and it wasn't really

intended to be "every man for himself," but to come from a chap that I knew well and believed, he certainly passed that message along to us. There must have been forty or fifty men by this time around Noah's Mission.

Some of the older fellows, and those who were not terribly well, decided to surrender. But I was young and very active and strong at that stage. I said, "No, I'm not giving up, I'm going into the bush."

All across the plateau, as the word of Scanlan's "orders" trickled from one scattered group to the next, Australians began to withdraw into the jungle. Some decided to not make any attempt to evade the Japanese, as Kollmorgen indicated, but self-preservation was a powerful motivator among the majority of Lark Force.

This included Carr. "In view of doubt regarding Colonel Scanlan's future actions," he later explained, "I had to give serious consideration to my own." He rationalized that he "would become commander of the guerilla force" if Scanlan surrendered, but there was no way to organize a resistance movement at this late stage. Nevertheless, he was convinced that his only recourse was to head toward the mountains. His first goal was to find Lieutenant Mackenzie, who was "known to be attempting to go bush with a wireless set from the vicinity of Malabunga." Carr must have realized that as soon as he left headquarters, all control of his battalion would be lost—but that's exactly what he did.

At Tomavatur, Captain Selby requested a meeting with Scanlan to discuss options. The NGA adjutant entered Scanlan's tent, then emerged a few minutes later and said, "The colonel's orders are that each man is to fend for himself." Shelby was stunned, not only by the message but by Scanlan's refusal to see him in person.

News of the encounter spread quickly among the troops gathered nearby, and many felt a sense of bewilderment. "Were it not for the seriousness of our situation, one could have been excused for thinking that this was some sort of a joke," recalled Gunner Bloomfield. "Here was the CO only a few days ago issuing the orders, 'EVERY MAN WILL FIGHT TO THE LAST' and 'THERE SHALL BE NO WITHDRAWAL,' telling us now that it was 'EVERY MAN FOR HIMSELF.'"

At approximately 1100, Scanlan and a party of five left Tomavatur and began walking toward the Baining Mountains. Carrying the colonel's large kitbag was Tovakina, a Tolai native who had waited on tables at the officers' mess before serving as his personal houseboy. The adjutant and a few other members of Scanlan's staff, including his regular batman, Private Eric A. Angwin, were also in the entourage. Scanlan even invited Bill Harry to accompany them, but the latter declined. Believing the colonel's departure was "somewhat premature," Harry decided to wait for friends.

The battle for Rabaul was not yet over when Scanlan quit the field and left his troops to fend for themselves. Weeks earlier he had called some of his subordinates "defeatist" because they wanted to hide caches of food in the jungle. More recently he had deliberately misled his men, telling them they were going on an exercise and preventing them from being adequately prepared to face the enemy. And now, mere hours after the invasion commenced, Scanlan abandoned his headquarters and walked into the jungle. For a veteran commander who had earned a DSO for gallantry in combat more than twenty years earlier, it was a spectacular capitulation.

Was Scanlan a coward? Probably not. His actions, however wrong, were preordained from the day he arrived at Rabaul. He was doomed to fail, thanks mainly to the War Cabinet's disregard for Lark Force and the other outlying garrisons. The unavoidable truth was that none of them could withstand the overwhelming power of the Southern Offensive.

AT VUNAPOPE THAT MORNING, THE ARMY NURSES SLEPT FOR A FEW HOURS in a nuns' dormitory while the orderlies monitored the patients in the native hospital. When the nurses arrived for duty shortly after dawn, they made two shocking discoveries. "We found there were only two orderlies left," Lorna Johnson remembered. "All the rest and the two doctors had gone. And we saw ships coming up Rabaul harbor; I can't remember how many, but there seemed to be thousands of them. There were about three aircraft carriers, and submarines, and troopships, and battleships, all together in this huge convoy. I don't think any one of us girls had ever seen an aircraft carrier or a submarine in our lives."

The nurses hardly knew which was more distressing—the sight of the invasion fleet or the sudden departure of the doctors. They could scarcely believe that Major Palmer and Captain Robertson had skulked away in the middle of the night. Even more insulting, the doctors had taken the two ambulances, eighteen orderlies, and a few patients with them. They knew Palmer had never fully approved of them, and his silent departure came as a bitter pill.

In actuality, the doctors' motives were anything but sinister. Palmer and Robertson knew there were plenty of good medical personnel at Vunapope, whereas the troops withdrawing into the jungle would have almost no help. Furthermore, Palmer had asked John May to stay at Vunapope and look after the nurses. The chaplain immediately agreed, though he knew it would guarantee his own capture.

Some seventy-five patients remained in the thatched-roof hospital by the beach, along with two orderlies from the 2/10 Field Ambulance who had volunteered to stay, Corporal Laurence A. Hudson and Private Reginald M. "Max" Langdon. No one had time to fuss about the situation, because a multitude of Japanese landing craft suddenly approached the beach. Chaplain May and Kay Parker walked outside to meet the enemy.

Later, Lorna Johnson described the first stressful hours of captivity:

> The Japanese jumped off the landing barges, ran up the beach, and came up to the hospital. They dragged all the boys out of the hospital; told them all to get out. The sun had started to come up, and it was getting very, very hot. They lined us up for about two hours. These soldiers looked like hundreds of little monkeys, with the shoes they used to wear, like sand shoes, with the big toe separated from the other four toes. They had these little khaki pants on, and khaki shirts, and funny little hats. They each had a gun with a bayonet, and they lined us all up.
>
> John May, who was our padre, stood with Kay. They had a white handkerchief tied onto something to say, "We surrender." There was nothing else we could do. The Japanese rushed up and down and they dragged the boys out of the hospital and slapped them across the face. Then they found the only lot of food that we had taken from Rabaul—a couple of cases of bully beef and things like that. They brought this food out in front of us, bayoneted

EVERY MAN FOR HIMSELF 119

it all, then made the boys dig a hole and throw it into the
hole. We couldn't understand their stupidity.

The patients were forced to remain standing in the hot sun for about
two hours. There were malaria cases with high fevers, burn victims from
the *Herstein*, and soldiers who suffered from tropical infections, including
Sergeant Gullidge. Several men collapsed, but the Japanese prodded them
back on their feet with bayonets. Finally, the patients and most of the medical staff were allowed to return to the hospital. John May and Laurie
Hudson were taken away by the Japanese, one of whom drew his sword.

Horrified, the nurses presumed the two men would be executed. A
few hours later, however, May and Hudson returned unharmed. They had
been driven a short distance down a side road to Vunapope's refrigeration
building, where they were made to sit in the sun. The escorts gave them
menacing looks, and the officer holding the sword demonstrated how
easily he could slice an inch-thick branch from a tree. But it was all an
act of intimidation. Nothing was done to physically harm the two
Australians, and they were given some lunch before the Japanese
returned them to the hospital.

ACROSS THE HARBOR, THE CIVILIANS IN REFUGE GULLY ENDURED A
frightening night. "[We] had little knowledge of what was happening along
the beaches; only the incessant rifle firing and bomb explosions indicated
that the invasion had started," recalled Gordon Thomas, editor of the
Rabaul Times. "Overhead, planes were zooming, and occasional bursts of
machine-gun fire, raking the hillsides where we were in hiding, showed
how trigger-happy were the Jap airmen."

At daybreak, Thomas set off with Nobby Clark and Hector Robinson,
the senior government official at Refuge Gully, to find the Japanese.
Carrying a white flag, the three men planned to lead a patrol back to the
shelter, their hope being that a voluntary surrender would prevent the
enemy from gunning down unarmed people. In that regard, their mission
succeeded. "Later in the morning," Thomas continued, "all civilians were
mustered onto the baseball oval, where we remained for the rest of the day,
foodless, and under a strong-armed guard, with machine guns trained on us
from every angle."

The civilian captives, more than two hundred in all, were made to swelter in the hot sun while the Tolai natives sat in the shade. It was an obvious manipulation by the Japanese to embarrass the former colonials. Everyone was compelled to listen while a Japanese officer loudly read a proclamation in English. It, too, was a piece of propaganda meant to curry favor with the Melanesians. "The soldiers of Japan," the officer stated, "have arrived here in order to improve your condition . . ."

After listening to the speeches, the captives were taken to the large Kuomintang Hall, headquarters of the Chinese Nationalist Party. Most had not eaten at all that day, nor were any meals provided during the night. Just twenty-four hours earlier, they had represented the upper echelon of their society; now, their lives turned suddenly upside down, they squabbled like children and scrounged for food.

THE LAST FIREFIGHT OF THE DAY WAS ONE OF THE FIERCEST. AT 0300 THAT morning, in compliance with orders from Colonel Scanlan, Captain Travers moved D Company to defensive positions astride the Kokopo Ridge Road near Taliligap. Upon arrival, he realized the Japanese could get behind him from Vulcan Crater, so he decided to concentrate his platoons on a ridge near the home of Albert Gaskin. Owner of the Cosmopolitan Hotel, Gaskin had joined the RAAF evacuation the previous afternoon and was currently at Wide Bay. Thus, he was out of harm's way when his handsome bungalow was shot to pieces.

The combat began at approximately 1130, when two natives wearing white mission garb led several Japanese soldiers out of the jungle directly in front of Lieutenant Alec Tolmer's platoon. Private Holmes, Tolmer's batman, saw the enemy and called out a warning, and Tolmer shot one of the natives dead. The rest of the platoon immediately opened fire, killing the second native and possibly a few of the soldiers. The surviving Japanese sought cover inside Gaskin's house, and dozens more attacked the ridge from several directions simultaneously.

Within minutes, D Company was cut off from the main road and its own parked vehicles. Travers had no communications with battalion headquarters or the other companies, and was therefore unaware that B Company had withdrawn from Three Ways. To ascertain what was happening, he sent a driver to contact Carr. The soldier never returned.

Travers next sent out a squad, followed later by a whole platoon, all of which ran afoul of the enemy. "They were attacked from all quarters by Japs in the kunai grass and scrub," stated Sergeant Desmond T. S. Ferguson in an official report. None doubled back to D Company.

Two other platoons, led by Lieutenants John G. "Geoff" Donaldson and boyish-looking Glenn Garrard, were also surrounded. The Japanese continued to close in, and by 1400, following more than two hours of enemy probes and skirmishes, Travers knew it was time to commence an organized withdrawal. He first sent Donaldson's platoon to counterattack along the Kokopo Ridge Road and recapture a few trucks.

Twenty-four-year-old Corporal Arthur B. Simpson, carrying one of the new Thompson submachine guns, distinguished himself by advancing toward the enemy in leaps and dashes "using all available cover," and firing into clusters of surprised Japanese. The platoon successfully retrieved two trucks, which they drove back to Travers' position through a hailstorm of small-arms fire and exploding mortar rounds. Miraculously, not a single Australian was lost. Donaldson claimed his men had killed fifty of the enemy, but actual Japanese losses were less than ten men.

Travers' company was still not out of danger. Two trucks were not nearly enough to carry everyone, so he ordered most of the company to withdraw southward on foot to the Glade Road. Shortly past 1500 they took off through the heavy kunai grass, vigorously pursued by enemy troops that closed to within a hundred yards. "The Japs were firing into the kunai from some hills to the left," Sergeant Ferguson reported, "and although their bullets whipped uncomfortably close through the grass, no one was hit."

During the withdrawal, several men fired Lewis machine guns and Tommy guns to the rear while they moved through the tall grass, keeping the enemy at bay. They could see the Japanese waving signal flags to communicate with aircraft overhead, and numerous strafing attacks ensued. The Australians suffered no casualties during their rush through the grass, and after a heart-pounding hour of evasion they stumbled across the Glade Road. Instead of calling a halt, however, Travers kept them moving south until they entered a *donga*, a deep gully near the base of Mount Varzin. The Japanese gave up the pursuit, and the exhausted men of D Company collapsed on the ground.

Similar actions occurred all across the plateau as groups of desperate Australians withdrew into the jungle. They had no provisions, no communications gear, and no training in the art of jungle survival. Most had either lost their weapons or deliberately dumped them during the withdrawal, keeping only what they wore: lightweight tropical uniforms and leather boots. Many also discarded their helmets, though a few wisely kept them.

BY MID-AFTERNOON ON JANUARY 23, THE JAPANESE WERE NO LONGER encountering resistance. An unnamed 3rd Battalion officer observed "places on the road where the enemy had abandoned vehicles, where ammunition was scattered about, and where due to the pursuit attacks of our high-speed *butai* [there] were pitiful traces of the confused flight and defeat of the enemy."

The victors carefully recorded their spoils, though much of it was damaged: five airplanes, two fortress cannons, two antiaircraft guns, fifteen antitank guns, eleven mortars, twenty-seven machine guns, 548 rifles, twelve armored cars, and nearly two hundred light vehicles. Someone even took the trouble to count all of the captured bullets, tallying 11,334 rounds of .303-caliber ammunition.

Taking such attention to detail into consideration, it is probable that the Japanese losses reported in various summaries are correct. For one thing, the dead had to be identified so that their families could properly honor their sacrifice. Some of the rituals were public and highly visible, such as periodic ceremonies to honor "fallen heroes" at the Yasukuni Shrine in Tokyo. If nothing else, they added another layer of legitimacy to the admitted losses at Rabaul. Sixteen men from the South Seas Detachment, all below the rank of warrant officer, were killed in action; and two officers and forty-six men were wounded. Among the naval forces, only one fighter pilot from the *Kaga*, Flying Petty Officer Second Class Isao Hiraishi, was lost on January 23.

According to the Australian nominal rolls, fifty-seven men were killed in action, of which forty-one belonged to the 2/22nd Battalion. Among the attached units of Lark Force, the antiaircraft gunners suffered the heaviest losses with seven killed.

Few specific details exist about individual casualties. Bandsman Jack Stebbings, for example, was simply listed as "killed while riding." Assigned as a dispatch rider, he was delivering messages at the time of his death, but whether he was the victim of a marauding Zero or Japanese soldiers was not recorded. Overall, the number killed in actual combat at Vulcan or Raluana Point is thought to be relatively low, which indicates that numerous casualties occurred on the roads. No matter how they were killed, the dead remained where they fell.

The number of Australians wounded that day has never been accurately determined. Some who could walk were able to escape into the jungle with the assistance of other troops. Graham Parsons, bleeding badly from bullet wounds in his chest and neck, had plenty of help as he made his way toward the north coast of New Britain. Those who were immobilized, however, had almost no chance of getting away—the terrain was simply too rugged. Most of the sick and wounded were therefore captured, sometimes along with a medical orderly or friend who volunteered to stay with them. Fifteen of the former bandsmen serving as stretcher bearers were taken prisoner in that fashion, including the only American-born member of Lark Force, Private Jim Thurst.

Inevitably, some of the captured Australians regretted their decision to stay rather than evade. None were prepared for the ruthless behavior of their captors, who deeply loathed Caucasians but abhorred the concept of surrender even more. Those emotions, combined with the Japanese soldiers' belief in their own superiority, made them capable of horrific brutalities.

There is no question that the Japanese acted savagely on January 23. Tolai natives witnessed an incident in which "some retreating Australians were killed in a fight and their heads were cut with axes, bellies sliced open, and limbs removed with bayonets." Although no other statements have surfaced to corroborate this particular incident, independent confirmation is unnecessary. Over the next several weeks, members of Lark Force would witness more than enough atrocities to give the account plenty of credibility.

THE JAPANESE WERE QUICK TO PUBLICIZE THEIR VICTORY, BEGINNING WITH an official statement from Imperial General Headquarters on the afternoon of January 24: "The Imperial Army and the Imperial Navy in cooperative fashion eliminated the enemy's resistance and successfully landed in

Rabaul, New Britain Island, in the east of New Guinea before dawn on 23 January. They are steadily extending their gains."

Despite the fact that several hundred Australians had escaped into the jungle, General Horii was certain his troops would hunt them down. So far the invasion had been conducted with almost surgical precision, and victory was guaranteed.

To honor their glorious campaign, the men of the South Seas Detachment composed an emotion-filled victory song titled "Nankai Dayori" ("Tidings from the South Seas")

> First to cross the Equator,
> Our unit of vigorous youth from Shikoku.
> Far from home, in the South Seas,
> The Rising Sun flag fluttering brightly
> Over Rabaul, New Britain.
>
> Like a maiden's breast,
> Rising kindly over the gulf,
> The fiery volcano beckons.
> The pure hearts of young brave men
> Think of the smoke in their homeland.
>
> Push on into the jungle,
> Bananas, papayas, and coconut milk,
> Enjoy the taste of bounteous nature;
> Nostalgic we would push on
> To our mothers in our villages.
>
> After a passing squall,
> A rainbow on Branch Gulf,
> When at last all the enemy bombs
> Are heard receding in the distant sky,
> Beautiful smokescreen blooms with the rainbow.
>
> Just below the Equator
> We are under the Southern Cross.

The warrior's blood runs hot
As the Rising Sun flag advances.
Ahead the enemy pleads for his life under a white flag.

A brisk divine breeze blowing
Towards Australia at the limit of the south.
The ultimate place to reach.
The dawn of a new world,
Not quickly but faintly.

CHAPTER EIGHT

YOU WILL ONLY DIE

*"Each day we felt ourselves growing
weaker . . ."*

—Captain David Selby,
Antiaircraft Battery

After Colonel Scanlan and his party left Tomavatur, Bill Harry was one of the few men left at the headquarters site. His decision to stay behind proved wise. Captain McLeod and Lieutenant Figgis showed up an hour or so later expecting to find the colonel still in charge; and shortly thereafter Major Mollard and ten more men arrived in an army truck and a civilian taxi. All were curious about Scanlan's whereabouts. Harry's answer was simple: The colonel and his staff had walked off, and he didn't know where they were.

As the senior officer on the scene, Mollard took charge of the group. He decided to conduct a recon to the rim of the caldera, and placed Harry on point as they moved along a narrow track that brought them to Blanche Bay just west of Kokopo. The view of enemy activity was astonishing. "Great quantities of Japanese shipping were in the harbor and minesweepers were methodically sweeping the area," remembered Harry. "Large numbers of enemy troops were ashore with trucks and armored fighting vehicles, and consolidation of the area they had so recently gained was well under way."

The party returned to Tomavatur at dusk. From the hilltop they could see the glare of headlights as Japanese vehicles moved onto Vunakanau air-drome. Obviously, the plateau was in enemy hands. To avoid capture, Mollard and his party would have to find a way off the island.

The most logical escape route from Tomavatur was south toward the coast. A network of roads led as far as the Warangoi River, from which point the Australians would have to walk or take boats to Wide Bay. There, rumor had it, the evaders might be picked up by the RAAF. The total distance to Wide Bay was more than seventy miles, and the Australians would be hunted every step of the way by Japanese planes and roving infantry patrols.

An alternative escape route was southwest to Malabunga Mission. From there, native footpaths led to Lemingi, a Roman Catholic mission high in the Baining Mountains. More trails branched out from Lemingi to Open Bay on New Britain's north coast or Wide Bay to the south.

Aside from Bill Harry, who had hiked among the mountains with the Reverend John Poole, few people in Lark Force knew enough about the territory to make an informed decision. For John Mollard, however, the choice was obvious: his primary goal was to find Hugh Mackenzie and the precious two-way radio, reported to be somewhere near Malabunga Mission.

Just as darkness began to settle over the hilltop, privates Webster, Kelleher, and Searle stumbled in, exhausted after escaping from the Japanese ambush on the Kokopo Ridge Road. They shared their story, then everyone boarded the two vehicles for the trip to Malabunga Mission. Starting up the Glade Road toward Vunakanau, they moved slowly past the airdrome under the cover of a heavy downpour. They encountered no Japanese patrols on that miserable night, but the road became so slick that the taxi skidded into a ditch just beyond Malabunga Junction. The whole group crowded aboard the truck, and the driver turned on headlights for a wild dash over the last few miles of road.

Arriving at Malabunga Mission, Mollard's party found the compound deserted except for two men holed up in an abandoned native hospital. Tom Connop, one of the oldest privates in the 2/22nd, had suffered a badly broken leg earlier in the day. One of Major Palmer's field ambulances had picked him up, but the bumpy ride had been excruciating. When the "meat wagon" reached the mission hospital, Connop was offloaded and doped with morphine to make him as comfortable as possible. There was no hope of moving him through the jungle, so Private Albert "Pop" Thomas, a London-born dental assistant, volunteered to remain at his side.

Mollard's party drove on for another mile and spent the night in a leaky native hut, then rose at dawn and continued on their journey. Soon the truck came to a fork in the road. To the right, a rough track led uphill to Kalas, the Methodist mission run by Reverend Poole. The main road, such as it was, continued a short distance to its terminus at the village of Rabata, situated on the upper reaches of the Warangoi River.

Getting down from the truck, "Tusker" McLeod, Peter Figgis, and Bill Harry hiked uphill toward Kalas to see if any friendly troops had gone in that direction. Soon they found an abandoned staff car, identified as Lieutenant Colonel Carr's, an encouraging sign that Mackenzie and the all-important radio were up ahead. But only a few paces up the trail they found the radio itself—smashed to pieces.

Disheartened, the three men continued to Kalas. At the large, well-maintained compound, they were met by what Harry described as "a concerned group of missionaries, all neatly attired in white and awaiting the arrival of the Japanese." John Poole and two other Methodist ministers, along with two businessmen from Rabaul, had decided to give themselves up. They shared a cup of tea with the soldiers, then explained what had recently happened. Mackenzie and Carr had indeed passed through Kalas, where they tried to hire native porters to help carry the radio. But none could be found, as most of the Tolai had disappeared into the jungle when the invasion started. With great reluctance, Mackenzie had destroyed the radio rather than let it fall into enemy hands.

The missionaries, afraid to be caught harboring Australian soldiers, were anxious to see the three men off. Bill Harry urged John Poole to join them, but the other two ministers interjected. The reverends Laurie McArthur, head of the Methodist missions on New Britain, and Laurie Linggood, who ran another mission station on the coast, explained why they were surrendering: four Australian women from the ministry had gone to Vunapope with the hospital staff two days earlier, and they were now prisoners. The pastors were determined to accept the same fate.

McLeod, Figgis, and Harry bid them all good luck and walked southward. The next day they caught up with Carr and Mackenzie in the village of Riat, swelling the total group to twenty-one individuals. In addition to Mackenzie and his naval signalers, the party included William B. "Bruce" Ball, the commissioner of police on New Britain, and two riflemen from the NGVR.

Mollard's group had not yet reached the village, which was fortunate. The men gathered at Riat had already run out of army rations and were subsisting on whatever they could barter from local villagers. Within two days of the invasion, the specter of starvation was already looming large.

Many soldiers were surprised to discover that the jungle, for all its lush vegetation, would not feed them. It was actually "a desert" in the words of Lieutenant Commander Feldt, who had spent twenty years among the islands. "At its best," he wrote, "the food the jungle can supply is only enough to sustain life, and under a prolonged diet of jungle food, mental and physical vigor decline until there is no ability left to do more than barely support life itself."

When their provisions ran low, evading soldiers turned to native-grown vegetables such as *kau-kau*, a close relative of the sweet potato, and taro, a broadleaf plant resembling a lily. The tubers were loaded with starch but lacked calories, and taro had to be cooked to a sticky paste in order to eliminate poisonous calcium oxalate. Other commonly grown foods included coconuts, papaya, sugar cane, and cassava roots, which yielded tapioca. There was very little meat available on the island, and although some villagers had pigs and fowl, they were not considered a regular part of the native diet.

McLeod, Figgis, and Harry could see that Carr and the others at Riat were in no hurry to move on. The general state of lethargy was made worse by heavy rains which had fallen for several days, and the combination of sodden conditions and lack of food was brutal on morale. Deciding to move on, the three newcomers hiked to Rabata on January 27 to look for John Mollard. The village was empty, but Mollard's vehicle was parked among a jumble of abandoned trucks, some of which still held plenty of canned rations. McLeod returned to Riat and obtained some help to transfer the food back to Carr and his dispirited group.

Figgis and Harry remained near the Warangoi River for a few days before returning to Riat on the 29th. However, despite the additional rations, there had been no improvement in morale among Carr's party. "The only plan," noted Harry, "was to eventually trek across the Baining Mountains to the south coast." No one had a timetable, and some of the men believed there was nothing to gain even if they crossed the rugged mountains. In their dejected condition, they believed it was better to simply wait for the Japanese to come. A few actually talked of returning to Rabaul under a white flag.

This was exactly what Major General Horii wanted. On the afternoon of the invasion, he had taken pains to dictate a warning to the retreating Australians. Printed on leaflets, the persuasive message was airdropped with remarkable efficiency and reached hundreds of Australians. Few, however, took the warning seriously:

> To the Officers and Soldiers of this Island!
> SURRENDER AT ONCE!
> And we will guarantee your life, treating you as war prisoners. Those who RESIST US WILL BE KILLED ONE AND ALL. Consider seriously, you can find neither food nor way of escape in this island and you will only die of hunger unless you surrender.
>> January 23rd, 1942.
>> Japanese Commander in Chief

Most Australians scoffed at the implied threats, though few would disagree with Horii about the lack of food in the jungle. Dick Travers, for one, believed there was little hope of successfully evading the enemy. Hiding near Mount Varzin with D Company, he hoped to arrange terms for a large-scale surrender. On the morning of January 24 he started toward Vunakanau with Geoff Donaldson, but after hiking for two hours without finding any Japanese, they returned to the donga. For the benefit of the troops, they outlined the situation as they saw it. "Travers called us together and told us there were only two things to do," remembered Lance Corporal William J. Neave. "[We could] either go back and give ourselves up or break up into small parties and try and make a break for it. He stated he would . . . go back with any troops who desired to give themselves up."

While Neave and several others struck out for the north coast, Travers waited with the rest for the Japanese to pick them up. The exact number of men from D Company who surrendered is unknown, but a Japanese soldier noted in his diary that approximately one hundred Australian prisoners were marched into Rabaul on the evening of January 27. Travers was not among them. When he surrendered, the Japanese executed him on the spot. Perhaps he was the first to pay with his life for miscalculating Horii's sincerity, but he was definitely not the last.

DEEP IN THE JUNGLE NEAR THE KERAVAT RIVER, PIP APPEL AND COLIN McInnes were acutely aware of their dire situation. During the afternoon of January 23 they safely led most of A and C Companies across the river, but none of the nearly three hundred men were prepared for a prolonged stay in the jungle. "Our first thought was for food and supplies for the troops," McInnes later stated, "but as none had been placed in dumps for a situation such as this, we had to depend on missions, plantations and native villages."

But such establishments were not equipped to cope with a sudden request to feed and shelter so many men. Therefore, the retreating Australians scrounged for whatever they could find, then continued walking northwest for mile after miserable mile. They worked their way around diamond-shaped Ataliklikun Bay toward the northern coast, where the terrain was slightly less demanding than in the mountains, but the going was still extremely slow.

Close behind them, the South Seas Detachment conducted the task of mopping up the plateau. Aware that many Australians were fleeing toward Ataliklikun Bay, Horii sent Lieutenant Colonel Tsukamoto's 1st Battalion to pursue them. Likewise, the 3rd Battalion, encamped at Kokopo, was ordered to intercept Australians retreating southward toward the mouth of the Warangoi River.

The Imperial Japanese Navy also participated, sending warships and floatplanes to patrol New Britain's coastline. They paid particular attention to the seaside plantations and mission stations, shelling some establishments—mainly for the purpose of intimidating the landowners—and destroying every seaworthy vessel that could be found. At Pondo, a large plantation owned by W. R. Carpenter and Company on the island's north coast, the Japanese bombed and sunk a sixty-foot schooner. A landing party then went ashore and wrecked the steamer *Malahuka*, which was under repair on a slipway. To make sure it never sailed again, the Japanese also punched a large hole in the hull and disabled the engine.

Pressed hard by the pursuing Japanese, the remnants of Lark Force separated into small, disorganized groups. Already smarting from the lopsided defeat, they found themselves caught in a nightmarish environment. The jungle—hot, sticky, dark, and smelling of decay—was their only shelter. The Australians slept on the wet ground, hunger pangs gnawing at their bellies and insects biting their faces, arms, and legs. They scratched mindlessly at the bites, which then became infected and began to suppurate, slowing the men even more as their malnourished bodies tried to fight off the illness.

When Japanese patrols caught up with slow-moving parties, the outcome was often brutal. On January 26, Doc Silverman and his leading orderly, Bert Morgan, were trying to get beyond Ataliklikun Bay with Len Henry and a few other soldiers, one of whom had malaria. About three miles past the Keravat River, just after entering a foul-smelling mangrove swamp, they were ambushed by an enemy patrol. Morgan pulled his malaria patient into the swamp and hid with him until it was safe to emerge. Silverman and Henry were captured after a brief exchange of gunfire near Mandres Sawmill, and Henry was immediately beheaded. Silverman was alive when taken to Rabaul, but according to information gathered later, the Japanese refused to recognize him as a medical officer and executed him on January 30. By that time, Bert Morgan and his unidentified patient had decided to surrender. Captured soon after recrossing the Keravat River, they were imprisoned at Rabaul.

FOR HUNDREDS OF OTHER EVADERS, IT TOOK EVERY OUNCE OF DETERMINATION to stay one step ahead of the Japanese while pushing through the seemingly endless jungle. Three days after the invasion, Appel and McInnes brought 285 tired, hungry men to Kamanakan Mission, twenty miles beyond the Keravat River. Appel, the senior officer of the group, called the men together for a pep talk. He urged them not to surrender and promised to organize camps in the hills. The troops perked up when he suggested the possibility of getting them fit enough to fight again. To improve their living conditions, he separated the men into four parties, each with a lieutenant or captain in charge, and divided the group's limited resources equally among them.

The day after Appel gave his talk, McInnes' party began walking toward Lassul Bay. Japanese warships shelled several plantations around the bay, then sent landing parties ashore. McInnes and his men would have been captured had they reached the coast a little sooner, but they heard the shelling and spotted the landing craft just in time. McInnes advised his men to split up into even smaller parties in order to slip past the enemy.

Appel and his group, approximately 120 strong, also tried to reach one of the plantations. Forced to evade Japanese patrols, they spent another rain-soaked night in the jungle, and by morning both Appel and McInnes had changed their minds. "The position," McInnes recalled, "appeared to me to be rather hopeless as we did not have sufficient food, and there did not appear to be any hope of getting away from New Britain, so Appel and myself decided to see what terms for surrender we could make with the Japanese."

Joined by three noncoms, the two officers headed for a plantation along the shore of Lassul Bay owned by former coastwatcher Ted Harvey. Japanese troops had been observed there the previous day, but when the Australians arrived at the plantation, it was no longer occupied. In fact, the entire northern coast had been abandoned. As suddenly as they'd come, the Japanese had gone.

The jungle, it turned out, was a great equalizer. Lieutenant Colonel Tsukamoto's battalion encountered several impediments as they pursued the Australians, not the least of which was the heavy rain that blanketed the Gazelle Peninsula. Similarly, Lieutenant Colonel Sakigawa's mechanized unit slowed to a crawl as they advanced around Ataliklikun Bay on January 27. "The *butai* could not advance as hoped," he reported. "The mountain roads went up and down and in some places [soldiers] walked in mud and water up to the knees. And also there were obstructions on the roads [such] as fallen bamboo and rotted trees."

Other units experienced even greater difficulty. One detachment of mountain artillery tried to drag their wheeled guns through the heavy jungle. They reached the Vudal River on January 25 only to find it impossible to ford, so the soldiers hacked out a road to a different crossing. They even labored to build a temporary bridge, but their progress was so slow that they were forced to leave the field guns in the jungle. By the time the detachment finally reached the western shores of Ataliklikun Bay, they had lost contact with the fleeing Australians.

As a result of such setbacks, the battalion commanders requested naval support. General Horii arranged for a destroyer and three transports to conduct a "sea pursuit," resulting in the aforementioned landings at Lassul Bay and Massawa Bay, but these proved to be only a minor threat to the Australians. The Japanese did not venture inland, mainly because the jungle quickly conspired against them. As the writer of an operational report later explained: "Practically every man of the 1st Infantry Battalion suffered from malaria owing to an eruptive outbreak of the disease at the time of mopping up . . . in particular, the pursuit action in the Ataliklikun Bay area."

The heavy rains and high humidity of the past several days had created ideal conditions for mosquitoes. Many of the men in Tsukamoto's battalion, poised to capture hundreds of Australians, were themselves laid low by malaria. That so many became infected was the result of "nothing but negligence," according to the report, which placed blame squarely on the "leaders, medical staffs and epidemic prevention staffs in particular." Days passed before the Japanese realized what had caused the outbreak. At least ten men died, and several others were "affected in the brain and became mad."

Within days, the combat strength of the South Seas Detachment was reduced by half. As a result, the 1st Battalion quit the jungle at Lassul Bay only a few hours before Appel and McInnes arrived with intentions to surrender.

Good fortune continued to smile on the Australians at the abandoned Harvey plantation. Although the Japanese had wrecked the house and two-way radio, they overlooked some hidden caches of food. Taking advantage of the windfall, Appel dispersed his men among several nearby plantations and divided the food among them, then rounded up the last stragglers still hiding in the jungle. Eventually he organized more than four hundred Australian soldiers along thirty miles of coastline, safe for the time being from Japanese pursuit. However, the conditions at most of the sites deteriorated quickly, and the Australians too began to suffer from malaria. Appel saved his limited supply of quinine for those with active infections, relying on his prewar experience as a pharmacist to aid the sick. Having nearly surrendered his men to the enemy, the thirty-seven-year-old captain proved to be "an inspiring and energetic leader."

ON THE OPPOSITE SIDE OF THE ISLAND, HUNDREDS OF LARK FORCE SOLDIERS made for Wide Bay. Many still believed the RAAF would evacuate them by seaplane, an idea that gained credibility when David Selby's party, consisting of two officers and around twenty men, came across a line of abandoned vehicles beyond Malabunga Mission. Some of the trucks bore RAAF markings, and there was plenty of canned food aboard. The soldiers gladly helped themselves. David Bloomfield ate a whole can of bully beef and another of peaches, then filled his haversack with extra tins.

Determined to deny the vehicles to the enemy, Selby divided his group into two parties with instructions to disable the entire lot. Keeping six men with himself, he started at one end of the line and sent the remainder with his second in command, Lieutenant Peter H. Fisher, to disable the trucks at the far end of the row. Somehow, the two parties became separated on the dark and narrow track. By the time Fisher's group finished slashing tires, draining oil pans, and running engines until they seized, Selby's party was "nowhere to be seen."

Fisher had a good prismatic compass for overland navigation, so he decided to lead his party independently into the Baining Mountains. He was unaware that Selby was actually nearby, casting about for Fisher's group in the jungle. The heavily forested slopes and lack of communication equipment kept the two parties separated for days. Thus, Fisher led his group up the footpath for several hours before they stopped to rest. The men shared a single fourteen-ounce can of bully beef, served with a stick into outstretched hands, then spread out to find a place to sleep.

Still hungry, David Bloomfield scratched out a shallow depression in the undergrowth and lay down, using his canteen for a pillow. A pelting rain woke him during the night, and he discovered that his "hip hole" was filled with water. It was an appropriate conclusion to a rotten day. "As I lay awake," he recalled, "I thought about how terribly unprepared we were. When we evacuated Frisbee Ridge all we were permitted to take with us was our rifle, bayonet, water bottle, respirator, and what we stood up in." Bloomfield's uniform—a khaki shirt and baggy shorts, underwear, boots, and socks—was inadequate for the jungle. No one in his group had a poncho, groundsheet, or extra clothing.

The men were poorly rested when the sun came up, yet Fisher spurred them on without breakfast. All that day they climbed progressively higher into the Bainings, alternately struggling up mountainsides that were nearly vertical, then carefully picking their way down the opposite slopes.

Invariably they would come to a fast-flowing river at the bottom of each narrow valley. The recent heavy rains had turned streams into rivers, and rivers into raging torrents. Overhead, Japanese planes circled above the rivers, waiting to machine-gun anyone who attempted to cross. The Australians discovered that if they dashed across just one man at a time, the enemy pilots were not inclined to waste the bullets or the fuel to dive down and attack them.

On one stretch of mud-slicked trail, Fisher's group met up with nine members of the 17th Antitank Battery. The two groups decided to pool their rations, and after crossing yet another river they made camp. They even allowed themselves the luxury of a small fire made from "damp paper and photo negatives and a lot of coaxing." The burning material gave off just enough heat to brew tea, which they savored along with one stale biscuit per man for supper. Soon thereafter it began to rain again, and that was the end of the fire.

Bloomfield awoke again during the night, this time to find his skin bloody from the bites of countless sand flies. Alarmed, he awoke the whole party and they retreated from the river. After pausing long enough to eat another biscuit, they started hiking in the darkness but soon became disoriented. Several frustrating hours later they ended up back at the original campsite—but at least they were no longer lost.

Starting out again, Fisher's party followed the river downstream, wading in the water until it became too swift and deep for safe footing. Then they scrambled up the sheer bank and clawed their way through tangled brush until someone located a footpath. Fisher used his compass to determine that it was the correct route, and on the afternoon of January 25 they staggered into Riat village. Their presence put additional strain on the resources hoarded by Carr's group, so the newcomers were offered nothing more than some cooked taro—a first for the militiamen. Nobody made room for them in the village huts, and after a night on the bare ground, Fisher and his group were ready to move on.

The trials they endured over the next several days continually challenged their resolve. On the afternoon of January 26, while working their way down the slope of a particularly steep valley, the men could hear the roar of a flooded river far below. By the time they reached its banks, the sound of the rushing water was nearly deafening. To attempt a crossing there would have been suicide, but half a mile upstream the men found a site that looked marginally safe.

They decided to rig a guide rope. Two men cut lengths of sturdy vine and spliced them together; then Lionel "Jack" Hawes, a twenty-year-old gunner from New South Wales, fought his way across the river and wrapped one end of the spliced line around a tree. Others did the same on the near shore, then pulled the line taut. Using the twisted vines as a handhold, the party inched across the river. There were tense moments when a few men lost their footing briefly, but everyone got across without mishap.

The reward for reaching the far side was another precipitous climb up the next mountain. That night, the men found shelter in an abandoned village, and scroungers even found a supply of taro to cook. "For the first time since Frisbee Ridge," Bloomfield remembered, "I slept well."

The next day brought more of the same torturous travel. Forcing their starved bodies to keep moving forward, the men stumbled along the ever-ascending track through the rotting jungle. Tormented by "mossies" (their nickname for mosquitoes), they also endured other frustrations. Normally the trail was used by barefooted natives walking in single file, but in recent days it had been soaked with rain and churned into a slick, muddy bog by dozens of boot-clad soldiers. Obviously, Fisher's party was not the first from Lark Force to use it.

The leader of one of the fastest-moving groups was Dick Hamill, whose squad had hiked until midnight on the day of the invasion. They slept in the jungle, then started out again before dawn with the aid of a flashlight. At midday on January 25, they were the first members of Lark Force to reach Lemingi, so high in the mountains the natives called it the "mission on top." By the end of the following day, some two hundred evaders had joined Hamill's men at the Roman Catholic compound, including separate parties led by Colonel Scanlan and Major Palmer.

The soldiers spread out and relaxed under the benevolent care of Father Alphons Meierhofer, a slender, bearded priest from Salzburg, Austria. Despite his heritage, he was no champion of the Nazi regime; to the contrary, he was generous with his supplies, and fed the Australians biscuits and strong tea upon arrival. The evening meal featured kau-kau and taro prepared by the mission staff.

Fisher's party did not reach Lemingi until the afternoon of January 27. Instead of spending a day or more to rest like the others, he and his men planned to get underway again the next morning. By this time, Meierhofer was anxious to see the Australians leave. Japanese floatplanes had been observing his station every day, and he was concerned about reprisals.

Meierhofer informed Fisher that his party was more than halfway to Adler Bay on the south coast. The bad news was that the terrain ahead was even more difficult. Normally it would take a day and a half for a strong native to walk to Adler Bay; but the soldiers were much weaker, and the hike would probably require several days. Fisher and his men departed on the morning of January 28, only a few hours before David Selby's small group arrived at the mission.

Unlike Fisher, Selby was in no hurry to move on once he reached Lemingi. He had fallen several times on the jungle track and painfully wrenched his knee. Thus, he decided to convalesce for a few days while conferring with Scanlan and other officers about their options. Rumors of rescue by the RAAF still dominated everyone's thoughts. "We discussed plans until late in the night," Selby remembered, "deciding that the best course was to push on with all speed for the coast where we thought there was every chance of being picked up by plane."

Meierhofer urged the Australians to take the northern trails to Open Bay. The terrain was less rugged, and the weary travelers would encounter more villages along the way. "He gravely doubted whether any of us would be able to make the south coast without guides, food and carriers," recalled Selby, "and warned us that even should we reach the coast, habitation was so sparse that we might all starve. For good measure, he told us that malaria, hookworm, elephantiasis and leprosy made this coast a most unattractive proposition."

Despite the warnings, Selby believed the south coast was the logical place to go, especially considering the possibility of an airlift. Others disagreed. Roughly half of the troops who passed through Lemingi followed the missionary's advice and walked north to Open Bay. Those who went south, including Selby, would later regret their decision to ignore the kindhearted priest.

After resting a full day at Lemingi, Selby teamed up with Scanlan (who still had Tovokina to carry his kitbag), Captain John R. Gray of the

Royal Australian Engineers, and a few other soldiers to begin the walk to Adler Bay. Within an hour of leaving, they made a near-vertical descent, sliding nearly two thousand feet down to the bank of a raging river. The mud-colored torrent was frightening to behold, and the thin cable someone had stretched across it for a handhold gave them no confidence.

Days earlier, Dick Hamill's party had reached the same river, whereupon Perce Pearson almost lost his resolve. "My first view of it," he remembered, "was to see a man hanging [from] the wire by his hands, and stretched out on the top of the water like a sheet in the wind." Pearson successfully crossed the river, but others evidently did not. "It was rumored," he continued, "that two committed suicide here. If true, I can quite realize their feelings."

Scanlan's party also made it across, each man "hanging on like grim death" and each experiencing at least one close call as the water pounded at their legs. The men rested for an hour, then started up the far side of the gorge, its slope just as steep as the one they'd descended. "Only by grasping vines and saplings and hauling ourselves up," Selby recalled, "could we avoid slipping back faster than we climbed."

At the top, the weary men shared a cold can of bully beef. The next day their only meal was a can of beans. After that, there was nothing to eat except moldy biscuits.

Later, Selby described the party's collective suffering:

> Each day we felt ourselves growing weaker from lack of food and the strain of climbing those towering mountains and crossing the racing rivers. Time after time we would miss our footing and fall, or a vine by which we were pulling ourselves up would give way, and we lay on the ground too weak to haul ourselves to our feet without the assistance of another member of the party. Our hands, never dry, were now cut and torn—it was painful even to close them to grip the rough vines—and our bodies were bruised and stiff from our innumerable falls. Our clothes, too, were never dry, for during the brief spells when we were not soaked to the skin by rain or river crossings we would be dripping with sweat.

The men lost count of the days as they struggled across the Bainings. At times it seemed as though the jungle had swallowed them in foul darkness; at others, they could not help admiring the spectacular views from atop tall mountains. Sometimes those same vistas depressed them, because they revealed many more ridges yet to be crossed.

The final leg of the journey was the most challenging. Having climbed to a high plateau, the men could see the ocean on the horizon. Far below, a slow-moving river appeared to lead toward the coast, but they could not find a way down. "Wherever we tried," Selby remembered, "we were stopped by sheer cliff faces with a drop of several hundred feet." Finally, someone discovered the cut of a watercourse in the face of a cliff, and they began a frightening descent. No one had mountaineering experience, let alone the proper equipment, so they simply lowered themselves from one precarious handhold to the next. Selby considered it "the most terrifying part" of the entire journey.

At the bottom, the group followed a path through the jungle to a village on the shore of Eber Bay. There they found John Mollard, whose party numbered about thirty men. Their camp was well stocked, including a supply of rice obtained from a nearby plantation, and the new arrivals were thrilled to receive a hot lunch. "It was our first real meal since leaving Rabaul," Selby explained, "and the feeling of satisfaction and delight with which we lay back and rested afterwards is quite beyond description."

To everyone's surprise, Peter Fisher and his group walked into the village later that afternoon. They had left Lemingi at least twenty-four hours ahead of Scanlan and Selby, but such was the maze of trails through the mountains that Fisher's group took a full day longer to navigate the unmapped terrain.

Arriving with Fisher, David Bloomfield learned that most of the gunners from the antiaircraft battery had gathered up the coast on Adler Bay. He and several friends continued walking and reached the abandoned plantation just as darkness fell. The additional effort was worthwhile. Compared with the conditions they'd endured on the trail, the situation at Adler Bay seemed idyllic. Approximately two hundred soldiers lounged among the huts of a large coastal village. A general store contained sacks of rice and flour, chickens and goats wandered about the plantation, and bananas and pawpaws grew in abundance. Bloomfield and the other newcomers enjoyed a large helping of stew, then fell asleep in a native hut.

Early the next morning, February 1, Bloomfield ambled to the beach to bathe in the ocean and wash what little was left of his tattered clothing. His shirt was rotting apart, his socks were in shreds, and his khaki shorts were ripped. "My underpants," he wrote later, "were the only garment intact." Bloomfield enjoyed a brief swim, but it ended abruptly when he spotted a white cloth tied to a length of bamboo. Returning to his hut, he asked what the flag was about. The answer caught him completely off-guard: everyone at Adler Bay had decided to surrender.

Bloomfield announced defiantly that he was not giving up, and pleaded with his friends to join him. None could be persuaded. Subsequently, Bloomfield learned that Scanlan, Mollard, and the large party down at Eber Bay were preparing to continue south to Wide Bay. He decided to follow them, and departed Adler Bay that afternoon with several civilians, including the Norwegian skipper of the *Herstein*, Captain Gotfred Gunderson.

Before leaving their campsite at Eber Bay, Scanlan and the others debated whether to order the troops at Adler Bay to join them. Nobody had a specific plan, and they knew that their rescue was far from guaranteed. As Selby later explained, "It seemed unfair to order the men to leave their food supplies, and their prospects of being repatriated after the war, for the uncertainties and privations which were all we could offer them if they came with us."

Walking southward along the coast, the Australians found the going somewhat easier than in the mountains, though not by much. Coral outcroppings tore at the soles of their boots, and every few miles the men were forced to climb one of the many ridges that ran at right angles to the shoreline. At the completion of one such climb on February 2, Bloomfield's group enjoyed a broad view of the sea. In the distance they could see a line of Japanese barges heading south. Someone speculated that they were en route to Gasmata, an old RAAF grass strip farther down the coast.

The next morning, catching up with a small group of soldiers near Wide Bay, Bloomfield learned that Scanlan's group was only a few hours ahead. To know the officers were breaking the trail made him even more eager to reach Tol plantation.

Up ahead, David Selby elected to follow a narrow track that meandered toward the shoreline. Just north of Wide Bay, he stepped into the open, hoping to get a glimpse of Tol.

That seemingly random decision probably saved his life:

> The plantation was plainly visible—a palm-covered tongue of land jutting out into the bay—but what I saw made me call to Fisher. A mile or so offshore were five barges towed by a steam pinnace. Through my binoculars I saw at the stern of each a Japanese flag, and they were crammed with troops. This was a cruel disappointment. For days Tol had been our goal, Tol was the word most often on our lips and at Tol we had anticipated the end of our wanderings [and] good food while we awaited the Catalinas which must surely be sent to our rescue. By a few short miles the enemy had beaten us to it.

The barges that Bloomfield had seen a day earlier were not headed for Gasmata, but for Tol. By a stroke of luck, Selby was in the right place at the right time to see the barges enter Wide Bay; otherwise he and the men behind him would have walked into a trap. He rushed ahead to warn Scanlan and Mollard, catching them just before they crossed a narrow river on the eastern border of the plantation.

The officers held back, but for almost two hundred others, the warning came too late.

Primarily composed of former Salvation Army musicians, the talented brass band was the pride of the 2/22nd Battalion. *Lindsay Cox*

Tanned and fit, the 2/22nd Infantry Battalion marched in a grand parade in Melbourne shortly before departing for New Britain. *Carl Johnson*

The officers of the 2/22nd Battalion during their first weeks of training at Trawool, fifty miles north of Melbourne. *Carl Johnson*

Lieutenant John D. Uzzell leads his company around the perimeter of the parade ground at Trawool in 1940. The men commonly referred to these marching drills as "square-bashing." *Carl Johnson*

Colonel John J. "Joe" Scanlan (left), the decorated combat veteran who commanded all Australian ground forces in the New Guinea Area, and Major John C. Mollard, second in command of the 2/22nd Battalion, during their imprisonment in Japan. *Carl Johnson*

On the day of his escape from New Britain's south coast aboard the *Laurabada*, Private George C. Russell was only twenty-four years old. His gaunt, haggard appearance is indicative of the acute starvation and illness experienced by most of the escaped Australians. *Lark Force Association*

Part of the Rabaul detachment of the New Guinea Volunteer Rifles (NGVR), a militia force raised in the territorial islands at the outbreak of World War II. During the invasion, most of the detachment saw action alongside A Company. *Carl Johnson*

Sergeant William Arthur Gullidge, leader of the 2/22nd Band, was renowned throughout Australia for his brass band compositions and renditions of popular music. *Lindsay Cox*

During their bid to escape from the Japanese, gunner Archibald N. Taylor helped to rescue a fellow soldier who fell from a cliff and suffered a broken leg. *Lark Force Association*

American-born Private James R. Thurst II, a cornet player in the 2/22nd Battalion Band, was the only "Yank" in Lark Force. *Bruce Thurst*

Private C. O. "Bill" Harry, a farmer from Victoria, performed a detailed survey of the Gazelle Peninsula in 1941 and was relied upon for his extensive knowledge of the area. *Lark Force Association*

Sergeant Bruce Perkins, Sergeant Arch Taylor, and Private Hugh Webster were reunited at Tol Plantation in 1945, just before the war ended. *Lark Force Association*

Private Frederick W. Kollmorgen, the only bandsman to survive the New Britain ordeal, was a tenor horn player who transferred to the 2/22nd because he hoped to see plenty of action. *Lindsay Cox*

Lieutenant Peter E. Figgis, the NGA intelligence officer, was instrumental in organizing the evacuation of soldiers trapped on New Britain's south coast. He later served as a coastwatcher. *Peter Figgis*

Japanese newspaper photo of combat on New Britain near Rabaul.
Osaka Mainichi Daily News

Tavurvur belches steam and ash behind the Rapindik Native Hospital near
Lakunai Airdrome. The hospital was badly damaged during the first Japanese
air attack.

The active volcano Tavurvur, located across Matupit Harbor from Lakunai
airdrome, erupted in mid-1941 and continued to plague the occupants of
Rabaul for the next two years. *Carl Johnson*

Junior Officers of the 144th Infantry Regiment, the primary combat element of the South Seas Force, photographed in a formal garden on their home island of Shikoku. *Carl Johnson*

The South Seas Detachment, en route to Rabaul, commemorates crossing the equator by honoring the Emperor and a tattered World War I battle flag. *Osaka Mainichi Daily News*

Zentsuji.

Sketch by Captain David C. Hutchinson-Smith, 17th Antitank Battery, of the POW barracks at Zentsuji, where the sixty captured officers from Lark Force were imprisoned for almost three years. *Roger Mansell*

Between January 1942 and August 1945, Rabaul and Simpson Harbor endured literally hundreds of air strikes, first by the Japanese, later by waves of Allied attackers. Miraculously, no Lark Force POWs were killed by friendly bombs. *National Archives*

The Rabaul Memorial at Bita Paka cemetery honors over 1,200 Australians who lost their lives on New Britain or New Ireland during World War II and have no known grave. *Lindsay Cox*

CHAPTER NINE

TOL

"Those who resist us will be killed one and all."

—Major General Tomitaro Horii,
South Seas Detachment

I n the days that followed the invasion, Major General Horii became increasingly frustrated. Like all officers in the Imperial Japanese Army, he was accustomed to instant obedience, yet hundreds of Australians had ignored his order to surrender. And they showed every sign of continuing to evade, despite the explicit warnings contained in his airdropped leaflets. Even more infuriating, thousands of his troops were incapacitated by an outbreak of malaria while chasing the Australians.

Within the South Seas Detachment, Lieutenant Colonel Kuwada's 3rd Infantry Battalion had been the least affected. During the first few days of mopping up, they collected more than two hundred Australian prisoners between Vunakanau and the Warangoi River. Some, like young "Norrie" Kennedy, were captured despite elaborate attempts at evasion. After escaping into the jungle with Lieutenant Dawson on January 23, Kennedy made his way to a native hospital near Kokopo. Nurses tried to hide him among the other patients by covering his skin with black shoe polish, but the Japanese saw through the disguise and took him prisoner.

After their initial successes, however, the 3rd Battalion was reluctant to pursue the Australians beyond the Warangoi River. Again, the deciding factor was malaria. Although the disease had not ravaged Kuwada's troops as badly as the 1st and 2nd Battalions, the mere threat of it was enough to deter Kuawada from conducting a prolonged overland pursuit. Instead,

Major General Horii implemented a change in tactics after Kuwada's men returned to Kokopo at the end of January. Relying on floatplanes, ships, and foot patrols for reconnaissance, Horii monitored the Australians' progress toward the south for several days. When he learned that a large force of Australians had gathered "in the forests north of Wide Bay," he ordered Kuwada "to carry out a pursuit by boats."

On the morning of February 2, approximately 150 soldiers of the 8th Company, led by Lieutenant Tadaichi Noda, boarded five Daihatsu landing craft at Kokopo. The boats were fitted with benches, canvas awnings, and facilities for cooking, and one of them even had a 75mm field gun lashed to its floorboards. Towed south by a larger vessel, the landing craft reached Wide Bay at dawn the next day. After rounding a promontory called Tongue Point, the small convoy turned north into a smaller inlet called Henry Reid Bay. In the middle of the bay, the landing craft cast off their towlines and surged ahead under their own power. As the Daihatsus approached the beach, Noda's men fired a few rounds from the field gun and sent several bursts of machine-gun fire into the branches of the palm trees.

DAWN ON FEBRUARY 3 FOUND MORE THAN TWO HUNDRED MEMBERS OF LARK Force in the vicinity of Wide Bay. Approximately seventy were living in the plantation house at Tol or at nearby Waitavalo, a smaller plantation approximately a mile beyond Tol on Henry Reid Bay. The rest were either camped in small groups among the vast coconut groves or were approaching Tol on native trails.

Those who had been at Wide Bay the longest were disheartened. Having struggled for days to reach Tol, where they had high expectations of rescue, they were bitterly disappointed that no had come for them. Little did they know that the War Cabinet had decided weeks ago not to attempt any relief missions.

The rabble had not posted lookouts. When the Japanese suddenly appeared and began shooting from their landing craft, the Australians were caught completely by surprise. Some ran into the jungle, but most were too demoralized to put up resistance. Twenty-two men, evidently led by Sandy Robertson, walked out to the beach carrying a white flag as soon as the firing stopped. They waited patiently near the water's edge, and within minutes were surrounded by Noda's soldiers.

Other Japanese troops fanned out and began rounding up the Australians. A few managed to escape, the largest group made up of four young privates who hid in the jungle for several hours, then started walking northward through the jungle. They crossed the mountainous spine of New Britain and walked all the way to Open Bay, where they were eventually rescued. They were the exception, however. Almost all of the hungry, unkempt Australians at Tol were captured with little or no difficulty.

The terrain itself made escape unlikely. The Henry Reid River was wide, swift, and deep—too hazardous to cross without a boat or canoe—and it had several winding tributaries that created a labyrinth of channels. About sixty men were trapped there, including Bill Collins of the 2/10 Field Ambulance. He and several other Australians were crawling in a shallow stream when they heard the sound of laughter behind them. Turning around, they saw several Japanese soldiers watching them with amused looks. With simple hand signals, the Japanese directed them to get to their feet and then escorted them to the beach. Shortly thereafter, the captured Australians were put aboard a landing craft and delivered to Tol.

By nightfall approximately 170 Australians had been locked inside a large hut at Tol that formerly housed native laborers. The prisoners were not abused, and they even received a hot meal of rice. Throughout the night, Japanese guards kept several bonfires going to illuminate the surroundings and discourage any ideas of escape, but the effort was hardly needed. The Australians were too weary and demoralized to mount any sort of organized resistance, and their first day of imprisonment at Tol ended quietly.

The situation changed dramatically the next morning. According to one account, Noda became impatient while the ration of rice for breakfast was being cooked. With much shouting and gesturing, he ordered the prisoners to line up outside the hut. A young lieutenant, possibly Glenn Garrard of D Company, was singled out and harshly interrogated by Noda, who was assisted by a mean-spirited interpreter known as Sungai. When Garrard failed to provide the correct responses, he was clubbed on the head and torso with a stout wooden stick until he collapsed. Revived with water, he endured more questioning and severe beating. Finally, too dazed to stand on his own, he was left shirtless in the scorching sun, his arms tied around a palm tree.

The rest of the prisoners were marched to the plantation house, where an attempt was made to identify the twenty-two men who had surrendered on the beach the previous morning. About forty soldiers claimed to have been part of that group, confounding the Japanese, but eventually two officers and twenty others were pulled out of formation and led away.

Next, the Japanese questioned the remaining captives as to name, rank, and serial number. They were thoroughly searched, and all personal items—identity discs, watches, rings, pay books, and photographs—were tossed in a heap on the ground. Finally, the prisoners' hands were tied behind their backs, most with their thumbs bound tightly together. The Australians were then arranged in lines of six to twelve men and tied together with assorted ropes, cords, or even their own belts. Allowed to sit back down, they received water, and some were permitted to share cigarettes.

The Japanese set up a two-way radio and established communications with a base unit, presumably headquarters at Rabaul. An exchange of messages generated much excitement among Noda's men, who then ordered the prisoners back on their feet. In ragged-looking groups, they were marched away from the house in different directions, each closely escorted by several soldiers armed with rifles and long bayonets.

In 1942 the great majority of Japanese troops carried the 6.5mm Arisaka Model 38, a long but relatively light rifle that boasted almost no recoil. The weapon also had another important attribute, as described in a U.S. Army intelligence bulletin: "The length of the Model 38 makes it particularly suitable for bayonet fighting. When the Japanese infantryman is armed with this rifle and the Model 30 (1897) bayonet, which is also unusually long, he feels that in close combat he is a match for his larger and taller enemies." The Imperial Army placed a heavy emphasis on bayonet fighting. Recruits spent hours practicing such moves as the "side-step thrust," the "low body thrust," and the "body contact thrust." At this point in the war, few members of the South Seas Detachment, if any, had personally experienced hand-to-hand combat. They didn't know what it felt like to pierce a man's body with the thin, fifteen-inch-long blade affixed to the end of their rifles. But on the morning of February 4, many of Noda's men would find out.

RIFLEMAN ALFRED L. "ALF" ROBINSON, THIRTY-EIGHT, A RESIDENT OF Rabaul who had joined the NGVR only three days before the invasion, found himself in a column of prisoners being marched single file into the coconut groves. For some reason the former clerk was not roped to the other captives, though his thumbs were bound tightly together behind his back. Observing the bayonets on the Japanese soldiers' rifles and the short-handled spades they carried, he suspected that the Australians were about to be executed. A terrible noise from a nearby grove confirmed his hunch. "An agonized scream was heard," he later remarked, "and the whole line halted to listen."

The escorts motioned for the column to resume marching. Soon thereafter, Robinson spotted a sharp bend in the trail up ahead. Heavy vegetation temporarily hid the captives at the front of the line, and when Robinson reached the bend he made a split-second decision. Jumping side-ways off the path, he ducked into the undergrowth. The man behind him whispered, "Lower, Sport," letting Robinson know that he needed to crawl deeper into the bushes. The other captives kept silent, and the guards passed by without noticing his absence.

Although he was safe for the time being, Robinson discovered that he could not loosen the bindings on his fast-swelling thumbs. Thus, a whole new ordeal began. The jungle was inhospitable enough for an able-bodied man, but now he was alone in the wilds with his hands tied behind his back.

AMBULANCE DRIVER BILL COLLINS WAS THE LAST MAN IN ANOTHER COLUMN of prisoners being marched into the coconut groves. The Japanese officer leading the way called a halt, and the Australians were directed to sit on the ground. Unsheathing his sword, the officer sliced the rope connecting the first captive in line with the others, but it was not for freedom's sake. The Australian was motioned to his feet, then a soldier with a fixed bayonet guided him into the underbrush. Collins heard a scream, and a few moments later the Japanese soldier reappeared, wiping his bayonet. One by one, the other prisoners were led away and executed. Finally, only Collins and two other Australians remained. The next captive in line suddenly jumped up and attempted to flee, but he ran awkwardly with his hands tied behind his back. The officer swiftly closed the distance, slashed the Australian with his sword, then drew his sidearm and shot the prisoner in the back.

At this, Private Thomas B. Clissold, an orderly with the 2/10 Field Ambulance, tried to protest by pointing to the Red Cross brassards he and Collins wore. The officer ripped them from their uniforms. Defiantly, Clissold indicated with his hands that he'd rather be shot than bayoneted. The officer complied, shooting Clissold where he sat.

Collins was now alone with the officer. "He put away his sword and took a rifle and motioned me to get up and walk," Collins later stated. "I took a few paces and he shot me through the shoulder. I fell to the ground and kept still. He fired again and hit me through both wrists and in the back. He decided he had finished me and went away."

After playing dead for as long as he could, Collins began to stir. He discovered that his hands were free. Miraculously, the second bullet had cut the cord binding his wrists. Although he was bleeding from multiple gunshot wounds, he managed to get on his feet and stagger away from the terrible killing grounds.

CLIFFORD MARSHALL, A THIRTY-ONE-YEAR-OLD LANCE CORPORAL FROM Prahran, Victoria, was in another group of prisoners taken deep into the coconut groves for execution. Like the others, his column was halted at a quiet spot, and then the killing began. One at a time the captives were led into the jungle by a Japanese soldier, and those left behind could hear the victims cry out. It was obvious the Japanese were using bayonets.

According to Marshall's later testimony, they were sloppy about finishing the job.

> When my turn came I was motioned to move off into the bush. There was a Japanese soldier walking behind me. I sort of turned, my hands being tied behind my back, to see what he was doing. I saw that he was making a rush at me with the bayonet. I received three wounds: one in the back just under the shoulder blades, not very deep, another through the arm and into the side, and another into the side lower down.

It came to me naturally to lie still and sham dead. I
could hear cries from the other men for a while and then
a lot of shooting.

Bleeding profusely, Marshall was able to squirm into the underbrush.
He eventually freed his hands, then began moving through the plantation
at dusk. After finding the bodies of several friends, he wandered among the
coconut groves in a state of shock, lost and alone.

THE PREVIOUS NIGHT HAD BEEN A LONG AND TROUBLING·ONE FOR SCANLAN,
Selby, and the others in their party. Warned in the nick of time about the
Japanese landing craft, they had debated late into the night about whether
or not to surrender. The realists argued that even if they got away from Tol,
the Japanese would simply set another trap along the coast. Also, their
families were anxious for any news, having heard nothing from Lark Force
in weeks; if nothing else, they would be relieved to learn that the men were
still alive, even as prisoners of war.

Selby refused to give up, but he almost changed his mind the next morning. While sitting alongside a stream to think about his options, he pulled
out his wallet to look at snapshots of his family and discovered the photos
were missing. Most likely they had washed away during one of the many
river crossings. Totally dejected, he considered the loss of the photos "an evil
and terrible omen."

Later that morning, he rejoined the party and was searching
through some old huts when he heard gunfire from the direction of Tol.
"An excited native rushed into the village," he explained, "and said
that the Japanese were killing all the pigs they could find, whereupon,
to our great disgust, they drove into the jungle the two pigs which had
been rooting around the village. (We had been casting greedy eyes at
the fatter of the two.) The firing which continued sporadically throughout the morning seemed to be unduly heavy for a pig hunt, but that
explanation sounded as plausible as any other and we did not give the
matter further thought."

Selby's intuition was correct. The Japanese were not shooting pigs at
Tol; they were murdering dozens of Australian prisoners.

THE KILLING WAS ALSO GOING ON AT WAITAVALO. IN ONE CASE, ELEVEN captured Australians were led into the undergrowth and lined up in front of a firing squad. The Japanese volley knocked them all down, but two young privates from D Company survived. One was Hugh J. "Nipper" Webster (no known relation to Norm Webster, the roughrider), from North Melbourne. Shot in the arm and side, he immediately lost consciousness, which probably saved his life. When he came to, the Japanese were gone. Nine of the men lying around him were dead, but Norman W. Walkley, shot in the arm, chest, and buttocks, was still breathing.

Webster stumbled away into the jungle. By the time he emerged from hiding, he could not find Walkley, who had evidently crawled some distance despite his grievous wounds. After searching in vain, Webster set off on his own to find help.

THE MORNING BEGAN WELL ENOUGH FOR GUNNER MAXWELL "SMACKER" Hazelgrove, a nineteen-year-old built like a fireplug. Traveling with a small group of six antiaircraft men, he arrived at the eastern boundary of Tol and came upon another party that had just killed a wild pig. The gunners received a portion of meat, then crossed the Balus River into Tol and built a fire, happily anticipating a feast. But while they were waiting for the meat to cook, a Japanese patrol took them by surprise. The captured group was marched to the Tol plantation house, where a white man addressed them. "All right, boys," he said, "you can put your hands down now." He looked and sounded Australian, but to this day his identity remains a mystery.

The prisoners were searched. One Australian carried a copy of Horii's leaflet, which supposedly guaranteed the lives of those who surrendered. The Japanese soldier who found it simply smiled and waved it in front of the captive's face.

The Japanese tied the prisoners' hands behind their backs, roped them together, led them away from the house for about a quarter of a mile, and without warning shot them in the back. All fell dead or mortally wounded except Hazelgrove, who was pulled down by the others. Hit in the left arm and shoulder, he managed to lie still while the Japanese covered the bodies with palm fronds. Hours later, after freeing his hands and untangling himself from the corpses of his friends, he stumbled to the beach.

PRIVATE WILLIAM COOK, AN ORDERLY IN THE 2/10 FIELD AMBULANCE, would never forget the brief conversation he had with one of his fellow medics that morning. As their party of eight approached the eastern boundary of Tol, Staff Sergeant Stewart C. Caston said he'd like to turn the calendar ahead two weeks to see "what had happened."

Cook replied, "You might be sorry."

A short distance along the trail they met another staff sergeant, Frank B. "Mick" Bauer, of the battalion Headquarters Company. He warned them that Japanese soldiers had been seen at Tol, and told the orderlies to hold their position while he scouted ahead. A native of London, Bauer was subsequently captured and executed; yet the orderlies waited dutifully for his return. After a while they decided to move off the trail and prepare some rice. Cook sat down to play cards with three of his friends, but their game was interrupted when one of the medics ran past yelling, "The bastards are here!"

Glancing up the path, Cook saw a Japanese soldier looking his way. Instinctively he fled into the jungle. "My shock must have been the greatest as I ran farther than the others and hid behind a fallen tree," he remembered. "I could see my mates walk out after a while with their hands up, so I followed."

While the Japanese were searching the orderlies, another Australian stumbled into their group. He was weak from fatigue, hardly able to walk, so two of the orderlies supported him as they marched under guard toward the plantation house. The sick man's progress was too slow for the Japanese, however, and they signaled for him to be left behind. One enemy soldier held back while the rest of the group kept moving, and a short while later he caught back up with them. The Australians had no doubt that the soldier had killed the ailing captive.

At the plantation house, the Japanese ransacked the prisoners' packs. They discarded all the medical equipment while looking for personal items to pilfer, thus ruining thousands of quinine tablets and other supplies. Next, recalled Cook, the Japanese searched the captives again:

> It took all our self control to stand and allow these
> yellow monkeys to dive their hands into our pockets and
> inside our shirts, but the worst was yet to come. Some

[Australians] had rings dragged from their fingers, [and] some, myself included, had their wrist watches taken. Next they collected our identity discs. The peculiar part was that some of the troops had religious tokens on their discs, but the Japs gave these back. I had been given a "Lucky Charm" on which was a cat descending in a parachute. Evidently the Nip thought this was holy, as I was given it back, and no other Nip would touch it.

While the searching was going on, I noticed two Japs grinning, and one gave the impression of shooting the other. They looked at us and laughed . . .

In what had become a familiar pattern, the Japanese lashed the captives' thumbs tightly behind their backs and roped all of the prisoners together. More prisoners arrived, swelling the group to about twenty-five men. The Japanese had to scrounge for belts and even native loin cloths to tie them all together. Finally, an officer signaled them to begin marching toward the coconut groves. "Well, fellows," said a prisoner, "this looks like it."

During the march an orderly tried to work his thumbs free, but an escorting soldier saw this and jerked hard on the rope. Several minutes later, in a clearing atop a small hill, the captives were ordered to halt. Cook could see Henry Reid Bay just four hundred feet away. The officer motioned for the captives to sit with their backs to the sea and forbade them from looking around. One prisoner tested the officer's sincerity and was promptly bashed in the face with a rifle butt.

At another signal from the officer, the first captive in line was ordered to his feet. He walked down the hill, followed by a soldier with his bayonet at the ready. Again, one of the prisoners pointed out the Red Cross brassards worn by the orderlies, and again the officer in charge tore them off. He then spoke a single, chilling word in English: "Next."

With remarkable calmness, two or three Australians stood and said, "Cheerio, fellows," then walked down the hill to their death. Sitting beside Cook, Private Trevor W. G. "Bill" Haines, one of the original Salvation Army bandsmen, "showed not a trace of fear." Cook was deeply moved. His mates were fatigued and hungry and helpless, yet in their final minutes they not only kept their composure, but gave each other the strength to face death calmly.

When the number of captives dwindled to five, the officer pointed from his sidearm to a nearby soldier's bayonet, as if to ask the Australians their preference. All of them indicated that they'd rather be shot than stabbed, but the officer was merely toying with them. Cook's turn came next. He stood with Bill Haines and another man from Victoria. "Well, Cookie," said Haines, "now we will know what the next world is like."

The three Australians walked resolutely down the slope. As they neared the bottom, three enemy soldiers converged from the left and fell in behind them. Fifty yards from the water's edge, the Japanese lunged, knocking Cook and his friends to the ground with their bayonets.

One of the soldiers stood over Cook, thrusting again and again with his fifteen-inch bayonet, each stab accompanied by snarls and grunts. Twice his bayonet pierced Cook's lower back, barely missing the spine; two more stabs broke ribs; another jab entered beneath Cook's shoulder blade; and the sixth blow was a slashing cut that bit deeply into his shoulder muscle.

Bill Haines and the third man went down without a sound. "I think that one of them must have died very quickly," Cook recalled, "and the other lingered a short time because, when the Japs started to leave us, he groaned a little." Hearing the sound, one of the Japanese returned and killed the victim with another stab.

Cook held his breath, feigning death, but he finally had to draw some air. In doing so, he either moved or made a sound, and the Japanese returned to finish him off. The unseen enemy plunged his bayonet into Cook's neck five more times. Thus far, Cook had seemingly been anesthetized due to shock, but the final stab was excruciating. The bayonet pierced his ear, entered his face near the temple, punched through his cheek, and then grated across his cheekbone. When the soldier pulled the bayonet out, Cook's head jerked backward. Blood from a nicked temporal artery gushed into his mouth. Feeling palm fronds being thrown on his body, he gave himself up for dead.

Somehow, after being stabbed eleven times, Cook did not lose consciousness. He desperately wanted to pass out, knowing it would relieve his agony, but the blackness did not come. "I just lay there waiting to die," he remembered, "and I heard two distinct shots followed by a scattered volley of rifle shots, which meant that the last two had been shot."

Cook remained under the fronds for an indeterminate time. Eventually the buzzing of flies began to bother him, and he also heard someone calling his name. "Although it was a voice in my imagination," he stated, "this saved my life and I decided that I would die trying to get away rather than stay as I was."

Cook freed himself from the native lap-lap that tied him to his dead companions, but could not undo the bindings on his thumbs. Rising unsteadily with his arms still lashed behind him, he stumbled toward the beach. He fell several times and did pass out briefly, but felt strong enough afterward to contort his body and stretch his hands past his legs. Once his hands were in front, he could chew through the bindings. However, all of the stretching had started his wounds bleeding again, and he suffered another blackout.

When he revived, Cook staggered to the beach. He walked into the water until it was waist deep, then did the almost unthinkable and immersed himself in the salt water. "This caused a lot of pain," he explained with amazing understatement, "but it just had to be done."

The agony of the dunking renewed Cook's energy. He stumbled northward through the shallows until he reached some rocks where he could move without leaving a bloody trail, then paused to sleep. When he awoke again he moved on, wanting to put some distance between himself and the Japanese. He also searched for a stream or river where he could slake his powerful thirst. As darkness fell he grew delirious. The stumps of trees began to resemble Japanese sentries, causing anxious moments as he fought against panic. Finally he found a river, and for a long time he "just lay there drinking." Soon, smoke from a distant campfire attracted his attention, but before he could reach it, exhaustion sent him to ground. Somehow, he had walked three miles from the scene of the massacre.

GLENN GARRARD'S BRUTAL TORTURE WAS NOT QUITE OVER. SURROUNDED by enemy soldiers on the front lawn of the plantation house, he was forced to dig his own grave. The former furniture designer scratched out a shallow hole, then was clubbed on the head and stabbed with a bayonet. The Japanese threw some dirt on the body, only half covering it.

WHEN THE LONG DAY OF KILLING FINALLY ENDED, NODA'S MEN HAD massacred 160 Australians. All were tied up, rendering them completely defenseless, before they were bayoneted or shot. The mass execution, sanctioned by Colonel Kusunose at Rabaul, almost certainly had the approval of Major General Horii. Afterward, the Japanese tacked a chilling message to the front door of the Waitavalo plantation house: "To Commander Scanlan—Now that this Island is took and tightly surrounded by our Air Forces and Navy you have no means of escape. If your religion does not allow you to commit suicide it is up to you to surrender yourself and to beg mercy for your troops. You will be responsible for the death of your men."

Leaving the bodies to rot in the sun, Noda and his troops boarded their landing craft and headed back to Rabaul, taking with them the twenty-two prisoners that had first surrendered on the beach. The 8th Company stopped at Adler Bay and picked up dozens of soldiers waiting there under a white flag, and also stopped at the Warangoi River for more prisoners, including Harold Page and Harry Townsend. All were delivered to Malaguna Camp, part of which had been wired off to form a prison compound.

WITHIN TWO DAYS OF THE MASSACRE, DAVID SELBY FOUND THE NOTE PINNED to the door at Waitavalo. Although he had not come across any corpses, he understood the message. Furthermore, a second note had been added directly below the first: "To Officers and Australian troops – Surrender yourselves. You will die of hunger or be killed by wild savages as there is no means of escape. You will be treated as prisoners of war and when the war is over you will be returned to your Motherland. Today we caught many prisoners but killed only those that attacked us."

The claim by the Japanese that they had been attacked was ludicrous. The prisoners were bound, and most of them had been roped together. Even more damning, the Japanese tried to erase the evidence by destroying the identification discs and other personal items they took from the victims, but their attempt was sloppy. They allowed several Australians to survive, for one thing, and many of the victims' ID tags were later recovered.

Initially, at least nine men survived the massacre. Bill Collins came out of hiding and found two Australians at Waitavalo suffering from bayonet wounds. They were unconscious, so he moved them into a shack and went to get help. But soon thereafter a Japanese warship entered Wide Bay and sent in a landing party, which found the two survivors. The Japanese dealt with them mercilessly, first smearing them with grease, then pouring flammable liquid onto the shack and setting it afire. Collins went into hiding again, and later met up with a group of civilian constables from Rabaul who were escaping down the coast.

BILL COOK SPENT THAT FIRST NIGHT IN MISERY. TORMENTED BY INSECTS that swarmed around his wounds, he tried to concentrate on anything that would distract him from the horrors of the day. When the sun rose, he discovered that the fire he'd seen the previous evening was only thirty yards away. The camp was occupied by Joe Scanlan's party, and within minutes Cook was receiving first aid and telling his gruesome story.

Scanlan replaced Cook's bloody shirt with one of his own, then sent Cook along with a native guide to find medical attention for his wounds. The islander, fearing the Japanese would kill him for aiding the enemy, promptly abandoned Cook on the track. Feeling helpless, Cook wandered on his own until he found another group of soldiers. "[One] can imagine my joy," he later stated, "when I saw three Aussies walking along."

After Cook shared his tale with them, they decided to take a wide detour around Tol. The terrain proved too rugged, however, and eventually they ended up back where they started. The only way to get farther south was to walk directly through the plantation. "We had to pass the spot where the massacre had been committed," Cook acknowledged, "and it took all my willpower to keep going. I carried a razor blade in my hand with the intention of committing suicide rather than be captured again. My mates could see my panic, and they kept me in the middle of the party."

As the foursome moved along the coastline, Cook's friends gave him plenty of encouragement. They told him his wounds "were healing wonderfully," but he wasn't so sure. The left side of his badly swollen face was discharging quantities of pus, the odor of which was difficult for all of them to endure.

Other parties of Australians passing through Tol discovered three more survivors of the massacre: Marshall, Webster, and Hazelgrove. Similarly, a trio of plantation owners found Alf Robinson wandering in the jungle, half out of his wits, his hands still tied behind his back. His physical appearance was hideous. Insects had tormented him for days, but he was helpless to ward them off. Now his face, arms, and legs were swollen from bites. Furthermore, his thumbs were black and grotesquely distended because of the fishing line that bound them tightly together. Once freed, he chose to remain alone, afraid of the reprisals that would befall any people who assisted him.

Fortunately for the survivors, Ted Palmer, the chief medical officer of Lark Force, was encamped only a few miles south of Wide Bay near a Roman Catholic mission. Friends carefully helped Cook, Marshall, Webster, and Hazelgrove around the bay and placed them under Palmer's care. Amazingly, despite their terrible wounds and the jungle's unforgiving conditions, all made a gradual recovery.

By February 7, a sizeable group of Australians had gathered near the mission, known as Kalai. John Mollard's party arrived prior to the massacres, and the numbers grew as additional groups straggled in. Two small parties were led by Ben Dawson and Bill Owen, who had each experienced several adventures as they trekked across the Baining Mountains. Their friends welcomed the newcomers warmly, especially Dawson, whom everyone thought had been killed at Rabaul.

Because of the recent atrocities, however, the general mood at Kalai remained somber. Scanlan was despondent when he arrived on February 8. John Gray, his traveling partner for much of the journey, had failed to return after conducting a recon of Tol on the morning of the massacre. A popular engineer, he had been among those captured and was taken by boat to Kokopo. Scanlan's houseboy, Tovokina, was also gone. One of the civilians in the party had decided to surrender, and the young native accompanied him back to Rabaul.

The news of the massacre was distressing enough, but the men gathered at Kalai were also troubled by the behavior of Father John Meierhofer, the local missionary. The biological brother of Alphons Meierhofer at Lemingi, he possessed none of his sibling's generosity or patience. Father John stubbornly refused to assist the Australians camped near his church; therefore, they simply helped themselves, even butchering some of his livestock. No one was happy about the situation, and the Australians decided to move farther down the coast.

Joe Scanlan did not accompany them. Defeated in battle, beaten by the jungle at every turn, he had finally reached the limit of his physical and emotional endurance. Blaming himself for the recent atrocities at Tol, he took seriously the latest warnings posted by the Japanese, and decided his only option was to surrender. On February 9 he announced his intention to go back to Rabaul. He was asked to speak to the assembled men that evening, but had nothing to say.

Suddenly, John Mollard stepped forward and said he would accompany Scanlan. Everyone was stunned, but he explained his decision with "sheer hard logic," at the same time urging the others to accompany him and Scanlan. Only a few troops decided to go, including Eric Angwin, who perhaps felt duty bound to the colonel. The rest were determined to keep moving south.

The next morning, the men at Kalai were amazed by the transformation in Scanlan's appearance. "There was the Commandant in a blaze of glory," recalled Selby, "complete with summer-weight uniform, collar and tie, red gorgets, and red cap band. He was wearing new boots and had cut his hair and shaved his beard with a razor borrowed from the missionary. He certainly looked every inch a colonel, and the effect was a startling contrast to our ragged shorts and shirts, battered boots, and stubbly beards."

Scanlan was determined to look dignified for his last act as the commander of Lark Force. Accompanied by Mollard, Angwin, and two others, he left Kalai on February 10 and began the long walk back to Rabaul.

CHAPTER TEN

ESCAPE:
THE LAKATOI

"... *after many adventures we arrived at*
Port Moresby."

—Sergeant Clive MacVean,
2/22nd Battalion

The mass murders at Tol and Waitavalo plantations on February 4 represented a turning point. Prior to that Bloody Wednesday, no one from Lark Force had successfully gotten off New Britain, which seemed to validate Major General Horii's warning that they could "find neither food nor way of escape." (About twenty troops had been airlifted with 24 Squadron two weeks earlier, but that was technically an evacuation, not an escape.) In the wake of the massacres, however, some 385 soldiers and sixty civilians escaped to Port Moresby or the Australian mainland over a period of ten weeks. They were the lucky ones. The accounts of their courage, ingenuity, and perseverance not only gave the Commonwealth something to cheer about, but rank among the most compelling escape stories of the entire war.

The dark side of their story is that they endured long weeks or even months of the harshest conditions imaginable before they reached safety. During that time, an estimated sixty-five evaders died from starvation or disease—more than were killed during the invasion itself. Most of those deaths could have been prevented with timely assistance from Canberra, but none came. No Australian warships were sent to rescue the remnants of Lark Force, no flying boats returned to pick up stragglers. The War Cabinet, aware for weeks that the troops were on the run, did nothing to help them.

In the absence of official support, a handful of individuals took charge of various rescue efforts. Some were soldiers, others lived on New Britain, and a few belonged to the Australia-New Guinea Administration Unit (ANGAU), which oversaw coastwatching operations.

One of the first to take action was Lieutenant Commander Feldt, stationed at Townsville. Soon after Lark Force went off the air, he contacted John K. "Keith" McCarthy, a coastwatcher at Talasea on New Britain's north shore, and asked him to transport a radio to Toma. McCarthy was to report on the situation at Rabaul, then coordinate an evacuation if possible. The mission would be long and hazardous, but Feldt believed the thirty-seven-year-old McCarthy had just the right stuff.

> I knew he was the appropriate man for the job. A tall, red-headed man of Irish descent, he was no cool, premeditating type. His affections and emotions governed him, but when his fine, free carelessness landed him in trouble, he could extricate himself, logic guiding his Celtic fervor until the danger was past. He had shown this capacity when ambushed in the heart of New Guinea by natives, coming safely out although wounded by three arrows, one of which he described as having ruined the beautiful symmetry of his navel. I could only hope that his long practice of improvising ways of escape from diverse and unorthodox difficulties had fitted him for coping with what lay ahead.

Accompanied by plantation owner George H. S. "Rod" Marsland (also a member of ANGAU) and sixteen native police boys to carry the AWA 3B radio, McCarthy left Talasea in the 36-foot launch *Aussi* and motored northward for nearly two hundred miles along New Britain's coastline. When he reached Open Bay, he learned that the Japanese occupied Pondo, one of the largest plantations on the northern shore. McCarthy directed Marsland to reconnoiter the coast on foot while he hid the *Aussi* a few miles up the Toriu River and established a base camp. He and the porters then began hauling the radio overland in the direction of Rabaul, but within days they encountered a steady stream of natives walking in the opposite direction. From them, McCarthy learned that Rabaul had fallen. The first part of his mission was therefore scrubbed, so he backtracked to the camp on the river.

Marsland walked as far as Pondo, which was no longer occupied, though its boats had been destroyed or disabled. There he found Captain Alan G. Cameron and nine troops from C Company, all in relatively good shape, and they followed him back to the Toriu River camp. They joined up with McCarthy on February 11, whereupon Cameron explained that nearly four hundred Australians under Captain Appel were gathered farther north along the coast.

This gave McCarthy something to work on. The base camp was moved up to Pondo, and by noon on February 14 the radio was ready for operation. Cameron transmitted the details of the Japanese invasion to Port Moresby, providing the first information received since Peter Figgis's cryptic message three weeks earlier. Cameron also claimed that he had important information to bring out, and indicated that he would attempt to reach New Guinea by boat. However, the headquarters staff at Port Moresby told him that McCarthy was in charge of the evacuation attempt, and was therefore the approving authority.

A battle of wills began immediately. McCarthy, who needed every available boat to evacuate Appel and his men, directed Cameron to set up staging sites at Talasea. But Cameron evidently resented taking orders from a civilian, even if he was an ANGAU officer, and ignored McCarthy's directive. Instead, he left New Britain on February 20 in the motor launch *Dulcy*, taking his troops with him, and landed on the coast of New Guinea. Feldt later called the action "ill-judged," but stopped short of accusing Cameron of dereliction or cowardice. "There was no lack of courage in this officer," he stated, "as both his earlier and later career proved."

However, Cameron's hasty departure was unnecessary. By the time his party docked at Salamaua, New Guinea, on March 3, other members of Lark Force had already reached Port Moresby, thus negating his justification for taking a vital boat away from McCarthy. Captain William G. Botham, the officer-in-charge of the Royal Australian Engineers at Rabaul, had led a small party on a fast trip down the south coast of New Britain. They had covered much of the distance in boats "borrowed" from missionaries, thereby getting beyond Tol prior to the massacres. Another party led by Captain Harold W. Nicholls of the NGA headquarters staff had done the same. The two groups sailed independently to the Trobriand Islands: Nicholls' party of nine aboard the launch *Goodava*, and Captain Botham's twelve men aboard the 20-foot-long *Maria*, her white hull hastily covered with black paint for camouflage. Both parties were airlifted to Port Moresby on March 1. Unfortunately, none of the escapees knew the whereabouts of the other scattered parties on New Britain; therefore, the authorities in New Guinea failed to convey to the War Cabinet the urgency of Lark Force's situation.

ON THE NORTHERN COAST OF NEW BRITAIN, PARTICULARLY AROUND Ataliklikun Bay, the South Seas Detachment played a waiting game. Instead of pushing into the jungle to flush out the Australian evaders, they set up outposts on the main trails that crisscrossed the Gazelle Peninsula, forming an effective cordon. The pickets snagged Australian prisoners almost daily. Many, like Bert Morgan and his malaria patient, simply surrendered at the first outpost they came to.

The Japanese officer in charge of the Keravat River outpost, an individual of unknown rank named Ayara Ogama, sent several messages to the Australians hiding in his sector. Native runners delivered the first message to Pip Appel on February 7.

> To officer in charge of Australian soldiers: You are herewith commanded to surrender all soldiers with you. Food stuffs have been left at Vunarima and at [Mandres Sawmill] to help you make your way towards Rabaul. Your lives will be spared. If you do not surrender you will all be killed.

Unaware of the massacres at Tol and Waitavalo, Appel ignored the message. Three days later Ogama tried a softer approach:

> Do not be afraid to be killed by us. Lots of your friends have surrendered to us. You cannot escape from this island and you will all die of starvation. You will be treated as

prisoners of war and only do enough work to keep your health. We will give you two days to surrender.

Once again there was no reply from the Australians, so Ogama included detailed instructions in his third note, delivered to Appel on February 14.

[All] sick Australian Soldiers and all other Australians who are at Mr. Harvey's bungalow tonight or early tomorrow morning are herewith commanded to be on the beach at Lassul at about 12 noon tomorrow. Put out a white flag and signal the ship to come in and pick you up. If no signal, ship will pass and leave you to walk back to [Vunakanau].

Rather than waiting for a reply, Ogama sent several landing craft filled with troops to Lassul Bay and nearby beaches over the next two days, taking numerous Australians by surprise. Captain David C. Hutchinson-Smith of the 17th Antitank Battery, whose small party fled from Harvey's plantation into the jungle, later described the struggle the Australians faced.

The Japanese had covered the distance between the beach and the plantation in a remarkably short time and opened up with mortar, light machine gun and small arms fire. My small group was soon sheltering in a donga and derived the maximum psychological and minimum physical protection from the leafy branches of a diminutive coffee tree.

At about dusk, contact was made with another small party and it was decided to have a scratch meal and camp till morning . . .

We had not been seated in a tiny clearing for more than 20 minutes when a surly, insolent Kanaka "boy" came through the gloom and handed me a note.* It was to

---

Australian soldiers often misunderstood the definition of *kanaka*, which is not a pronoun describing nationality but simply means *villager*.

the effect that he had been instructed to state that if we gave ourselves up our lives would be guaranteed, that the Japanese knew where we were, and that if we did not surrender, all troops in the area would be killed. That they did know our whereabouts was evidenced by the fact that the "boy" had delivered the note, and we were thus faced with a problem which was one for individual decision.

Hutchinson-Smith pondered his choices only briefly. His group possessed just enough food for one or two "very scanty" meals, and none of his men had the strength to walk more than a few miles. Thus, he and two enlisted men followed the native back toward the plantation. They were taken prisoner and escorted to the main house, where approximately sixty other captured Australians were already sitting on the lawn. The prisoners were somewhat surprised to be served a meal of steamed rice, bully beef, and canned beets—more food than they'd seen in weeks.

But their gratification, recalled Hutchinson-Smith, was tempered by the sight of a local half-German individual who was helping the Japanese. "[Joseph] Rokker was ingratiating himself with the Japs and was overbearing and insolent in his attitude to us. He had always been surly when he held the contract for the supply of firewood to Malaguna Camp before the attack, and from his frequent visits to the camp he was probably in a position to give quite a deal of information to the Japanese on local military matters."

That night, the captives were ferried out to the *Duranbah*, a large copra vessel. The next day it moved slowly toward Rabaul, stopping at several points along the way to pick up more prisoners. Ogama's dragnet had captured approximately 160 soldiers, including four officers of the 17th Antitank Battery and four from the 2/22nd Battalion. Delivered to Rabaul in the *Duranbah*, they found themselves back in their former camp on Malaguna Road. "And so," added Hutchinson-Smith, "the prodigal sons returned to the fold."

Evidently satisfied with bagging such a large number of prisoners, Ogama discontinued the pursuit and sent his troops back to their encampment near the Keravat. However, with a little more effort they could have captured twice as many Australians. Trapped between the mountains and the sea, Pip Appel and nearly two hundred others were critically low on food. They were separated into several groups, each of which faced conditions that grew ever more intolerable.

AT PONDO, KEITH MCCARTHY LEARNED THAT MORE AUSTRALIANS WERE IN hiding than he'd originally thought. In addition to the men still holding out on the north shore, there were hundreds of Lark Force soldiers scattered among several plantations on the south coast. Eager to rescue as many as possible, he approached Frank Holland, a local timber merchant, and asked him to hike across the island to Wide Bay. He was to contact any soldiers he could find there, then guide them back to Pondo. A superbly fit individual of many talents, Holland immediately accepted the challenge.

With six armed police boys and several native carriers, Holland started out from Open Bay on February 20. If it seemed a large party for such a short journey—it was only twenty miles to Wide Bay on the opposite coast—there was good reason. The mountainous terrain was the domain of the Mokolkol tribe, a mysterious band of warriors feared for their exceptional ferocity and stealth. The precautions were justified. On the third day out, Holland's party was attacked by axe-wielding warriors, and one of the police boys was badly cut on the arm. The warriors struck again the next day, but two of them were killed and three others wounded. The Mokolkols attempted no more attacks during the rest of the journey.

Just north of Wide Bay, near the Mavelo River, Holland came upon Alf Robinson, still scrounging on his own while waiting for his mangled hands to heal. Holland learned that Lieutenant Colonel Carr and Police Commissioner Ball were camped only six miles down the trail at Ril plantation, so he pressed ahead with two of the police boys and left the others to care for Robinson. During the next several days, Holland tried to catch Carr's party but was unable to gain ground. The soldiers kept moving south, always staying a day or two ahead. Holland sent a runner with a message, but the attempt failed because the recipients thought the native was trying to deceive them. To Holland, it began to appear as though his trek across the island had been in vain.

IRONICALLY, CARR'S GROUP HAD PICKED UP THEIR PACE SHORTLY BEFORE Holland approached the south coast. Previously, they had moved down the island with slow deliberation. As Peter Figgis later put it, "We weren't racing down the coast like the rest of them, who were unfortunately in a bit of a panic." Indeed, they spent a whole week at Riat before an advance party consisting of Figgis, Bill Harry, and Ivan Smith departed for Lemingi. Arriving on the morning of January 31, they found Father Meierhofer caring for a few men in bad health; otherwise, dozens of soldiers had already passed through the mission and were gone. The remainder of Carr's party reached Lemingi a day later, and once they discovered the luxuries of hot food and solid roofs over their heads, they decided to linger for several more days. Figgis and Hugh Mackenzie moved on, anxious to find the two-way radio that was allegedly at Tol plantation.

Accompanied by Rifleman K. C. J. "Ken" Stone, a former AWA telegraph operator who had enlisted in the NGVR and was later seconded to naval intelligence, they reached Tol on February 14. There was no radio, of course. Instead, they found only the terrible detritus of the slaughter that had occurred ten days earlier. As they searched through the plantation they uncovered more grisly evidence of the atrocities, and Figgis found Norm Walkley. Remarkably, the twenty-two-year-old private was still alive but in dreadful shape, his wounds having become infected. The newcomers thought he was the only survivor, and were dismayed that he was beyond saving.

By this time, the conditions among the coconut groves at Tol and Waitavalo were appalling. The bodies strewn on the ground had been decomposing for ten days in the tropical heat, and though they still held a human shape, they were too bloated and blackened for identification. Handling the corpses for burial was out of the question. Whatever was left after being scavenged by birds, insects, and small animals was swarming with maggots; and if such corruption wasn't repugnant enough by itself, the very atmosphere was polluted with the stench of hydrogen sulfide and methane gases. "It wasn't very nice," admitted Figgis with typical understatement. He, Mackenzie, and Stone collected several "meat tickets," as they called the metal identification tags, but there was nothing else the living could do for the dead. Within a few weeks, nature would reduce the corpses to clean skeletons.

Next, while searching the buildings at Waitavalo, Mackenzie and Figgis made another gruesome discovery: inside one charred structure was the body of a soldier, and the evidence clearly showed that he had been alive when the building was torched. "We lifted out several sheets of iron and found a corpse that had been burned," Mackenzie told an investigating committee later. "The corpse was within a few feet of the back entrance of the house and was on its hands and knees with one arm flung around a watering can. The attitude was that of a man attempting to crawl out of the house. There was a smell as if there was another corpse in the house but I did not see it."

The search party was unaware that several Australians had survived the massacres. In due time, the full extent of the Japanese atrocities would be revealed to the world.

HIGH IN THE MOUNTAINS, MEANWHILE, THERE HAD BEEN A CHANGE OF leadership among the Australians at Lemingi. Howard Carr, officially the ranking officer, gradually assumed a secondary position. "The Bodger" had already lost the respect of his men before the war started, then behaved irrationally during the invasion. In the jungle, he was just another lost soldier on the run. Fortunately for the rest of the party, a few capable individuals were prepared to step forward when their talents were needed.

One notable example was Chief Yeoman Stephen Lamont. Born near Belfast in 1898 and said to be "as Irish as Paddy's pig," he was a veteran of the Royal Navy during World War I. Later he became a coastwatcher in the mandated territory, and by coincidence had retired from that duty only a few days before Rabaul fell. He was awaiting transportation to Australia when the Japanese spoiled his plans.

Bruce Ball, the police commissioner, had served in the British Army during World War I, and was likewise more than competent in the jungle. And there was Richard E. P. "Larry" Dwyer, a rifleman in the NGVR who had worked in the New Guinea Department of Agriculture before the war. The others relied on his expertise regarding "all matters edible."

Between them, the three men had accumulated dozens of years of practical experience in the islands. They were familiar with the local customs and, most importantly, could converse with the natives in Pidgin English. Over the past twenty years, missionaries and territorial administrators had promoted its use to the point that Pidgin English bridged many of the innumerable dialects spoken by different tribes. The sing-song language had a surprisingly large vocabulary, and the soldiers of Lark Force benefited from learning basic words for day-to-day survival. *Kaikai* (food), *wara* (water), *haus* (hut), and *balus* (airplane) were among the most vital.

Ball, a no-nonsense character and tough policeman, gradually became the leader of the Australians at Lemingi. They remained with Father Alfons Meierhofer until February 7, then walked to Adler Bay. By that time only one small party remained nearby at Sum Sum plantation, and Bill Harry hiked there with Ivan Smith on February 12. They found Colin N. M. Stirling, a lieutenant from R Company, living with several other soldiers in relative comfort. They had plenty of rice and livestock available, and therefore declined Smith's offer to join the southbound group. Stirling and his party would later regret their decision.

Smith and Harry rejoined Ball's party, which resumed the journey south. A day or two later, Harry was scouting ahead with Larry Dwyer when they came upon a quiet freshwater stream. After washing the remnants of their uniforms, they bathed in the cool water while their clothing dried in the sun. Howard Carr suddenly appeared at the edge of the stream, and without preamble inquired, "Well, Larry, have you found any *kaikai* around?"

Momentarily befuddled by Carr's abrupt question, Dwyer recovered quickly. He rose slowly until he stood naked in the stream, then extended his arm and pointed at the canopy of a massive tree high above. "There is a fungus up there," he said deadpan, "which the natives sometimes eat. Good food, too—chock full of carbohydrates and protein." Carr simply ambled off without saying another word.

Back on the move again, Ball's group was just north of Tol plantation on February 14 when they met Scanlan's party walking in the opposite direction. The colonel was sullen and withdrawn, so John Mollard did most of the talking. After first explaining that their party was headed back to Rabaul to surrender, he tried to persuade Ball's group to join them. "Mollard stressed that there was no hope of evacuation from the island," recalled Harry, "and by surrendering to the Japanese there was a chance they would live." No one from either party changed their minds, and the groups went their separate ways.

Next, Ball's party stopped at Ril plantation, halfway between Tol and Kalai. They found the emaciated Alf Robinson, who declined an invitation to join their group. Until the telltale wounds on his wrists healed, he was fearful of leaving the relative safety of the plantation.

While the party rested at Ril, one of the young naval ratings died from malaria. The death of Signalman Arthur E. Francis on February 24 seemed to echo Mollard's warning. As a result, the men decided to continue southward at a faster pace than before, unaware that Holland was trying to catch up with them. Near Kalai, they came upon six warrant officers living in an old copra shed. All were former policemen from Ball's jurisdiction in the New Guinea constabulary. Although they knew each other well and were invited to join Ball's party, they preferred to remain at Kalai for the time being rather than head south.

Moving on without delay, Ball's group arrived at the village of Milim, approximately fifteen miles south of Kalai, on February 26. The villagers had fled after a gang of laborers from a nearby plantation took over their huts. Such changes were not unusual after the invasion, as most white plantation owners had abandoned their properties, leaving the native workers with no supervision. Islanders from the Admiralties and other "outside" areas frequently formed into gangs, some of which were influenced by Japanese bribes and rewards. In exchange, the gangs reported on local activities and pressured other natives into turning pro-Japanese.

The unruly gang at Milim, mostly natives from Manus Island, immediately showed their resentment of the Australians. Purely by coincidence, Frank Holland's messenger arrived at this precise moment and handed Ball a note. It simply stated that the party was to return to Kalai, which made the Australians suspicious. After questioning the runner, Ball decided the message was a ruse and called for the Manus gang's leader.

The situation quickly turned ugly. The boss-boy, full of defiance, threatened to "send talk" to the Japanese. Ball silenced him with sharp words, but the native began backing slowly toward a jungle trail. Suddenly he turned and ran. Ball drew his revolver and fired, badly wounding the native. The fight went out of his "sulky cohorts," who picked up their leader and carried him into the jungle.

The Australians moved on to the small village of Setwi on the afternoon of February 28. Another runner appeared with a message, and this time Ball recognized the scrawl of Arthur S. "Sandy" Sinclair, one of the warrant officers back at Kalai. His note read: "Advise return immediately. New plan."

The group conferred briefly and decided the message was too cryptic to act upon in blind faith. Dysentery and malaria were beginning to weaken some members of the party, and more information was needed before everyone would commit to going all the way back to Kalai. It made more sense for one individual to attempt a fast trip to the warrant officers' camp and get the complete story.

The obvious choice was Bill Harry. Still in good health, he had demonstrated his cross-country abilities on numerous occasions. The total journey was estimated to be forty miles, virtually all of it over rough terrain, and no extra rations could be spared. Harry would have to scrounge for native foods along the way. Could he do it in four days? If he failed to return by then, the group would continue south. Harry did not pause to think about it. Arming himself with a handgun, he started immediately on the path to Kalai. Only a few hours of daylight remained, and he wanted to make the most of it.

Darkness was falling by the time he approached Milim, where the "dust-up" had taken place two days earlier. Concerned that the Manus natives would seek retribution against the next white man they saw, Harry approached the village cautiously. On the path he met an islander who identified himself as the *tultul*, advisor to the *luluai*, the local headman. He gave Harry the good news that Milim was back in the hands of the villagers. The Manus ringleader was still alive, but remained hidden in the jungle with his gang.

The change in fortune was a boon to Harry. He promptly arranged for several natives to paddle him across Wide Bay in an outrigger canoe, thereby reducing the length of the trip by several hours. Arriving at Kalai before dawn, he walked into Sinclair's camp just as the constables were beginning to stir. None had expected such a fast response to the note, and they were duly impressed when Harry announced: "Good morning, I'm from Ball's party."

Sinclair asked where the rest of the men were.

"Still a couple of days down the coast," answered Harry. He explained that Ball had sent him "to get the story."

"Hell," Sinclair grumbled, "What's the use of that? This really puts the lid on it—we haven't a hope of holding Holland any longer."

"But who is Holland," Harry asked. "What is on, and where does he fit into it?"

Sinclair outlined the rescue attempt. Frank Holland was waiting near Ril to guide them all across the island to Pondo, where an evacuation was being organized. He was also caring for two survivors of the recent massacre, Alf Robinson and Bill Collins, and was impatient to get going. More importantly, Sinclair added, the Japanese occupied Gasmata, cutting off the escape route to the south. "We will do our best to hold Holland," he promised, "but there must be a limit."

After a breakfast of boiled kau-kau served on a leaf, Harry got back on the path. The natives who had brought him by canoe were gone, so he took the long way around the coast, walking nonstop throughout the day. Once again he reached Milim just before dark, and again the native advisor met him. This time, he took Harry aside and begged him to finish off the wounded gang leader, claiming the Manus natives had "whiskey galore from the plantation house, and large quantities of rice and tinned meat."

Harry wisely refused to get involved. After noting the location of the supplies, he arranged for another canoe to speed him on his way. At about 2200 on March 1, he walked into Ball's camp, having completed the round trip in just thirty hours.

The camp was abuzz. During Harry's absence, Peter Figgis, Hugh Mackenzie, and Ken Stone had rejoined the group. The entire party now commenced a late-night planning session. Figgis reported that there was an opportunity to evacuate even more Australians: his small party had found approximately two hundred members of Lark Force encamped in the vicinity of Jacquinot Bay. They were trapped when the Japanese landed at Gasmata on February 9, and now faced severe food shortages.

New plans were drawn up that night, and Figgis outlined the details in a coded message. The next morning, Ivan Smith and James C. H. "Connel" Gill, one of Mackenzie's sub-lieutenants, set off for the north coast to deliver the message directly to Keith McCarthy. Harry informed them of the food cache at Milim village, which indeed contained supplies that helped them in their effort to cross the island.

The rest of Ball's party also prepared to get underway. Most would hike back to Ril and join Frank Holland, but the new plan also called for several volunteers to stay behind and attempt to coordinate a southern evacuation. Well aware that they were passing up a good opportunity to get off the island, a total of six agreed to help the stranded troops. Peter Figgis, Bill Harry, Hugh Mackenzie, Ken Stone, and two of the naval ratings divvied up the few remaining tins of food and set off for Jacquinot Bay.

Ball led the rest of his party, which included Howard Carr, "Tusker" McLeod, Steve Lamont, and eight naval ratings, back to Wide Bay. They succeeded in finding Holland at Ril plantation, where Sinclair and the other constables joined them, as did the three civilian planters who had originally found Alf Robinson in the jungle. Holland then guided the collective group to his remote camp, where Bill Collins was still recovering from the wounds he had received at Tol.

The party now numbered twenty-five Australians. However, before they could get underway from Holland's camp, two of the naval ratings fell gravely ill with dysentery. Yeoman George P. Knight and Writer Thomas I. Douglas were too sick to travel, so Chief Lamont nobly volunteered to take care of them until they were able to move. The three navy men remained in the jungle camp while the rest of the evacuees started across the island. Thanks to Holland's expert guidance, the group joined Keith McCarthy at Pondo on March 8.

By then, both Thomas and Knight were dead, but not because of illness. Soon after the main party left the camp, they were captured along with Lamont and taken to Rabaul. Lamont was imprisoned at the Malaguna Camp stockade, but Douglas and Knight were executed on March 5.

KEITH MCCARTHY SEEMED TO BE EVERYWHERE AT ONCE. AFTER SENDING Holland across the island, he proceeded north to Cape Lambert and searched for scattered groups of Australian soldiers. At a plantation called Seragi, he found two noncoms, both sick with malaria, who led him around the cape to Langinoa, another plantation. There, thirty soldiers languished, slowly starving, but within yards of where they sat was a huge crop of untouched cassava. McCarthy could scarcely believe the soldiers' ignorance. The cassava roots would yield plenty of life-giving tapioca, but the soldiers had no knowledge of their surrounding habitat.

Near midnight on February 21, Pip Appel learned that McCarthy was in the vicinity. The timing could not have been better. Appel had recently received additional messages from the Japanese stating that they would round up all Australian troops at Lassul Bay on February 22. He was on the verge of giving up, but the news of McCarthy's arrival saved the day. Appel pulled his men back into the hills. He met face-to-face with McCarthy in the morning, and together they planned an evacuation.

The plan's success depended entirely on Appel. Because the Japanese controlled the waters off Lassul Bay, he had to move his men overland to Pondo, twenty-five miles from Harvey's plantation, in order for McCarthy to evacuate them by boat. Appel told McCarthy that he could have 145 men at Pondo in seven days. His most difficult task was leaving behind those who were too sick to travel. At this, John Ackeroyd stepped forward and volunteered to remain with eight men at St. Paul's Mission, knowing that all of them would eventually become POWs. Later, Ackeroyd was decorated with a Member of the British Empire for his selfless devotion.

Meanwhile, those who could walk were in bad shape. Appel noted a long list of ailments among them, including "acute tinea, tropical ulcers, ringworm, diarrhea, dysentery, swollen glands, [and] infected sores, with over 80% developing malaria." Despite their poor physical condition, he got them all to Pondo as promised—and in five days, not seven.

The arrival of Holland's party on March 8 brought the total number of soldiers and civilians on the north coast to well over two hundred. McCarthy intended to move them in stages down the coast using boats, but he had only the *Aussi* and a few other small craft available. He therefore assigned several men to repair the steamer *Malahuka*, which still sat on the slipway at Pondo. Leading the effort was Lincoln J. Bell, another timber merchant. His team repaired the hole in the hull easily enough; the bigger problem was the damage to the boat's engine, which proved difficult to fix. After five days of intensive work, the vessel was deemed ready to launch, and the process of ferrying men to Talasea began under the cover of darkness. But on three successive nights the *Malahuka's* engine broke down, forcing McCarthy to radio Port Moresby for assistance.

Enter the "Harris Navy," a motley flotilla of launches and schooners gathered by Gwynne C. "Blue" Harris, a member of ANGAU on New Guinea whose nickname came from the fringe of bright red hair surrounding his otherwise bald head. Lieutenant Commander Feldt, who later described Harris as "a collection of contradictions," instructed him to support the evacuation being organized by McCarthy.

Harris's fastest vessel had a top speed of only eight knots. "It would have been hard," Feldt recalled, "to find a more pathetic task force than this haphazard little group of launches." But the boats were adequate to move the troops away from the clutches of the Japanese. McCarthy directed the men who were weak with malnutrition or illness to be ferried aboard the flotilla while the fittest troops walked. He was constantly in motion during the journey from Pondo, sometimes browbeating demoralized troops to keep them going, other times rushing off to attend to some organizational requirement: canoes for a river crossing, food at the next plantation, radio messages to Port Moresby. By mid-March he had succeeded in moving the Australians approximately two hundred miles to Iboki plantation, an achievement that could not have been accomplished without his boundless energy.

There was ample food at Iboki, and even better, a tireless widow named Gladys Baker who volunteered to treat the sick and wounded men. Bill Collins was among the worst cases, but there were plenty of others who also needed her attention. "I worked all night and day caring for them and feeding them," she remembered. "In sixteen days I could only snatch thirteen hours sleep." At the start of the war, Baker had abandoned her own plantation on Vitu, fifty miles north of New Britain, and moved to a camp upriver from Iboki. She was accompanied by two crewmen from the Burns-Philp vessel *Lakatoi*, which the captain had decided to hide along the coast at Vitu.

Upon learning of the *Lakatoi*, Keith McCarthy sent an armed party to commandeer it, and the timid captain readily agreed to cooperate. The decision was made to keep the *Lakatoi* hidden at Vitu, which would minimize the possibility of its detection by the Japanese. The logistics were therefore more complicated, but the Harris Navy helped out again, successfully ferrying all of the Australians from Iboki to Vitu on the night of March 20.

The next day, the *Lakatoi* sailed for Australia with a total of 214 souls aboard, of whom 162 were members of Lark Force. The remainder consisted of civilians, ANGAU representatives, and crewmen. When the vessel docked at Cairns a week later, Keith McCarthy slumped in utter exhaustion. He had plenty of company: only six men from Lark Force were still fit for duty. "All the rest were sick," recalled Eric Feldt, "debilitated by poor and insufficient food, weakened by malaria and exposure. Most had sores, the beginnings of tropical ulcers, covered by dirty bandages. Their faces were the dirty gray of malaria victims, their clothes in rags and stinking of stale sweat."

For their extraordinary roles in the successful evacuation, Keith McCarthy, Frank Holland, and Gladys Baker were decorated as Members of the British Empire, and Pip Appel received a Military Cross.

ANOTHER NOTEWORTHY ESCAPE FROM THE NORTH COAST TOOK CONSIDERABLY longer to accomplish. Colin McInnes and a party of soldiers from B Company, including Graham Parsons (who had been shot in the neck and still suffered bouts of hemorrhaging), moved overland from their hideout near Cape Lambert to Rangarere plantation. There, owner John McLean had hidden a thirty-two-foot motor launch named the *Lottie Don* in a shallow creek. Over a period of days, the boat was provisioned with food and fuel and her white hull was camouflaged with dark green paint.

The first attempt to get the *Lottie Don* past the reefs failed on February 15. The next night, McLean himself decided to join the escape attempt and brought along his personal servant, Bombangi, along with a soldier from C Company, Private Norman J. Burgell. A skilled boatman, Mclean urged the party, now numbering eleven, to make for New Ireland rather than risk the long journey to New Guinea. Everyone decided to accept his recommendation, and the *Lottie Don* carried them across St. George's Channel in the dark without incident. Two days later, as the men worked their way south along the coast of New Ireland, they were met by coastwatchers Alan F. "Bill" Kyle and Gregory N. Benham, who had periodic radio communications with Port Moresby.

However, before a rescue could be arranged, Japanese ships arrived in the nearby harbor. Troops landed in force, sending the Australians pell-mell into the jungle. Separated into small parties, they spent weeks moving up and down the narrow island, scrounging food where they could, relying on native runners to occasionally send messages to each other, and always endeavoring to stay one step ahead of the Japanese.

All of them suffered at various times from tropical ailments. McInnes became so ill with malaria that he had to be watched constantly to prevent him from wandering mindlessly into the jungle. He recovered, but another victim of malaria, Warrant Officer Neale E. Evans of the RAAF, died on March 20. A helpful native dug most of the grave, because none of the Australians could wield a spade for more than a few minutes at a time.

At last, McInnes' small party met a Chinese captain named Chin Pak who owned a battered, ungainly-looking boat named the *Quong Wah.* They negotiated with him to buy the craft, and he proved to be a wily trader. Part of the agreement included the purchase of thousands of cigarettes. The cartons were colorful and attractive, but the cigarettes turned out to be an Egyptian brand made during World War I. After twenty years in the tropics, none would light. "[On] that point at least," recalled Douglas A. Aplin, a corporal from B Company, "the Chinaman had the last laugh."

With the assistance of coastwatchers Kyle and Benham, the scattered parties were reunited after five miserable weeks of jungle survival.* They departed New Ireland on April 30 aboard the *Quong Wah* for what should have been a two-day voyage to New Guinea. However, multiple break-downs slowed their progress, and they spent fifty-seven hours adrift before making landfall on May 5, by which time they were 120 miles off course. Motoring down to Buna, McInnes made radio contact with area headquarters on May 6. Then, after resting at Buna for several days, the entire party proceeded to Milne Bay. A small coastal vessel picked them up and delivered them to Port Moresby on May 26, ninety-nine days after they had escaped from New Britain.

Amazingly, for all the hardships they experienced, McInnes and his men did not endure the most difficult circumstances. That distinction went to the approximately two hundred Australians trapped near Jacquinot Bay on the south coast of New Britain, where conditions were even worse.

---

* Kyle and Benham did not leave New Ireland. They received RAN rank and were compelled to stay behind as coastwatchers. Later, they were betrayed by natives and executed by the Japanese.

CHAPTER ELEVEN

ESCAPE: THE LAURABADA

"We could do nothing but wait."

—Gunner David Bloomfield,
antiaircraft battery

In early March, a few days after volunteering to stay behind on the south coast of New Britain, Peter Figgis and the five men with him walked into a village at the tip of Cape Orford. There they found Ben Dawson and seven soldiers from Lark Force, most of whom looked sick and dejected. Their party had left Kalai in a commandeered motor launch on February 10, and moved down the coast as far as Pul Pul. However, within two weeks everyone except Dawson was infected with malaria, and one man died. After resting for several days, the men had worked their way south to Marau plantation, from which they set out again in the launch on February 26. Strong winds blew them onto a reef near the village of Baien, wrecking the boat, and that was where Figgis found them— out of hope and planning to surrender. However, when Figgis informed Dawson of the evacuation being organized on the north coast, Dawson thought his group would be able to walk to Pondo. With directions for finding the stash of food at Milim, he and his ailing men set off across the island on yet another arduous journey.

Figgis' party continued south for another thirty-five miles to Waterfall Bay. They took shelter in an abandoned sawmill, near which a large garden of sweet potatoes was ready to harvest. Other foods included pawpaws ripening on numerous trees. Four men rested there while Figgis and Mackenzie walked farther south to look for the main body of troops on the far side of Jacquinot Bay. A few days later they located Bill Owen and numerous Lark Force soldiers living in squalid conditions.

As the ranking officer on the south coast, Owen had performed admirably in moving the troops southward after the departure of Scanlan and Mollard. It was to Owen's credit that so many had traveled so far, but after they reached Jacquinot Bay the situation turned nightmarish. The incidence of malnutrition and disease increased dramatically, and although Ted Palmer helped the soldiers as best he could with his limited medical supplies, some individuals had died.

Palmer was grateful for the aid of Father Ted Harris, the local priest at Malmal Mission. Tall and slender, Harris possessed "a wonderfully eloquent gift of expression, a delightful Irish brogue, and a frank and infectious smile." In short, he was a parody of the typical Irish priest. Working out of his church—naturally called St. Patrick's—he cheered the sick men and provided native foods. It was a losing battle, however, as both he and Palmer constantly fought another enemy that affected the troops. "Morale gradually deteriorated," recalled Palmer, "the jungle itself seeming to depress the men quite apart from the massacres and the deaths from malaria."

The men lived at two plantations: Wunung, about a mile from Harris's mission, and Drina, twenty miles farther down the coast. Palmer used Wunung as an aid station, checking the condition of each man that arrived. He sent those deemed "fit" to Drina, while the sick remained at Wunung for treatment in his makeshift hospital.

At Drina, Bill Owen strived to keep the healthy ones busy. He organized the men into three platoons, each with a rotating schedule: one day of camp duties, a day of rest, and then a day of gardening. They planted the flat terrain of an unused airstrip with sweet potatoes, which would eventually improve their food supply, but in the meantime men began dying at an alarming rate.

Palmer was forced to divide his time between both plantations. "With one exception," he wrote later, "every man of more than 150 was infected." He had a limited amount of quinine, so he administered small doses only to the worst cases, giving each man 50 grams daily for a maximum of four days. Soon he had to stop using even that insufficient amount. "I decided to use the minimum of quinine and only when I thought the patient would die without it. This should have produced black water fever but I do not think any occurred." Suffering his own malaria attacks, Palmer watched helplessly as the men endured the debilitating infection with virtually no relief.

One vivid portrayal of malaria's mind-bending effects appears in a book written after the war by David Selby. Appropriately titled *Hell and High Fever*, it describes a feverish episode that occurred on the porch of the Drina plantation house:

> From where I lay on the floor I could see, further down the veranda, the legs of a table which, together with an upturned box, comprised the Adjutant's office. Those table legs acquired a peculiar significance with the approach of delirium. As the fever rose, they would grow and grow until, colossal giants, they floated towards me. I struggled in my mind to keep them back but nothing would hold them. One was kneeling on my chest, crushing my lungs and, as I panted for breath, it seemed that no breath would come.
>
> Iron fingers were grasping my throat, choking me, and red-hot bands were pressing in my temples, splitting my skull. I felt my struggles against this intangible menace growing weaker, and at last a black abyss opened up behind me and I slipped headlong down through waves of undulating darkness. Then a gigantic face floated down on me, and I tortured my brain to think where I had seen that face before as names drifted through my brain but seemed to elude my grasp . . . and a voice a thousand miles away would offer me a drink. I tried to answer but my tongue was sticking to the roof of my mouth and only horrible sounds issued forth.
>
> Then the mists cleared and I felt that by an enormous effort of will I could force the table legs back to their place as they dwindled to their correct size. I realized that it was not months, or years since I had last seen them, but perhaps minutes, and that I was still lying on the veranda floor at Drina.

The attacks of chills and fever would periodically wane, and the infected men could accomplish some limited work. However, by the end of March at least a third of the men had positive symptoms at any given time, including daily rigors and a temperature above 102 degrees. Virtually everyone was anemic, and many soldiers suffered edema of the feet and ankles. Some of the sickest men appeared almost skeletal, with shreds of filthy uniforms hanging from their bony frames. Dysentery was another endemic problem, mainly because of poor sanitation. Although latrines were dug, the afflicted individuals were often too weak to reach them before diarrhea struck.

Overwhelmed by the number of sick and dying men, Palmer was forced to make difficult choices. "There were some deaths," he admitted, "owing to the difficulty of deciding which men were in immediate danger." Remarkably, the four men in Palmer's care who had been so terribly wounded by the Japanese—Bill Cook, "Smacker" Hazelgrove, Cliff Marshall, and "Nipper" Webster—all pulled through.

Not only did the soldiers at Wunung and Drina battle malaria and dysentery, they also suffered from an acute shortage of food. Their diet was limited almost exclusively to taro and rice, and the sick men did not receive enough nutrition to recover. Many of those who died actually succumbed to a combination of disease and malnourishment.

The garden in front of the Drina plantation house was used as a cemetery, but eventually all the space was taken up. A new burial plot was started adjacent to a pig sty behind the house. There was good reason for choosing both locations: the ground was relatively soft to begin with, and elsewhere it took hours to dig even a shallow grave. With so much death and misery at Drina, the men came to despise "every stone and tree on that plantation."

FOR ALL THEIR DREADFULNESS, DRINA AND WUNUNG REPRESENTED SAFE havens for the Australians who managed to stumble in from the jungle. Some arrived with harrowing tales of their journeys down the coast.

David Bloomfield, slowed by malaria as he traveled with a party of soldiers and civilians, did not reach Jacquinot Bay until March 29, fully seven weeks after the massacre at Tol. Suffering from exhaustion and malnourishment, he was one of the lucky ones. Several of his friends had collapsed along the trail, then gradually faded away until they slipped into a coma. It was terribly depressing to watch them draw their final breath in a dark and foul-smelling hut in some lonely, abandoned village.

Perhaps the most compelling adventure was the one endured by three young friends. On February 19, gunners Archibald N. "Arch" Taylor and James W. R. "Bob" Hannah of the 17th Antitank Battery, along with Jack Hart of the antiaircraft unit, attempted a shortcut across a rugged section of the southern coast. They made good progress until they came to a cliff overlooking jagged coral rocks near the shore. While Taylor went to search for a vine to use as a rope, Hart decided to climb down on his own. After a few minutes Taylor returned and warned Hart to be careful, but an instant later the rock Hart was holding onto suddenly broke. As his friends watched in horror, he detached from the cliff face and "turned over about three times" before hitting the rocks below.

By some miracle, Hart was not killed. It took Taylor about fifteen minutes to descend the cliff and run to his friend, by which time Hart was alert. Blood ran from a deep gash in his face, and despite his agony he managed to say, "Arch, my leg is broken." A moment later Hannah appeared, having nearly fallen himself as he climbed down the cliff. He helped Taylor fashion a crude splint from driftwood and strips of cloth, which they used to stabilize the broken leg.

Taylor started hiking along the coast to get help, and found two natives in an otherwise-abandoned village. When he reached their hut, located on a tiny island formed by the tributaries of a fast-flowing river, he was pleased to see that they "had very kind faces and were both of a good build." The one named Lao spoke passable Pidgin English and promised to seek help for Hart in the morning. Meanwhile, they were already caring for an Australian soldier with malaria.

Later that evening, another soldier was brought to the little hut. Thirty-four-year-old Private George P. Harris of C Company was half-drowned, having attempted suicide in the river. Known as "George the Greek" (his birthplace was Polamon, Greece), he was out of his mind with fever. "He was absolutely exhausted," Taylor remembered, "so exhausted that a sort of paralysis had set in and he had no control over his limbs . . . George was delirious and I couldn't get to sleep because of his cries."

In the morning, Lao appeared with six natives. Taylor led them to where Hart lay, and they built a stretcher from saplings and empty copra sacks. The natives stumbled often as they carried the injured man over the rough terrain, but each time someone slipped, the others instantly lowered themselves to keep the stretcher level. At the swift river, they made a crude raft from driftwood and tied Hart's stretcher to it, then floated him five hundred yards downstream. Later, describing their effort as "the most wonderful piece of teamwork" he had ever witnessed, Taylor felt ashamed at giving each native one coin when they reached the village. They seemed pleased, however, and that was how the system worked.

Compassion kept Hart alive. The natives reset his broken leg, then Taylor and Hanna nursed him while Lao and others delivered food. For six weeks the three Australians stayed in the rat-infested hut. Hart was immobilized on a bed of bamboo rods, his back tortured by bedsores, his body wracked by malaria. But he survived whereas "George the Greek" died on February 24, just five days after being brought to the village.

Taylor tried again to compensate the natives for helping Hart. One day, a wounded youth from the Nakanai Mountains was carried down to the coastal village following a Japanese attack. The boy's knee, filled with shrapnel, was badly infected. With nothing but "great trepidation" and a rusty pair of scissors that he disinfected in boiling water, Taylor dug out the shards. They were accompanied by "heaps of blood and pus," and Taylor was astounded when the Nakanai people chewed ginger root and then spat it into the wound before carrying the boy back to the mountains. Having gained the confidence of the natives for miles around, Taylor told them to hate the Japanese.

Eventually, word got back to Father Harris about the three gunners. He sent them tins of sardines, but it was all he could give, his other supplies having been used up long before. Later, Bill Owen conveyed a message to Taylor and Hannah, urging them to bring Hart to Wunung. In early April, they arranged for several natives to carry Hart to a village where they obtained a canoe for a night crossing of Jacquinot Bay. A storm lashed the coast of New Britain that night, terrifying the occupants of the canoe as it bucked across the large bay. The team safely reached the far shore and finished the journey on foot, traveling an estimated forty miles in just seventeen hours. As a reward, the natives received a bag of rice and some tobacco.*

The three wayward gunners soon learned why Owen had sent for them. At long last, there had been a breakthrough in communications with Port Moresby. It turned out that Ivan Smith and Con Gill had successfully reached the north coast of New Britain, where they found Keith McCarthy. He promptly informed headquarters about the Australians trapped near Jacquinot Bay, to which ANGAU responded by sending patrol officer Allan T. Timperley from the Trobriands in the fast launch *Mascot*. Although it was too small for the evacuation of troops, it carried plenty of food and a two-way radio.

When he reached Palmalmal plantation on April 5, Timperley was met by several ragged-looking men from Lark Force. Thinking the *Mascot* had come to rescue them, they were dismayed by its small size—though they didn't hesitate to consume some of the bully beef and tea on board. For his part, Timperley was anxious to contact Figgis and Mackenzie, who had written the original note forwarded to Port Moresby, in order to coordinate the actual evacuation effort.

FOR THE PAST THREE WEEKS, FIGGIS'S PARTY HAD BEEN ENCAMPED AT BOVALPUN, a native village near the northeastern shore of Jacquinot Bay. Happily distant from the miserable conditions at Wunung and Drina, they tinkered with a steel-hulled lifeboat, said to be a relic from the SS *President Johnson*, with hopes of sailing it to the Trobriands. "It was all a diversion," admitted Bill Harry, but the days spent on the secluded beach reaped rewards later.

One day in early April, a charismatic native named Golpak arrived to address the villagers of Bovalpun. They had begun to show timidity in the Australians' presence, and Golpak, the "paramount *luluai*" or headman representing many southern villages, was concerned that the people were being persuaded by the increasingly influential Japanese. Calling the natives together, he "jerked them into line with a great demonstration of oratory." Wiry and strong, estimated to be sixty years old, Golpak wielded enormous influence over the natives. In his youth he had worked as a boss-boy and was loyal to the Allies, a fact that would be invaluable to

*The natives had done more for Jack Hart than anyone realized. Later, in Australia, an x-ray of his leg revealed that the broken bone had been set "spot on" and was healing perfectly.

New Britain's coastwatchers in the years to come. Soon after Golpak departed, the Australians at Bovalpun were informed of Timperley's arrival. Immediately they dropped what they were doing and made their way to Palmalmal.

Down at Drina, Bill Owen had also received an urgent-sounding message on the afternoon of Timperley's arrival:

> Send all men that can travel over to Wunung, including all sick if you can get them over. They must be here today as tonight is the night. It is imperative that you come and you will get all details. C.E.G.

The initials were those of Captain Christopher E. Goodman, the ranking officer currently at Wunung.

With great excitement, speculating freely on what sort of evacuation might be pending, Owen and his men set off for the overnight journey to Wunung. However, the twenty miles separating the plantations began to feel like a hundred. Virtually everyone had malaria, and there were numerous stretcher cases among the men. Enough were capable of walking to provide two relay teams for each stretcher, but the so-called "healthy" individuals could walk only a few hundred yards before stopping to rest.

The greatest challenge for Owen and his starving group was the ascent of a steep mountain in the darkness. The slope was slick with rotten coral and numerous loose rocks, forcing the men to manhandle the stretchers up one ledge at a time. At the top, the stretcher bearers and relief teams stumbled forward on legs that felt like "brittle sticks." When they could walk no farther, they sagged to the ground, panting for breath against the damp earth until someone rose and cursed the others to their feet. The trek went on like that for hours: men walking as though in a stupor, falling often, despairing that their progress was too slow, that their opportunity for rescue would be lost.

Just after midnight, a group of natives carrying flaming torches met the Australians on the trail. They had been sent to guide the soldiers directly to Palmalmal. Grinning with excitement, they picked up the stretchers and led the weary soldiers forward. David Selby was "near to weeping with relief" as he moved off with renewed energy. At Palmalmal, however, when the soldiers saw the tiny *Mascot*, their spirits tumbled again. Finally they learned the whole story: Timperley was merely a relay. His boat carried a radio with which to call in a larger vessel.

On the morning of April 6, a Sunday, Timperley established contact with Port Moresby and was informed that the HMAS *Laurabada*, the former yacht of the Papuan administrator, would arrive on Wednesday. The three-day delay not only strained the patience of everyone involved, but also meant that the hurried march from Drina and Wunung had been unnecessary. Even worse, three men had fallen critically ill immediately after the march. None had been stretcher cases—in fact all three carried their share of the burden—but the strain had been too great for their weakened bodies. One was Colin Dowse, the entertainer who had charmed everyone with his animated honky-tonk piano playing back in happier times. He lasted only two days, and died on April 7.

Then, before the *Laurabada* arrived, another of the sick men passed away. Death had become almost routine during the past few months, but the men at Palmalmal became intensely frustrated as they grieved for the two latest victims. "They had come so far, and so near to rescue," wrote David Selby, "only to be snatched away at the last minute."

The overall mood improved greatly when Captain Ivan F. Champion, a well-known local explorer from an influential family, brought the sleek-hulled *Laurabada* into Palmalmal on April 9. He anchored the yacht in the lee of a small island to hide it from prowling Japanese boats and aircraft.

After a closer look at the yacht, the anxious Australians onshore were skeptical. The *Laurabada* was certainly larger than the *Mascot*, but with just four small cabins she couldn't possibly accommodate the number of people who waited ashore. The diesel-powered vessel was barely a hundred feet long and displaced only 150 tons. In short, a pleasure craft had been sent to rescue the entire contingent. The *Laurabada*'s only armament consisted of a few Vickers guns arranged on a temporary platform extending fore and aft over her deck from the main cabin. It made the yacht appear top-heavy and spoiled her rakish lines.

Champion was under orders to sail that night, but he decided to keep the boat hidden as long as possible. There was good reason for delaying the departure. A few days earlier, radioman Dave Laws and several other men had departed for Awul, a Roman Catholic mission near Gasmata, with hopes of repairing the transmitter there. The party had not yet returned, and the crew of the *Laurabada* waited anxiously while scanning the skies for Japanese planes.

Several Australians tried to convince Father Harris to come with them on the *Laurabada*. The kindly priest, more concerned with the welfare of the local natives than his own skin, refused. What kind of Christian would he be, he asked rhetorically, if he abandoned his "children" in their hour of need?

Late that afternoon, Champion moved the *Laurabada* to the plantation's jetty to embark passengers. Almost as if scripted, a dark-looking storm approached that afternoon, but boarding was accomplished quickly thanks to a plan devised by Selby. A few civilians occupied one of the four cabins, and stretcher cases went into the other three plus the dining room. The rest of the troops filed onto the outer decks, squeezing into every available inch of space. Ridiculously overloaded, the *Laurabada* listed to starboard. Built to accommodate eight passengers and a handful of crewmembers, she was packed with 157 escapees, of whom an estimated 135 were from Lark Force.

As the hour for sailing approached, Dave Laws and his party failed to appear. The radio was pulled out of the *Mascot* and left with Father Harris, so that when Laws returned he could contact Port Moresby. Otherwise there was nothing for Champion to do but to leave the small party behind. Every minute that the *Laurabada* stayed at Palmalmal, the risk of discovery by the Japanese increased.

Providentially, the storm broke at 1700 and pelted the *Laurabada* with "black torrents" of rain. It was a perfect shroud for hiding the boat, and Champion promptly got her underway. Standing at the crowded rail, David Selby savored the moment as the shoreline of New Britain slowly receded from view.

David Bloomfield's parting glimpse of the unforgiving island was more somber: "My last memory of New Britain was the figure of Father Harris . . . standing on the wharf in the rain, waving us goodbye. Within minutes the rain became so heavy that we lost sight of Father Harris. It was as if a curtain had been drawn between us and our adventures on New Britain."

Unfortunately for the priest, Bloomfield's metaphor proved all too accurate. Sometime during the latter half of 1942, the Japanese came to his

Harris' mission and took him aboard a vessel, ostensibly to send him to Rabaul. Instead, they executed Harris and dumped his body overboard.

On April 10, mere hours after leaving New Britain, the last of the three men who fell sick at Palmalmal died aboard the *Laurabada*. Private Ivor P. James had gotten married just before shipping out from Australia, with Bill Harry serving as his best man. Now, the survivors listened as Champion performed a brief memorial service for James. The decks were too crowded for most of the passengers to observe the proceedings, but there was no mistaking the splash as James' canvas-wrapped body was committed to the deep.

After a queasy voyage across the Solomon Sea, the *Laurabada* rounded the tip of New Guinea at Samarai and motored slowly northwestward to Port Moresby. As the boatload of sick and weary troops neared the end of the three-day voyage, Bill Harry found something to laugh about. His haversack still held a few cans of "panic rations," and for weeks he and Figgis had entertained themselves by trying to guess the contents of a can that had no label. Now that they were safe, Figgis could no longer resist. "Look," he said, "we'll open that mystery tin of yours and see what it's all about. It looks as though we won't need to keep it." Harry pried the lid off. They looked inside, then shook their heads with a mixture of amusement and disdain. Tropical fruit salad. The irony wasn't lost on them.

IN ADDITION TO THE MEN WHO ARRIVED ABOARD THE *LAURABADA*, A FEW smaller parties from the south coast of New Britain also reached friendly lines, some after amazing adventures. Their stories are likewise worth noting.

One party walked almost the entire length of New Britain's south coast. Dick Hamill, Fred Kollmorgen, Perce Pearson, and three other soldiers had been part of larger parties led by Botham and Nicholls, but the groups fractured into three smaller parties over a period of weeks. Botham's and Nicholls' groups escaped independently by boat, and another led by Lieutenant Edward W. "Ted" Best nearly did. However, Best's party was captured at Gasmata on February 10, the day after it was occupied by the Japanese.

Dick Hamill's group of six men successfully skirted Gasmata and made it all the way to Arawe. "We got down almost to the end of the island," remembered Kollmorgen, "then faced the open sea. To get across to the New Guinea mainland was about sixty miles over water, but we did get across."

In a small launch crewed by several natives, the Australians crossed the Dampier Straits and reached Finschhafen on March 2. After stocking up on food, they split up into pairs—Kollmorgen stayed with Hamill—and successfully crossed the rugged Papuan Peninsula over a period of weeks. All were infected with malaria, and the journey nearly killed them. "On New Guinea more than on New Britain, the mosquitoes were shocking," Kollmorgen stated. "We finished up, myself in particular, with a very bad dose of malaria coming back. Even when I got to Melbourne, I was sent straight to [the] hospital from the train. I was in and out of Heidelberg, the military hospital in Melbourne, and was never fit for duty after that."

KOLLMORGEN, A TENOR HORN PLAYER, WAS THE ONLY MEMBER OF THE 2/22nd Battalion band to reach Australia. At least seven other bandsmen managed to avoid capture on the day of the invasion, but one by one their luck ran out. Bert Morgan (tenor horn), the only band member known to have tried evading toward the north coast, was the first to be taken prisoner. Six others headed south with various parties. Stanley R. Parker (E-flat bass) was hobbled by a leg infection which resulted in his capture at an unnamed mission station. Ronald H. Cook (trombone) and Bill Haines (tenor horn) were captured at Tol and murdered on February 4. William E. Edwards (drummer) was taken prisoner with Lieutenant Best's party at Gasmata six days later. Austin Creed (trombone) avoided the massacres and made it past Wide Bay, but then fell ill with malaria and died in a remote village on February 20.

One additional bandsman almost made it off the island. After traveling for a while with Dick Hamill's group, Frederick J. Meyer (tenor horn) ended up in Dave Laws' party as they attempted to find the radio at Awul. The group had almost reached the Catholic mission when word came about the arrival of the Laurabada, so they raced back to Palmalmal only to learn from Father Harris that the boat had departed four days earlier. Meyer became despondent, and his health plummeted to the point that he was unable or unwilling to fight off a bout of malaria. He died at Wunung on April 27.

A month later, Laws finally escaped with seven men. They left New Britain aboard a repaired motor launch and landed on the coast of New Guinea, then walked over the rugged peninsula to Port Moresby.

But even that amazing odyssey was eclipsed by Ben Dawson. After departing from Marau plantation on the south coast, Dawson and his party walked across New Britain in mid-March. They reached the north coast only to find that the *Lakatoi* had sailed days earlier. There was no faulting Keith McCarthy, who was unaware that another party was trying to reach him; Dawson's attempt at crossing the island had been a long shot to begin with.

With the aid of various missionaries and natives, Dawson and his men moved from village to village until they reached Talasea in late March. There they found Lincoln Bell, who had stayed to serve as a coastwatcher rather than evacuate on the *Lakatoi*. He transmitted their names and status to Port Moresby, but there was little that ANGAU could do. By that time, the Japanese had captured Lae, Salamaua, and Finschhafen, expanding their influence over the entire Bismarck Archipelago. They also patrolled the seas and skies, making it extremely hazardous for the Australians to attempt a rescue effort.

Leaving two men to help Bell run his boat and radio, Dawson moved to Iboki, where his party lived off the land for a month. On April 24 they moved out to the Vitu Islands using Bell's boat. After three weeks at a plantation there, they moved again to Unea Island and were picked up by "Blue" Harris in the schooner *Umboi*. Harris wanted to take them directly to Port Moresby, but in early May a clash between Japanese and American carrier forces in the Coral Sea turned the entire region into a hornet's nest. Harris therefore pointed the *Umboi* westward and delivered Dawson's party to the village of Bogadjim on the coast of New Guinea.

The big island presented numerous challenges to Dawson and his men. Lieutenant Reginald H. Boyan of ANGAU led them on a wild excursion along the Ramu River valley and through the rugged Bismarck Mountains. At a tiny airstrip near Kainatu, they found several American crewmen from a crashed B-25 bomber. With them were two U.S. Army dive bomber pilots, one of them badly injured. They and another pilot had been dispatched from Port Moresby to rescue the B-25 crew with three Douglas A-24s, but all three planes cracked up while trying to land on the rough field. One pilot had been killed and another had both legs broken. For an entire month, the combined group stayed near the remote airstrip while awaiting transportation.

Finally, an odd-looking RAAF De Havilland Dragon Rapide biplane arrived. Out jumped Flight Lieutenant John R. "Jerry" Pentland, who matter-of-factly stated that the runway was too short to lift anyone out. They would have to walk twenty-five miles across the Ramu valley to Bena Bena, he said, where there was a better airstrip. Pentland kept his promise, and when the party reached Bena Bena several days later, he evacuated the injured American pilot along with one of Dawson's noncoms. Returning for a second trip, he flew out another Australian; but when he came back the third time he stated that only Americans could be airlifted.

Dawson was appalled. According to Pentland, someone at Port Moresby had declared that the RAAF wasn't responsible for transporting Australian soldiers: that was ANGAU's job. Dawson was instructed to take his party on foot to Wau, then down to the south coast where an administration vessel would pick them up. Having already endured more than five months of incredible hardships, Dawson and his men were compelled to walk another two hundred miles, much of it across the island's most rugged mountains. Not only had snobbery and service rivalry sunk to an all-time low, but Dawson and his men had become castaways.

Having no other options, Dawson's party followed the Ramu and Markham valleys for more than 130 twisting miles, reaching Wau on July 15. There, an administration officer ordered them to continue on foot to Bulldog, a camp thirty torturous miles farther across the steep mountains. Once there, they would have to canoe down the Lakekamu River, known for its hoards of mosquitoes and giant sago swamps.

Hearing this, Dawson refused to push his men any further. He sought out the medical officer of the local NGVR contingent, who agreed that the men were unfit for such a journey. All had malaria, and the doctor stated that they were virtually guaranteed to get blackwater fever if they made it as far as the Lakekamu River.

Eventually, Dawson's men were airlifted to Port Moresby. Instead of going with them, however, he joined the 2/5th Independent Company and remained in the jungles until late September. At last, illness forced him to leave, but the indefatigable lieutenant walked to the coast of New Guinea on foot. Battling dysentery, he crossed mountains that soared to 8,500 feet as he trekked more than seventy-five miles to the mouth of the Lakekamu River. From there, he traveled by boat to Port Moresby, and later was hospitalized in Australia. After recovering, he returned to active duty and even served on New Britain again in 1945.

The stamina exhibited by Dawson was truly unique. Of the 385 soldiers rescued from New Britain and New Ireland in 1942, very few reached safety with their health intact. When the *Lakatoi* docked at Cairns on March 28, only six men aboard were deemed fit; two weeks later the *Laurabada* reached Port Moresby with even fewer able-bodied soldiers. Among the smaller parties, virtually everyone was in bad shape. The great majority of returnees, like Fred Kollmorgen, spent weeks or even months in Heidelberg Military Hospital. Tragically, one of the *Lakatoi*'s soldiers was so sick that he did not make it to the hospital. Colin Dowse, the enthusiastic honky-tonk pianist, completed an incredibly difficult trek across New Britain while battling malaria and escaped from the north coast, but the rigors of the disease proved too much. He died at the Albury railway station, just hours short of the hospital in Melbourne.

Ultimately, only a few of the soldiers who escaped from New Britain got back in the fight. The rest, although technically not wounded in action, were casualties nonetheless because of prolonged illness and malnutrition. Throughout the entire garrison, therefore, the casualty rate exceeded 96 percent, including those killed or wounded in action, those who were executed by the Japanese, and those who died of various causes while trying to escape. Based on that statistic alone, Lark Force suffered one of the worst defeats of World War II among Australian units of battalion size or larger.

Make no mistake: other units, especially those of the Malay Barrier, likewise suffered heavy casualties. Gull Force lasted only three days after the Japanese invaded Ambon on January 30, and approximately 800 of the 1,100-man garrison became POWs. Some remained on Ambon, but most were eventually shipped to labor camps on Hainan Island in the South China Sea. Collectively, the Gull Force prisoners endured such brutal treatment that fewer than 25 percent survived captivity.

Sparrow Force fared only slightly better. After two days of heavy fighting on Timor, Lieutenant Colonel Leggatt surrendered the 2/40th Infantry

Battalion to the Japanese on February 23. The battalion lost 84 dead and 132 wounded, and approximately 160 others died in captivity.

In the Egyptian desert, the 2/28th Infantry Battalion was nearly annihilated on the night of July 26-27, 1942. As the forward element of an attempted breakout through Afrika Korps positions near El Alamein, the 2/28th advanced up a rocky hill called Ruin Ridge and was surrounded by Axis tanks and mechanized infantry. After an intense but hopeless fight, the battalion lost 65 dead and 490 captured.

But those bitter defeats were not nearly as disastrous as the one suffered by Lark Force, and the casualty rate was only part of the equation. The contemptible actions of the top two officers and the indifference shown by the War Cabinet also factor heavily, making the fall of Rabaul arguably the worst defeat ever suffered by Australia in any war.

And, as the POWs at Rabaul would discover, the most terrible event was yet to come.

CHAPTER TWELVE

OUTCRY

*"Why were reinforcements and equipment
withheld from New Britain?"*

—*Smith's Weekly*, May 16, 1942

A s might be expected, the defeat of Lark Force made headlines across Australia. Little was known about the garrison's fate after the radios on New Britain were knocked out, and the first information to appear in the papers was misleading. "Militia Holds Out In Rabaul," boasted the *Sydney Sun* on Wednesday, January 28. Under the subtitle, "RAAF Shocks Japs: New Air Blows Likely," the article explained that a strike from Port Moresby had left two enemy ships ablaze in Simpson Harbor. In truth, a handful of Catalina flying boats had dropped their bombs haphazardly through the clouds, causing little damage. The scant information known about Lark Force itself was presented with less enthusiasm. "The besieged garrison is still holding out west of Rabaul," invented the writer, "and is believed to be strongly contesting every attempt by the Japanese to mop up the island."

The effort to save face was almost laughable. Whether it was a case of propaganda gone wild or something more devious—a deliberate attempt to hide the disaster from the public, for example—the reality was that the garrison had been overwhelmed in a matter of hours. The remnants of Lark Force weren't contesting anything; they were simply trying to survive.

After the first sketchy articles were published, the Australian press revealed nothing more about Lark Force for several weeks. Even after Botham and Nicholls reached Port Moresby on March 1, the story of what had happened was kept under wraps for more than a month. Finally, on April 6, a detailed account of the invasion appeared in the *Sydney Morning Herald* under the banner headline: "Terrific Odds Faced at Rabaul."

Once again the accompanying article was heavily fictionalized. The garrison, it claimed, "fought against odds of more than 10 to one and they did not give in until the Japanese landing force, comprising between 17,000 and 20,000 men, had suffered at least 2,000 casualties." Details of the battle were similarly distorted. "They were squealing like pigs," one defender allegedly said of the Japanese. "Hundreds of them had been killed as they tried to get across the wire, and their bodies were slumped there in all sorts of grotesque positions."

The *Sun* went on to claim that Australian casualties numbered "about 700," including POWs, which implied that approximately half of the garrison was safe. The paper published vivid details of the "nightmare trek" that Nicholls and Botham endured, but those two groups had escaped relatively quickly. Thus, they did not suffer nearly as much as the men who escaped months later. The real horrors were not revealed until the *Laurabada* and *Lakatoi* delivered another 300 members of Lark Force. When the numbers of rescued soldiers from the other small parties were added up, the total didn't equal 700, or even 400.

Public outrage followed. One of the strongest national voices belonged to *Smith's Weekly*, a periodical that billed itself as "The Public Guardian." The editors demanded an official investigation into the "New Guinea Affair," as they dubbed it, and reported "evidence of serious bungling." They appealed directly to Prime Minister John Curtin, asking him "to discover why, in the year the island has been garrisoned, nothing had been done to give the AIF and [militia] forces even a gambler's chance against the invading Japs."

Aside from pressuring the government, however, there was little that *Smith's* or anyone else could do. It was all too apparent that hundreds of men were unaccounted for, but no official explanation was given. With each passing week, the public's anxiety grew.

IN THE WAKE OF THE DEBACLE, MOST OF THE RETURNED SOLDIERS WENT BACK to some semblance of their former civilian life. David Selby resumed the practice of law and eventually became a prominent judge in Papua New

Guinea. Fred Kollmorgen worked for a vegetable grower and drove a produce truck to the Melbourne market three times a week. Others served as civilians in military groups. After spending more than a year in and out of hospitals, David Bloomfield joined a detachment of the American Small Ships and served on the north coast of New Guinea for the duration of the war.

Of the few who were healthy enough to return to active duty, most eagerly accepted combat assignments. Bill Owen was promoted to lieutenant colonel and fought in the brutal campaign to hold the Papuan Peninsula against the Japanese. In late July 1942, just three months after escaping from New Britain, he was killed during a firefight on the Kokoda Track. "Jungle Ted" Palmer, something of a legend for his battlefield medicine, was likewise promoted to lieutenant colonel. He commanded a field ambulance unit for the rest of the war and was awarded an Order of the British Empire. Dave Laws joined ANGAU and was attached to the Allied Intelligence Bureau as a commando. During service in New Guinea, he was killed in action on May 5, 1943. Bill Harry was more fortunate: he served with the ANGAU intelligence section at Port Moresby and later worked with American forces in the Admiralty Islands. Peter Figgis was promoted to major and became a commando, after which he joined the Allied Intelligence Bureau (AIB). In March of 1943, a year after escaping from New Britain, he returned to the island aboard an American submarine and spent the next twelve months in various jungle camps as a coastwatcher.

Three other members of Lark Force also returned to New Britain during the war. Arch Taylor, now a sergeant, was back in action against the Japanese with the 1st New Guinea Infantry Battalion. So was Sergeant Bruce L. Perkins, who had come off the south coast with Taylor in the *Laurabada*. The two men helped to flush Japanese troops from Tol plantation in 1945. In a remarkable reunion, they met up with one of the survivors of the 1942 massacre, "Nipper" Webster, now serving with a transportation unit. Together they posed for a photograph, but none felt like smiling for the camera. Instead, their faces relected the horrors of what had happened to so many of their mates.

CHAPTER THIRTEEN

INSIDE THE FORTRESS

"I am a prisoner-of-war in New Britain . . ."

—Sergeant W. Arthur Gullidge,
2/22nd Battalion

R abaul had never been so busy, or its streets so crowded. By mid-afternoon on the day of the invasion, troops of the South Seas Detachment offloaded from various transports jammed against the wharves and jetties in Simpson Harbor. The streets of Rabaul were chaotic, as described by historian Peter Stone: "Japanese soldiers fanned out to inspect their prize. Battalions branded their names on the doors of buildings as they forced them open and claimed what was inside. Tinned food was not touched for fear of being poisoned but it was later issued to prisoners . . . Cars, trucks, machinery and other useful equipment were stockpiled, while houses and buildings were ransacked. Furniture was thrown into the streets for fear of booby-traps, and valuable books and records were burnt. Natives found looting were shot on sight."

Order was soon established by the 81st Naval Garrison Unit, but there was still plenty of plunder for the conquerors to indulge in. Rabaul's department stores were filled with dry goods, the cold storage warehouse held plenty of meat, and the pubs in Chinatown yielded all sorts of alcoholic beverages. Once the pickings were gone, however, the Japanese were left to cope with severe overcrowding, which only worsened as additional personnel came ashore.

Support units of the South Seas Detachment included the 1st Field Hospital, the 55th Division's Medical Corps, the 55th's Veterinary Depot

(to care for approximately forty-five hundred army horses), a water supply and purification unit, and the 47th Field Antiaircraft Artillery
Battalion. Conditions ashore became so crowded that many personnel
were forced to live aboard the transports. "I was left to work on board the
ship," noted Private Akiyoshi Hisaeda, a member of the field hospital.
He remained aboard the *Venice Maru* for an entire week before making
his first visit to Rabaul.

At the time of the invasion, Rabaul consisted of approximately 330
structures of all types, including warehouses and commercial buildings.
The Japanese would eventually triple that figure, constructing more than
six hundred wooden structures for an aggregate floor space of 2.8 million
square feet. The demand for lumber was so great that both the army and
navy put local sawmills back into operation and constructed new mills.
Ultimately, twenty-nine sawmills were in operation on the Gazelle
Peninsula under Japanese supervision, with a combined monthly output of
more than seven hundred thousand board feet of lumber.

Initially, however, the Japanese had to use whatever materials were
available, and even tore down old copra sheds to obtain wood. As a conse-
quence, most of the new structures were crudely built. It pained longtime
resident Gordon Thomas to see the Japanese turn his once-lovely town
into an unsightly mess. "On every vacant piece of land within the township portable huts were erected," he remembered, "and into the sides of the
hills, surrounding the town, air-raid shelters were dug; and these later were
enlarged to cave-like dimensions."

Taken prisoner at Refuge Gully, Thomas was among the many
Australians forced to work for the Japanese. The captors refused to recognize the 1929 Convention with Respect to the Laws and Customs of War
on Land, better known as the Geneva Convention, and sidestepped the
article prohibiting the use of prisoners as slaves by "paying" the POWs a
few yen each month. Not that the captives received any money—the
Japanese simply alleged the payments with falsified documents.

At Rabaul, most of the Australian POWs and civilian internees
served as stevedores. "The days . . . were filled with working on the wharves,
unloading some of the many transports that had arrived with the invasion
convoy," wrote Thomas. "Each day our numbers grew as more and more
civilians and soldiers were brought in from outlying areas, until the

accommodation in Chinatown was inadequate, and both civilians and military prisoners were moved to the camp previously occupied by the AIF on the Malaguna Road."

The Japanese no doubt appreciated the irony of imprisoning the Australians in the same barracks with the asbestos siding they had occupied before the invasion. Instead of gathering on the parade ground for marching drills or other familiar activities, the prisoners hurried outside twice each day, spurred by the raucous shouts of Japanese guards, and lined up for roll call.

Hardly a day passed without the Kempeitai (the military police and counterespionage branch of the Imperial Army) or naval guards bringing in more prisoners. Most were captured at one of the outposts that cordoned off the Gazelle Peninsula, but large groups were occasionally brought in by ship. On February 3, for example, a destroyer arrived with approximately 130 captured commandos of the 1st Independent Company.

Their adventure had begun eleven days earlier on New Ireland, when the Maizuru 2nd Special Naval Landing Force went ashore at Kavieng. The defenders were quickly overrun, and Major James Edmonds-Wilson withdrew with his company down the southern coast of New Ireland. At a village called Kaut, where the *Induna Star* had been hidden, the Australians began working on the ketch's damaged hull. Ready to sail in a week, she carried the survivors down the coast to Kalili Harbor on the night of January 30. There, a local planter informed Edmonds-Wilson about the fall of Rabaul, so he decided to sail straight for the Woodlark Islands, 350 miles due south.

The perfect opportunity to sneak down St. George's Channel past the Japanese came two nights later, when a storm lashed the archipelago. By daybreak on February 2, the *Induna Star* was already more than seventy miles south of Rabaul, seemingly in safe waters, but a Japanese patrol plane came along and attacked with bombs and machine guns. One bomb struck amidships, killing three men and destroying the only lifeboat. More enemy aircraft began to circle overhead, and the *Star*, her hull leaking badly, turned toward New Britain. All available hands were needed to man the pumps just to keep her afloat. Later that morning, a Japanese destroyer took her in tow. The commandos were transferred over to the warship which delivered them to Rabaul.

Another large group of 160 ragged-looking prisoners, all captured on the north coast of New Britain, arrived at Rabaul aboard the *Duranbah* on February 16. Among them was Captain Hutchinson-Smith, who would later write a marvelously detailed account of his experiences as a POW. Although never published, it stands alone as the only comprehensive narrative among the many prisoners from Lark Force. The manuscript contains a wealth of detail, such as the fact that the volcano Tavurvur welcomed the prisoners' return to Rabaul "by roaring and emitting large columns of smoke."

Ferried from the *Duranbah* in Daihatsu landing craft, the POWs were met by a committee of Japanese officers wearing "magnificent swords, white gloves and acres of service decorations." The eight Australian officers were then taken by truck to the former residence of William Phillpott, manager of the Burns, Philp & Company store, who was now among the civilian internees. They were ordered to sit outside on the lawn, but after an hour or so they were led across the street to Harold Page's bungalow. Here they were ordered to write down their name, rank, and serial number, after which a guard called for the senior officer. Hutchinson-Smith stepped forward and was immediately escorted into the house for interrogation.

He soon discovered that he had much to learn about Japanese customs:

> Behind the table sat a wizened worm of a man, in the full uniform of a Lieutenant, and at his left was another Nip who proved to be an interpreter.
>
> The interpreter opened the proceedings by losing his temper when, through ignorance, I failed to bow, and he experienced much difficulty in explaining my lapse in the etiquette department. A deft cuff or two clarified his meaning unmistakably, but my execution of this formal Japanese greeting was, I am afraid, perfunctory and gauche. The stooge then said, "Senior Officah? So you are Scanlan?" I hurriedly explained that I was not the Officer Commanding, New Guinea Area, but merely the senior officer of my group. The interpreter was very, very disappointed.

During the course of the interrogation, the interpreter asked Hutchinson-Smith point blank if he wanted to die. He ordered the Australian to kneel on the floor. Hutchinson-Smith shivered when the blade of a sword was laid across his neck, but it was merely a warning to not stray "from the narrow path of veracity." Afterward he was allowed to sit in a chair while the Japanese questioned him about his background, military career, religion, and family.

Suddenly the questioning became more direct. The Japanese wanted to know why he didn't commit suicide from shame; they asked about "women for the use of the officers and soldiers" and wondered why the Australians didn't have them; and they especially wanted to know where Scanlan was. Hutchinson-Smith didn't have the answers they were looking for, but he found the questions "easy to stall."

A few minutes later, in a different room, he was interrogated by a Japanese captain named Harada, who said he had taught English literature at a university in Tokyo. Hutchinson-Smith stated that he was "shockingly tired and weak from hunger," so Harada obliged him. A bottle of iced beer was brought in along with a plateful of delicious food: a meatball covered with onion sauce and "the biggest pile of white rice" he had ever seen.

When the interrogations ended, the Australian officers were driven to their former AIF camp. The barracks and storerooms previously used by B Company and the antiaircraft unit were now fenced with barbed wire, forming a separate compound. The newcomers were searched, then ordered to report to the officers' hut. They were introduced to Major Edmonds-Wilson, the ranking Australian, who briefed them on the current situation.

For starters, the officers held no status among the Japanese because they "had not done the decent thing and committed suicide." Instead, the prison staff recognized Mac McLellan, the forty-one-year-old warrant officer, as the senior Australian. During roll call, he always tried to frustrate the guards by making it nearly impossible for them to get an accurate count of prisoners. At any given time there were men in the hospital, or sick in their huts, or helping in the cookhouse. Even the benjos were always busy, thanks to a high rate of dysentery and other intestinal ailments. The Japanese never seemed to allow for such absences when taking roll call, and McLellan, much to the delight of his fellow prisoners, invariably got them to start over again when the numbers didn't add up.

The newcomers were dismayed by the small helping of rice they received that first evening. It wasn't the clean, white variety Hutchinson-Smith had eaten earlier that day, but "Kanaka issue plus weevils, stones and rat-droppings." Accompanying the meager portion was a cup of watery soup, and a number of prisoners became sick after eating it.

The new prisoners were also briefed regarding the camp personnel. The commandant, a heavyset former banker nicknamed "Tubby," boasted of beheading an American officer on Guam with one stroke of his sword. Although only a lieutenant, he wielded absolute authority.

Another key figure was the chief interpreter, known only as Matsui, who claimed he had worked in a Tokyo shirt factory before the war. His speech had an impressive range of inflection, often zooming down to a deep pitch and then rising back up as he struggled with the English language. His gravelly voice sounded somewhat like an airplane, and he was therefore nicknamed "The Dive Bomber."

A second interpreter, Kawaguchi, spoke with a distinctly American accent. The quartermaster, "a tiny, delicate-looking army lieutenant with hands like a young girl," wore boots that were several sizes too large. He liked to stand on the back of a truck and read propaganda bulletins to the prisoners. "He was very bitter towards Britain and America and was loud in his praise of Hitler and the Nazis," recalled Hutchinson-Smith, who referred to him as "Puss in Boots."

The guards were equally colorful. One lance corporal wore comical-looking glasses with blue lenses, and was nicknamed "Four Eyes." Like all the guards, he demanded that the prisoners bow low at every encounter. Those who failed to show respect discovered that he had a volatile temper and was "a fiend when roused."

The prisoners were awakened at 0500 every day for muster, or *tenko*. "Hurry! Hurry," yelled Matsui. "All men come with running." After they gathered on the parade ground, McClellan made certain they were counted several times. Breakfast for the working parties was served at six, after which the officers ate. The meal was not only the same as the night before, but had obviously been prepared at the same time. Flies swarmed over the food and the rice was coated with pumice dust. Despite its unappetizing appearance, there was no option but to eat what was served, primarily because the Australian officers received only two meals per day, while the troops got three.

The reason was simple. Edmonds-Wilson, a firm believer in the Geneva Convention, insisted that the officers would neither work nor assist the enemy in any other way. It was a gallant gesture of defiance, but the Japanese had the final say. One day, as Matsui struggled to translate Edmonds-Wilson's latest refusal to work, the commandant got the impression that the officers were mutinous. Outraged, he singled out Edmonds-Wilson for execution. The other officers kept their composure, and after several tense moments the commandant calmed down. "The atmosphere was electric," remembered Hutchinson-Smith, "and we realized that they would have no compunction in executing anyone if they desired. Their local record in recent weeks had proved that beyond all doubt."

Edmonds-Wilson was spared, but from that day on the officers labored alongside the rest of the men. Work parties were sent out daily to the wharves, various storage dumps, and the Imperial Navy headquarters building (the former Crown Law office); others chopped wood for the camp kitchen or mowed grass. The dockside labor was especially heavy, and although the workers received three meals a day, the measly rations provided only a few hundred calories a day rather than the thousands necessary for sustained physical effort. Not surprisingly, the POWs' health declined steadily.

Dressed in the shaggy remnants of their uniforms or civilian clothing, the Australians unloaded an astonishing amount of war material in the ungodly heat of the caldera. Cargo ships brought thousands of bombs, drums of gasoline and aviation fuel, all sorts of weapons and ammunition, food, vehicles, tools, and numerous aircraft components, from complete engines to replacement wings. The vehicles alone numbered more than four thousand, including trucks, light tanks, staff cars, and even captured American vehicles such as a GMC truck and a pink Studebaker brought from Guam. When the ships were empty, the prisoners loaded them with copra, lumber, crates of empty bottles, and booty from Rabaul. The prisoners were amazed at the array of pilfered goods sent to Japan, including furniture and even the glass countertops from the downtown stores.

But the art of scrounging worked both ways. The prisoners' health and morale would have been much worse were it not for their ability to filch supplies, especially foodstuffs. The dockworkers had by far the best opportunities to steal food, and it was alleged that they sometimes enjoyed "gargantuan meals" at the wharves. Prisoners kept an eye out for Australian army rations—tropical fruit salad was even back in favor—and they invented clever ways of sneaking it into the stockade to share with the sick men. Dry goods were the easiest to acquire. Countless handfuls of sugar and coffee were hidden in pockets and the insides of shoes.

Next to food, cigarettes were also in huge demand. Thanks to an active theft ring, "fags" were available for almost everyone who wanted to smoke. "The cigarette racket was really extraordinary," wrote Hutchinson-Smith, "and revealed the stupidity of our captors." The Japanese confiscated all tobacco and cigarettes when they brought in new prisoners, and there was no place in camp where the POWs could purchase cigarettes—yet most of them smoked incessantly. "It did not dawn on the Japanese for almost five months," added Hutchinson-Smith, "that we were smoking *their* cigarettes."

The Australians might have continued to get away with the stealing, but eventually the thieves took so many cigarettes that there weren't enough left for the guards. The commandant threatened to execute anyone caught in the act and had a cage built to store the cigarettes in. But the tobacco continued to disappear. The prisoners quickly discovered that the cage's wooden bars were far enough apart for an arm to fit through, making it easy to grab a handful of cigarettes when the guards weren't paying attention.

Keith M. "Shorty" Berwick, a twenty-four-year-old antitank gunner from New South Wales, was reputedly the best scrounger. Despite being a "rather nervous little fellow," he smuggled impressive amounts of loot into the camp. One night, as he returned from a work party with four other soldiers, his clothing positively bulged with cigarettes and cans of food. A Japanese NCO pulled him aside at the gate and ordered him to stand near one of the huts to await a more thorough search—but as soon as the guard wasn't looking, Shorty bolted around the corner. He made it safely to the enlisted men's quarters and delivered his "groceries" to the men who were sick.

A few Japanese admired the captives' efforts to help each other. Jiro Takamura oversaw several prisoners who were sent to his shop to repair broken communications equipment. He liked their ability to fix things, but was even more impressed by their solidarity. "They work hard with little rest," he wrote in his diary. "I felt sorry for them. They probably do not get much to eat in the stockade. At least while they are here I do all I can for them, and they appreciate it and work harder. They stay till about 1600 hours, eat and then go back. They put the food that is left over into empty cans and take it back to their comrades. That feeling of brotherly love is the same everywhere. Tears welled up in my eyes."

Softhearted overseers were the exception. Most of the Japanese guards were, at best, indifferent to the terrible conditions endured by the POWs. In turn, the Australians extracted some revenge and boosted their own morale through minor acts of sabotage. They tossed tools and equipment into the harbor, loosened the plugs on drums of fuel to let the contents leak out, and soaked bundles of copra with seawater in the hope that the wet material would spontaneously combust in the jam-packed hold of some merchantman.

The Japanese never seemed to notice the prisoners' meddlesome behavior, but the POWs could never relax their own vigilance, mainly because the guards were completely unpredictable. For days on end they would seem almost friendly, entering the prisoners' huts to share cigarettes and try a few words of English; then, with shocking fury, they would commence "beating, bashing and bludgeoning everyone in sight." Just as suddenly, the Japanese would stop their brutish behavior and act as though nothing had happened.

History would later reveal that their behavior, especially the bullying, was the same at virtually every POW camp. It usually came on the heels of military setbacks, even minor defeats that occurred in far-off places, because the Japanese were embarrassed at losing face. In response, they took out their frustrations on the POWs, not unlike some curmudgeon who kicks his dog.

At Rabaul, the prisoners saw several such cracks in the Japanese façade of invincibility. The stockade was practically in the center of the fortress, giving the POWs a ringside seat to the night strikes conducted by the RAAF. It was worth the beatings the POWs received to see the Japanese react nervously. During the first raid, conducted by a handful of Catalinas on the night of January 24, antiaircraft fire from warships in Simpson Harbor landed among Japanese positions on the plateau, resulting in casualties. As additional strikes followed—generally every other night for the next two weeks—the prisoners themselves began to feel the strain, sleeping fitfully on nights when there was a "bomber's moon." When the attacks came, they spent hours lying in slit trenches while the antiaircraft guns blasted away at shadows.

Aside from the occasional night raids, no other attacks on Rabaul were attempted by the Allies for nearly a month after the invasion. Early in the afternoon of February 20, the prisoners were assembled on the parade ground for an announcement by the interpreter, whose boastful words Hutchinson-Smith later parodied: "Matsui came out and said very sympathetically, 'Ah, so sorry! So sorry! Japan airplane go out—bomb Americah aircraft carriah! So sorry!' and grinned broadly. Shortly after, eighteen heavy bombers went off and he said, 'Japan airplane sink carriah. So sorry!' We did not share his delight . . ."

The carrier Matsui referred to was the USS *Lexington*, flagship of a U.S. Navy task force steaming to attack Rabaul at dawn the next day. However, a pair of Kawanishi H6K flying boats had located the American force while it was still nearly four hundred miles from Rabaul. Shortly after 1400 on the 20th, seventeen Mitsubishi G4M1s of the newly arrived 4th *Kokutai* took off from Vunakanau for a preemptive strike.*

Matsui's glee proved to be short-lived. Fighters from the *Lexington* shot down both of the Kawanishi flying boats, and the Mitsubishi bombers fared poorly. En route to the target they split into two formations due to heavy weather. All nine aircraft of the first wave were shot down by tenacious F4F Wildcats and shipboard antiaircraft, and the second wave was badly mauled by one pilot, Lieutenant Edward "Butch" O'Hare, who was officially credited with five planes destroyed. He earned a Medal of Honor for his remarkable gunnery, though in actuality only four of the eight bombers were shot down, one of which was finished off by the *Lexington*'s antiaircraft guns. Of the four survivors, one later crash-landed near a small atoll east of New Ireland, another ditched in Simpson Harbor with several dead and wounded crewmen aboard, and only two landed safely at Vunakanau.

Having lost the element of surprise, the Americans called off the raid. But the Japanese losses had been appalling: fifteen Mitsubishi

---

* Hutchinson-Smith had miscounted slightly. The Air Echelon Combat Log of the 4th *Kokutai* shows that the the 1st Chutai, normally a nine-plane division, was short one bomber.

bombers were shot down with the loss of more than ninety crewmembers; and twenty more airmen were killed aboard the two flying boats. A third H6K failed to return from its patrol that night, which brought the grand total of dead airmen to more than 120, all in a single day. Meanwhile, the *Lexington* escaped with barely a scratch, having lost two Wildcats and one pilot.

Oddly enough, although the raid had been a disaster for the Japanese, they did not harass the POWs afterward. The entire camp was distracted the following day by the arrival of the most important prisoner of all. An unnamed Kempeitai officer recorded the details in his diary on February 21: "Sergeant Okazaki and others captured Colonel Sukanron, Major Norado, one sergeant and two privates near the Warangoi River. The sergeant was sent to the hospital with malaria. Colonel Sukanron and the other three [were] sent to Rabaul."

Although their names were phonetically butchered, the individuals were obviously Scanlan and Mollard, last seen walking toward Rabaul with three enlisted men a week before they were captured. A few days later, Jiro Takamura read Scanlan's POW file and was impressed by what he saw. "Colonel Scanlan was interrogated. Looked at his record taken by staff officer Tanaka and was surprised at the resolute answers he made, even though he is a reserve officer. After all, if one becomes a commander, one must have considerable ability. He manifested the ideal that the Englishman has of respecting appearance by wearing his service uniform and by requesting special quarters."

It is particularly interesting to note that Scanlan asked for private quarters, but Takamura misinterpreted his motives. If anything, Scanlan was ashamed, not arrogant. Undoubtedly he wished to be separated from the men because he was reluctant to face them. Some had been captives for nearly a month already, and most would have held him accountable for their present situation.

As NOTED BY THE KEMPEITAI OFFICER, THE SERGEANT WITH MALARIA WAS taken to Vunapope, where the native hospital near the beach was still being used by POWs. A civilian doctor, two orderlies, and thirteen military and civilian nurses treated the ailing captives under the watchful eyes of Japanese guards.

In early February, Sandy Robertson was brought back to Vunapope after surrendering on the beach at Tol. He was lucky to be alive, but the six army nurses were not happy to see him. Still bitter about being abandoned on the morning of the invasion, they were unsympathetic about his capture. Like Scanlan, he was a pariah. "We just ignored him," recalled Lorna Johnson. "We thought, we'll get our own back, this time. He was very put out by that, but he knew he couldn't expect any other treatment. He would have been very surprised if we'd been delighted to see him."

In addition to avoiding Robertson as much as possible, the nurses also learned to conduct their business with a degree of indifference toward all of the men at Vunapope. If they acted too friendly, their behavior was likely to invite lewd gestures and insinuating looks from the Japanese. The nurses were afraid of being raped, and on several occasions, inebriated soldiers banged on the doors of the women's dormitory at night, terrifying the occupants.

The worst episode coincided with the fall of Singapore on February 15, which the victors celebrated with gusto. "Drunken Japs," noted Alice Bowman, "made the night hideous with screams and cheers accompanying Japanese marching songs." Some of the nurses kept vials of morphine hidden in their clothing, preferring suicide to rape—at least in theory. And virtually all of them slept fully clothed, which had the added benefit of saving time when attacks by the RAAF necessitated a midnight dash to the nearest bomb shelter.

Ten days after the fall of Singapore, at the request of the nuns, the nurses were permitted to move into the convent. Ironically, the harassment of the Australian women was mild compared to the mistreatment of the Catholic staff. Colonel Kuwada and his 3rd Battalion showed no regard for Christianity, nor did they respect the sanctity of the buildings at Vunapope. In their eyes, the campus was merely a collection of structures suitable for occupation, as Kuwada demonstrated by taking the bishop's residence for his own. Apparently, the Japanese didn't care that The Most Reverend Leo Scharmach and his staff were Germans; they were treated with the same contempt as the Australians. Adding insult to injury, the Japanese converted the cathedral into a stable for the battalion's horses.

If the bishop was mortified about the desecration of his church, he never showed it. Slightly built, with an enormous nose and round specta-

cles that made him resemble Groucho Marx, he was an intellectual with
the courage of a crusader. He flummoxed the Japanese at every opportunity, according to one correspondent, and deliberately maintained "an
appearance of sublime self-confidence, an arrogance that not even the
most fanatical follower of the bushido code could match."

But Scharmach could do little to prevent the Japanese from abusing
the women at Vunapope. Nuns who rebuffed the guards' sexual advances
sometimes received severe punishment. A favorite method was to force
them to kneel on the ground, and a bamboo pole was laid across both legs
behind the knee. Soldiers or collaborating police boys would then stand on
both ends of the pole and bounce, mashing the victim's kneecaps into the
ground. One nun allegedly suffered permanent disability from such torture.

The women at Vunapope were in a constant state of fear, and
Scharmach lodged complaints with the Japanese high command.
Eventually Major General Horii took steps to stop the abuses by issuing a
directive known as the "Guide to Soldiers in the South Seas." It consisted
of five simple commandments:

> Do not needlessly kill or injure the local inhabitants.
> Behavior such as looting and violating women is strictly forbidden.
> Buildings and property in enemy territory must not be burned without
>   permission.
> Scrupulously keep secrets and maintain security.
> Treat ammunition carefully, and reduce waste to a minimum.

Although the edict deterred common soldiers from raping and pillag-
ing, it did not put an end to executions or indiscriminate atrocities.
Natives, Asians, and Australians alike were punished—sometimes with
utter brutality—for minor infractions. The Rabaul market was the site of
numerous public executions, which served the dual purpose of demon-
strating Japanese domination over the civilian populace and deterring
would-be rebels. In one example, the Japanese rounded up several
Chinese officials from the local chapter of the Nationalist Party, accused
them of "underground activities," and summarily executed them. On
another occasion, three natives charged with cutting telephone wires
were publicly beheaded.

To most Westerners, execution by decapitation seemed barbaric, a horrible method of killing. But among the Japanese it was an honored method, not only for death sentences but also as an element of ritualistic suicide. Swords were issued to all officers and many NCOs in the Imperial Army, and they were encouraged to perform a beheading as a "trial of courage."

The army-issue swords, often referred to as Showa swords, were representative of the ubiquitous samurai sword, but their quality was only average. Many officers either purchased their own high-quality swords or received them as gifts, and they were fond of giving them pet names. If a soldier sought a "cutting test" to demonstrate his prowess, there was no shortage of prisoners to experiment on. Those who cut off a head with a single stroke, like the commandant at Rabaul boasted of doing, gained prestige.

Some of the executions at Rabaul were photographed. One pair of images that survived the war shows the beheading of a native catechist in a public area. In the first photograph, a dark-skinned native sits straight-legged on the ground with his back against a thick post. His feet are tied to a stake between his ankles, and his wrists are shackled. Several uniformed Japanese stand nearby, while numerous onlookers peer over a cloth barricade. In the second image, the executioner is off balance, having just swung his sword. Twin fountains of blood jet into the air from the victim's carotid arteries, and his decapitated head lies near his outstretched feet.

The total number of beheadings at Rabaul is unknown, but there can be no doubt that plenty of Japanese executed captives with their swords. There were literally hundreds of victims, from individual sentences to mass executions. In one incident documented by historian Peter Stone, no fewer than thirty islanders were beheaded merely because "they *discussed* giving food to another native suspected of aiding the Allies." Obviously, the edict about killing natives "needlessly" was open to interpretation.

At Rabaul, captured soldiers and airmen were subjected to some of the worst atrocities. John Gray, the engineering officer captured at Tol, was the victim of a particularly heinous crime committed by members of the 3rd Battalion. Taken to Vunapope rather than imprisoned at the Malaguna Road stockade, he was tied to a palm tree outside Lieutenant Colonel Kuwada's residence and questioned for hours in the blazing sun. Periodically the Japanese slapped him with a length of rope, beat him with planking, or sprinkled biting ants on his body. When they grew tired of the interrogation, they took Gray to a distant hill where missionary students witnessed his execution. First, a doctor named Chikumi, whose reputation for malevolence had earned him the ironic nickname "Sunshine Sam," administered an injection that rendered Gray semi-conscious. Next, Chikumi performed a vivisection and removed Gray's still-beating heart, for no better reason than "to study his reactions."

In the first weeks after the invasion, the Japanese murdered at least five officers from Lark Force: Glenn Garrard, Len Henry, Herb Silverman, Dick Travers, and John Gray. James Edmonds-Wilson nearly joined them when he refused to allow the officers to work; and when other Australians were threatened with execution, they knew to take it seriously.

Conditions for other prisoners on New Britain were just as grim. Soon after the fall of Singapore, tens of thousands of Malaysian and Indian captives were sent to Rabaul to build roads and perform other heavy labor. Proof of their service as slaves was discovered after the war in documents written by the 18th Army commander, Major General Hatazo Adachi, whose instructions stated that "prisoners and coolies" of the 31st Field Road Construction Unit were to rebuild a "motor vehicle road" in the vicinity of Kokopo. Month after grueling month, the work parties toiled under oppressive and appalling conditions, then returned to overcrowded, disease-riddled camps.

Shingara Singh, a *jemedar* (junior officer) captured with the 5/11 Sikh Regiment at Singapore, reported that about six thousand Indians were imprisoned near Kokopo along with "several thousand" Chinese. At Tanoura prison camp near Tunnel Hill Road, another two thousand Malaysians and Burmese were kept in a single compound. Brutalities were routine. Prisoners caught trying to escape were mutilated, their toes or the lower parts of their feet sliced off with swords to prevent further attempts. Those who were too sick to work were simply executed and tossed aside. As the war progressed, untold thousands of Asian and Indian prisoners died of neglect, malnutrition, exhaustion, or murder in the pestilential camps scattered around the Gazelle Peninsula.

DESPITE THE JAPANESE PROCLAMATION, THE FEMALE PRISONERS AT Vunapope did not feel safe until they saw dozens of kimono-clad women in the area. In Rabaul, Gordon Thomas observed them in the streets immediately after the invasion, and he later speculated that they had been aboard the fleet to serve the officers. Ultimately, some three thousand conscripted prostitutes were sent to Rabaul to provide a sexual outlet for the military in the separate army and navy districts. They were known as "comfort women," but the friendly sounding name was deceptive: the vast majority were enslaved Koreans and Formosans taken forcibly from their homes or "hired" under false pretenses.

Each service maintained its own brothels. The Imperial Navy operated three establishments in Rabaul, fancifully named the East, West, and North Magnificent Love Lines. The first served officers and senior administration officials, the second served NCOs and below, and the third was for laborers and "military coolies." Sailors were permitted four hours of shore leave per week, during which they could purchase a ticket at their representative "Special Purpose House" for a maximum of thirty minutes with a prostitute. Enlisted men and civilian workers were charged two yen per ticket; commissioned officers paid half a yen more.

The army also operated three brothels in town—but their privilege system was oddly different. The enlisted men were served until 1600, the NCOs until 1900, then the officers visited until 2200 or later. Naturally there were far fewer officers, which meant they had a more leisurely schedule, but many of the women had been forced to perform throughout the day.

Okyron Pak, a Korean who worked in an army brothel in Rabaul, recalled having intercourse with the rank and file, NCOs, and officers all on the same day. An hour was supposedly allotted for each customer, but no one dared take that long because of the queue of impatient men waiting outside the door. Sundays were the worst, with soldiers arriving by the truckload. "On those busy days," recalled Pak, "we couldn't find time to put on underwear. My private parts were all swollen and ached. Exhausted, I begged a warm-hearted officer to [send me] home."

The road that led Pak to Rabaul was not unusual. Born in the province of North Cholla, she was married at age sixteen, then ran away and became the concubine of a wealthy man. She married him and had a child, but husband number two often beat her. He eventually sold her to an employment agency, which in turn sold her to a bigger agency in Seoul. She was put aboard a ship with other women, none of whom learned the truth about their "employment" until they reached Rabaul six weeks later. "We had never dreamt that we would have to serve soldiers," she stated. "What we expected to do was wash clothes or care for soldiers. How terrified we were when soldiers broke into our rooms and raped us. We resisted with all our strength, but it was hopeless."

In February, the 3rd Battalion set up a brothel at Vunapope, after first evicting the Brotherhood of the Sacred Heart from their dormitory. Alice Bowman and the other nurses watched the proceedings from the balcony of the nearby convent.

> One morning after breakfast we looked out from the upstairs verandah to see a moving mass of color spreading from the lawn below us to the front of the cathedral. There were hundreds of tiny women in bright kimonos flitting about like swarms of butterflies . . .
>
> Opposite our residence was a three-story building where the Brothers of the Mission lived, and it was painfully clear that they were moving out. Missionaries from the building were carrying cases and baggage; we saw Father Barrow, whom we'd met at Christmas, reduced to an undignified role among the porters. While the girls waited demurely on the lawn, the Japs looked on from a distance.
>
> As the last of the Brothers left their home, the visitors on the lawn gathered up their handkerchief bundles and hurried inside. We felt a deep sympathy for the missionaries over this humiliation, yet, at the same time gained comfort from the realization that, with so many of their own women on the premises, the Japanese would no longer pay undue attention towards us.

Soon after opening the brothel at Vunapope, the Japanese heaped even more indignities on the Catholic staff. First, troops led the horses out of the cathedral, then they scooped the straw and manure off the floor. When the church was sufficiently clean, a long procession of soldiers filed inside for a special ceremony to honor their war dead. "The cathedral had already been desecrated when it was used for a stable," continued Bowman, "and now it was being further defiled by what could only be regarded, by our Christian missionaries, as a pagan ceremony."

AT THE MALAGUNA STOCKADE, PRISONERS DIED FOR LACK OF PROPER MEDICAL care. The Japanese blamed the deaths on malaria and did not send sick men from the prison to the hospital at Vunapope. A few men such as Bert Morgan had basic medical training, but little could be done for the sick except to give them extra food.

Some of the deaths among the close-knit Victorians were especially heartbreaking. Bespectacled baritone player Stanley A. French, a native of England and the oldest member of the battalion band, died in the stockade on February 15 at the age of thirty-nine. His passing was mourned by Morgan, Arthur Gullidge, and sixteen other captured bandsmen who had been together for almost two years. Most of the musicians were firmly committed to their Salvation Army roots. Although somewhat parochial, the "Salvos" happily accepted Jim Thurst (Methodist) and drummer William E. Edwards(Church of England) as part of "their" band. Vocalists as well as musicians, they all sang numerous hymns as a way of sharing their faith with their fellow POWs.

Initially, the Japanese prohibited religious gatherings, but several weeks after the invasion, they began to allow a short prayer meeting after the morning roll call. Upon securing that small victory, the clergy imprisoned at Malaguna sought permission to conduct worship services on Sundays. There was no shortage of preachers: John Poole and Laurie McArthur were among the eight Methodist ministers, and others included a Roman Catholic priest, a Seventh Day Adventist, several lay ministers, and the battalion's Catholic padre, Victor Turner.

Soon after the advent of religious services, the Japanese allowed another opportunity for music in the stockade. In early March, the Imperial Navy's 8th Base Unit accepted responsibility for the military control of the occupied islands in the Bismarck Archipelago. Rabaul was considered sufficiently developed for the establishment of a civil administration, or *minseibu*, which meant that representatives of the Imperial government would be headquartered in the region. In what was regarded as an important advancement of the Greater East Asia Co-Prosperity Sphere, the Japanese officially established the *minseibu* at Rabaul on March 10. They decided to commemorate the event with a huge celebration and reception at the Regent Theater.

This was the moment that Alexander "Lex" Fraser, a captain in the 1st Independent Company, had been hoping for. An accomplished pianist who was also fluent in Japanese, he had been approached earlier by a Japanese officer who wanted him to transpose a book of army songs into conventional sheet music. Fraser not only agreed to cooperate, but arranged to have Arthur Gullidge join him. Together they spent several days in Rabaul writing music and getting "plenty to eat."

Soon after, an officer named Kishida arranged for the Australians to provide the music for the gala event. Several instruments were available, including the Regent theater's piano, and the two Australians picked some of the former battalion bandsmen to play them. With great cunning, Fraser also arranged to have some of the sick men attend rehearsals. By pretending to play different instruments, they received extra food. During the grand ceremony at the Regent, the Japanese drank so heavily they never realized half the orchestra was phony.

The real musicians made up for it by playing their hearts out. The evening affair, as described by Hutchinson-Smith, was a triumph for the Australians:

> The sake flowed freely, and many were the unorthodox dances to the prisoners' music. The only occurrences which marred the proceedings were the thrashing of a Japanese belle by her escort who was mad with liquor, and the unexpected arrival of a decrepit truck which was driven into the theater by an intoxicated officer in the middle of the dance.
>
> The band, however, had an extra meal with what was given them and what they could lift unseen, and they voted the function a success at which a good time was had by all. The Japs failed to realize that much of the music was a jazzed-up version of such songs as the National Anthem, "Advance Australia Fair," "Rule Britannia," "Waltzing Matilda" and similar numbers. A great hit was

"Auld Lang Syne," our knowledge of which surprised the Japanese, who stated that it was a Japanese melody. We never found out what their words were, but every time they heard the piece they became sentimental and wistful.

As a reward for their performance, the musicians were allowed to take the instruments—even the piano—back to the stockade. For a few pleasant days, the Fibro huts echoed with the strains of popular music, mostly played for the benefit of sick prisoners. The effect on the POWs' morale was profound, and when the Japanese realized how much the captives were benefiting from the music, they took the instruments away.

AS THE WEEKS STRETCHED INTO MONTHS AT MALAGUNA CAMP, THE POWs suffered continuously from the compounding effects of heavy labor, malnutrition, and neglect. In addition to hunger and sickness, the majority of prisoners also endured personal indignities. Harold Page was singled out because of his former government position. While he struggled to unload cargo, the guards cajoled and sometimes physically mistreated him. Many other Australians were similarly abused, though the civilians generally endured less than the soldiers. "The Japanese never lost an opportunity to ridicule and humiliate prisoners, particularly officers," recalled Hutchinson-Smith. "Beatings and invective in the presence of Kanakas and Japanese troops were designed to lower the prestige of the white men."

Despite all the persecution, the vast majority of POWs remained indomitable in spirit if not in body. There was nothing the Japanese could do to completely crush their resolve or their natural sense of humor, in part because the Australians took pleasure in stealing whatever they could carry off and sabotaging what they couldn't.

Best of all, for those few memorable days in March, the prisoners at Rabaul enjoyed an unexpected lift from Lex Fraser, Arthur Gullidge, and the other musicians who played their favorite anthems and popular songs right under the noses of the Japanese.

CHAPTER FOURTEEN

CRUEL FATES

*"They marched out with cheerful grins
and banter . . ."*

—Captain David Hutchinson-
Smith, 17th Antitank Battery

A t dawn on February 23, 1942, exactly one month after the Japanese invaded Rabaul, American bombers attacked the harbor for the first time. The mission had started before midnight, when six B-17E Flying Fortresses of the 14th Reconnaissance Squadron (RS) took off from Garbutt Field outside Townsville and flew north toward Rabaul. One bomber became lost in a heavy squall and turned back. The remaining five, led by Hollywood-handsome Major Richard H. Carmichael, reached Simpson Harbor in two separated groups and dropped their bombs from thirty thousand feet. Due to an almost solid cloud cover, made worse by large quantities of steam from Tavurvur, the bombardiers had a difficult time picking out targets. Thus, the raid did no material damage.

The Fortresses were intercepted by several Zeros that zoomed up from Lakunai, and although both sides claimed aerial victories, no planes were actually shot down. One B-17, low on fuel, crash-landed in a swamp near the New Guinea coast. The crew survived and spent five torturous weeks in the jungle before they reached Port Moresby on foot. The other bombers returned safely to Australia, but within a matter of days more than half the squadron's aircrews were grounded by an outbreak of dengue fever. Weeks passed before another attempt to hit Rabaul was made.

In the interim, the RAAF continued their haphazard night raids. The next occurred before dawn on February 24, as noted by Private Hisaeda of the 1st Field Hospital: "3 enemy planes dropped two bombs in the sea and one on the Sakigawa unit; there was no damage and one enemy aircraft was shot down." His information matches RAAF records exactly. On that night, three Catalinas attacked Rabaul at 0500, and the aircraft piloted by Flight Lieutenant Ernest V. Beaumont failed to return.

By the middle of March, the fortunes of Carmichael's B-17 squadron had not changed. An attempt by five Fortresses to raid Simpson Harbor on Friday the 13th was a dismal failure, with only one aircraft reaching the target because of foul weather. The next day, the outfit was redesignated the 40th RS and transferred into the 19th Bomb Group, which was being re-formed at Townsville. The squadron's luck finally began to improve during the second half of March. Two B-17s picked up General Douglas MacArthur, along with his family and important staff members, at Del Monte Field on Mindanao and delivered them safely to Australia on the 17th.

The day after MacArthur's arrival in Australia, the 40th RS flew its next mission to Rabaul. Led once again by Carmichael, four B-17s took off from Port Moresby at dawn to attack shipping in Simpson Harbor. All four aircraft dropped their bombs over the target area and returned safely to Port Moresby, but the plane piloted by First Lieutenant James R. DuBose was grounded, its number four engine having disintegrated in flight.* Carmichael led the other three B-17s to Townsville, where he reported that they had sunk a Japanese cruiser. The lead bombardier initially argued against the claim, but Carmichael refused to back down, and credit was duly given. (The Japanese suffered no such loss that day. The simple truth was that many a bombardier was fooled by the formation of rocks called "the Beehives" that jutted from the middle of Simpson Harbor. From five miles up they looked just like a ship, particularly when the wind and tides created the illusion of a wake.)

B-17s conducted three more raids during March and finally got the attention of the POWs, whose reactions were considerably different from those of the Japanese. Alice Bowman recalled, "[In] March, giant planes appeared in the sky over Rabaul and caused a great deal of frenzied activity among the Japs. We had never seen anything like them before; previous

---

* The author's uncle, 2LT John J. Steinbinder, was the navigator aboard DuBose's aircraft. During eleven months with the squadron, Steinbinder flew forty-three combat missions, eight of them against Rabaul.

raids were with Catalinas. From the excitement created among the Japs these planes were quite definitely something new to them as well. They were the magnificent American Flying Fortresses and this was the greatest air raid on Rabaul since the invasion. It was a wonderful boost to our morale . . ."

The women at Vunapope needed all the psychological advantages they could get. Despite the army's edict, they still endured physical and verbal harassment from the Japanese. A favorite punishment among the guards was slapping, but this actually gave the women something to laugh about—at least in private. One of the officers was so short that in order to get eye-to-eye with Kay Parker, he had to climb onto a stool before slapping her. Whenever the Japanese were out of earshot, the women jeered them as "little monkeys."

At both Vunapope and the Malaguna Road stockade, the guards and prison staff continued to be unpredictable. During the last week of March, the POWs were pleasantly surprised when they received permission to write letters home. They became skeptical when an officer told them the letters would be dropped over Port Moresby "instead of a bomb," but the prisoners were eager to let their families know they were alive.

Not surprisingly, the Japanese told them what to write. Virtually every letter began with a phrase such as, "I am a prisoner-of-war . . . and am very well treated." Most of the men added very little else, because any additional information had to pass strict censorship. Arthur Gullidge, however, wrote about his loneliness and included a poignant message about his faith journey: "We must trust in the Heavenly Father . . . I am confident in Him now more than ever and am experiencing an inward peace that amazes me . . . I am so happy to be able to write at last and hope that soon letter-writing will be needless . . ."

Several bags of letters, dated between March 22 and 24, were dropped as promised over Port Moresby a month later. One bag allegedly fell into the sea, but approximately four hundred letters were delivered to grateful families in Australia.

Two weeks after the POWs wrote home, their safety was again threatened, this time by American medium bombers. On April 6, aircraft of the 22nd Bomb Group attacked Simpson Harbor in what proved to be the combat debut of the Martin B-26 Marauder. The attackers claimed a transport as sunk, but no corresponding loss was recorded by the Japanese. One B-26, badly damaged by antiaircraft fire, crash-landed in the water near the Trobriands, killing the flight engineer and wounding the bombardier. An RAAF Catalina picked up the survivors in one of the first documented air-sea rescues of the Pacific war.

A week and a half later, a POW work party was sent to the Government Wharf to begin the long task of unloading the *Komaki Maru*, an 8,500-ton navy transport that had arrived from Bali on April 16 with a mixed cargo of bombs and aircraft parts. The ship also carried the Zero pilots and ground personnel of the Tainan *Kokutai*, transferred from the Netherlands East Indies to Rabaul as part of a major reorganization of naval air groups.

The day after the *Komaki Maru*'s arrival, eight olive-drab Marauders took off from Townsville and flew to Port Moresby. Armed and refueled, six of them launched early the next morning for the group's second strike on Simpson Harbor. Although half of the bombers turned back for various reasons, two of the B-26s that reached the target made straight for the *Komaki Maru*.

By a stroke of luck, the POWs unloading the ship had been ordered off the Government Wharf only five minutes earlier. They were seated on the ground for lunch when the two B-26s swept in low over Tunnel Hill Road at 1059 and released their bombs. Some landed forward and aft of the ship, but three 500-pounders hit the *Komaki Maru* squarely, starting fires that soon reached the volatile cargo of munitions. Explosions ripped open the hull, sending a river of burning fuel onto the harbor's surface. Soon the ship was fully ablaze, and the shrieks of Japanese sailors trapped inside could be heard over the roar of the inferno. Eleven crewmen died, yet by some miracle not a single POW was hurt.

The attackers did not get away unscathed. A pair of Zeros briefly pursued one Marauder as it pulled away over the harbor; then the fighters shifted their attention to the B-26 flown by Captain William A. Garnett, commanding officer of the 33rd Bomb Squadron. Chased almost fifteen miles, the bomber took fatal hits in one engine and crashed in the water off Cape Gazelle. Only two crewmen managed to bail out. Both were taken prisoner, as recorded by a Kempeitai officer in his diary: "An enemy plane was shot down near Higashisaki [East Point]. No. 9 Company captured a

signal sergeant and engineer corporal who had parachuted from their plane
. . . Sent the two captured airmen to Rabaul."

The unnamed officer's information regarding the crewmen was accurate. The flight engineer/tail-gunner, Corporal Sanger E. Reed, and the
radio operator, Technical Sergeant Theron K. Lutz, became the first
American airmen captured at Rabaul. They were later sent to Japan for
thorough interrogation, presumably because they possessed significant
knowledge of the B-26. At war's end Reed was one of approximately two
hundred Americans liberated from Camp 5-B in the city of Niigata, but
Lutz's ultimate fate remains a mystery.

The POWs, meanwhile, had a ringside view from Malaguna Road as
the *Komaki Maru* burned uncontrollably throughout the night. The massive fire was visible from as far away as Vunapope, remembered Alice
Bowman, and "looked to be out of control, threatening Rabaul." Flaming
debris rained down on nearby structures, igniting a warehouse and consum-
ing additional war material. Some of the prisoners cheered, prompting one
indignant Japanese to write: "They must all be very happy after seeing
today's bombing. Among them were some who clapped their hands. All
the members of my unit who heard this agreed that it was better to kill
them off one after another."

No prisoners were executed, but two Australians were punished
severely for laughing in front of the guards. "That night at muster,"
wrote Hutchinson-Smith, "we witnessed the most brutal bashing we had
seen to date." The entire population of the camp was assembled on the
parade ground to watch as Lieutenant Jack L. Burns and an antitank
gunner were "beaten for half an hour by five or six guards armed with
pick handles and battens."

Several days after the destruction of the *Komaki Maru*, the brutalities
endured by the POWs at the hands of the Imperial Japanese Army finally
came to an end. First, all male prisoners were consolidated at the Malaguna
Road stockade. The patients from Vunapope, along with John May, Sandy
Robertson, and other men being held there, were moved to Rabaul on
April 27. Two days later the administration of the stockade was handed
over to the Imperial Japanese Navy. It also happened that April 29 was
the 41st birthday of Emperor Hirohito. Everywhere across his empire, the
Japanese people made a great ceremony of honoring the occasion of

Tencho-setsu for His Majesty. They gathered to pay homage in the direction of Nippon and shout "Banzai!" The prisoners also benefited, each receiving a small loaf of bread.

With the changeover to navy administration came minor improvements in the daily rations. Stewart G. Nottage, a captain in the heavy artillery, was assigned to oversee the preparation of meals. He made it a priority to provide ample food for the sick men, but was forced to give them portions that were "still terribly meager." Nottage pleaded with the Japanese for more rations, but was told bluntly that the staff was "too busy to be bothered with sick men."

The new commandant was fifty-three-year-old Captain Shojiro Mizusaki, the officer in charge of the 81st Naval Garrison Unit. According to Hutchinson-Smith, he "was six feet high, not very Japanese in facial characteristics, immaculately dressed, spoke English carefully but not fluently, and advertised himself as a member of the directorate of Nippon General Electric." The Australians came to despise Mizusaki, who was not only arrogant and contemptuous, but continued to farm the prisoners out to labor parties on a daily basis.

TOWARD THE END OF APRIL 1942, THE DOCKSIDE WORKERS NOTICED A tremendous increase in harbor activity at Rabaul. Something big was obviously afoot, but they could only speculate about what might be happening.

Unknowingly, the POWs were being used to help the Japanese resume the offensive. Pleased that the South Seas Force was "making better progress than expected," Imperial General Headquarters had ordered Vice Admiral Inoue to "capture various important points in British New Guinea and in the Solomon Islands . . .as quickly as possible." The general idea was to gradually expand the Empire's control over the Southeastern Area, thereby cutting the lines of supply and communication between Australia and the United States and forcing the Commonwealth to sue for peace.

The orders called for the second stage of the Southern Offensive to begin with MO Operation, a bi-directional thrust from Rabaul. First, a small invasion force would head six hundred miles southeast to Tulagi, the capital of the British Solomon Islands Protectorate; a few days later, an even larger force would move southwest against Port Moresby. The Japanese had already gained control of the northern Solomons by establishing forward air bases on Bougainville and nearby Buka, along with Faisi in the Shortlands. Once Tulagi was occupied and a new airfield was constructed on the coastal plains of Guadalcanal, twenty miles to the south, the Japanese would dominate the entire Solomons chain.

Admiral Isoroku Yamamoto, who ultimately commanded MO Operation from his headquarters in Tokyo, did not like the concept of dividing his forces for the two-pronged attack. However, he viewed it as an opportunity to lure the carriers of the U.S. Pacific Fleet into a decisive battle, and reluctantly gave approval to commence the operation. Vice Admiral Inoue dispatched the Tulagi Invasion Force from Simpson Harbor on April 30, after which the next fleet of transports began loading men and equipment for the assault on Port Moresby.

Laboring at the wharves for days on end, the Australian POWs were duly impressed by all the harbor activity. The Port Moresby Invasion Force included twelve transports carrying a total of six thousand troops, and on May 4, "a sleek Jap aircraft carrier" was seen sailing down St. George's Channel in company with four powerful cruisers. This was the light carrier *Shoho* and her escorts, part of the Close Support Force. In all, the Australians counted twenty-seven Japanese ships leaving Rabaul on the 4th, known thereafter as the "Day of the Armada." That evening, one of the guards at Rabaul boasted, "Japanese take Moresby, then Australia, you go home."

The Tulagi Invasion Force achieved its objective with relative ease, but the invasion of Port Moresby was foiled by the American carriers. The Battle of the Coral Sea began on the morning of May 7, when Japanese planes crippled the American oiler *Neosho* (later finished off by friendly torpedoes) and sank the destroyer *Sims*. A few hours later the *Shoho* was sunk by dive bombers and torpedo planes from the *Lexington* and *Yorktown*.

The following day, American planes damaged the heavy carrier *Shokaku*, scoring two bomb hits on her flight deck and another on the bridge. She withdrew from the battle after sending forty-six aircraft to land aboard the *Zuikaku*, whose own pilots were simultaneously attacking the American task force. The *Lexington*, struck by two torpedoes and two bombs, seemed initially to have weathered the damage. However, fumes from leaking high-octane aviation fuel tanks ignited a few hours later, gutting the carrier with massive internal explosions. Torpedoes fired by the American destroyer *Phelps* finally sent her under that night.

Meanwhile, the *Yorktown's* flight deck had been damaged by a heavy bomb. The Japanese, thinking both American carriers were sunk, congratulated themselves on yet another victory. They had scored a tactical win, sinking three American ships in exchange for the *Shoho*, but both the *Zuikaku* and the damaged *Shokaku* were withdrawn, leaving the transports of the Port Moresby invasion force without aerial protection. Inoue had no alternative but to postpone the invasion for the second time in as many months.

At Vunapope, the captive women noticed that the guards had suddenly become quiet. Some even looked depressed. The reason soon became clear as "a battered and dirty replica" of the fleet returned to Rabaul. Watching from the shoreline, Alice Bowman was mesmerized by the sight of the *Shokaku*—her superstructure blackened and the flight deck empty—as she limped slowly past Kokopo.

Soon after the sea battle, plantation owner Ted Harvey and his family were arrested by the Kempeitai and charged with espionage. For the past three months they had been hiding in the hills above New Britain's north coast, but suddenly they became scapegoats. Ted, a former coastwatcher, was charged with signaling the enemy "by radio telegraphy and fires." No specifics about the alleged espionage were given, nor did the charges state why his wife Marjorie and his eleven-year-old stepson, Richard, were also arrested. Perhaps the Kempeitai discovered that the Harvey plantation had been used earlier by Australian soldiers, but the more likely explanation is that informers revealed the family's hideout. Whatever led to their arrest, the Harveys were no threat to the Japanese.

At the time of Ted Harvey's recruitment as a coastwatcher in 1940, he was given a military-channel crystal for his two-way radio. A few months later, his supereriors deemed him unreliable and repossessed the crystal, terminating his assignment. However, he continued to use the transmitter on a commercial frequency. After the Japanese invaded New Britain, Harvey continually sent what one AIB officer described as "all sorts of silly reports" from his jungle hideout. Considered an oddball by the AIB, he ignored repeated warnings to stay off the air, and probably contributed to his own downfall.

Within days of their arrest, the Harveys were handed over to the 81st Naval Garrison Unit. They were confined in a small compound in Chinatown while Vice Admiral Inoue convened a court-martial to try them for espionage. He appointed Captain Mizusaki as the senior member of the tribunal, and named three other officers to the prosecuting panel. The accused received no legal representation for their defense.

During the three-day trial the Harveys underwent intense questioning. An interpreter was provided to assist them with presenting a defense, but the verdict was already decided. The entire family was found guilty of espionage, and the prosecuting panel recommended the death penalty. Their statements were forwarded to Inoue, who approved the findings and issued an order for execution. Lieutenant Yoshio Endo, adjutant of the 81st Naval Garrison Unit, was directed to "dispose of them by shooting."

On June 5, a truck carrying several sailors armed with rifles pulled up in front of the compound. The Harveys were placed aboard, and the truck drove east out of Rabaul, following the road that led around Simpson Harbor to the base of Tavurvur. A short distance from the volcano, near the town dump known as the Malay Hole, the Japanese had established a crematorium and "war cemetery." The volcanic earth was soft and easily excavated, an ideal location for disposing of bodies.

A number of officers, including Mizusaki and Endo, were already waiting at the site. They watched as the family was lined up in front of the armed sailors, and when all was ready, the master-at-arms barked commands to the firing squad. A volley of shots rang out. Later, during a postwar interrogation, a member of Mizusaki's unit testified: "I remember hearing some seamen say it was a really miserable scene, and the parents had clasped hands with the young boy standing between them. I thought at that time it was not possible a young boy could be guilty of any crime."

At the time, neither Mizusaki nor Endo could have known that Richard Harvey would be the youngest Australian executed during World War II. If they had any objections, they did not make them public; they simply followed orders. Indeed, there were many more executions yet to come over the next few years, and the three bodies buried at the foot of Tavurvur would have plenty of company.

JUNE 5 WAS A DAY OF IMPORTANT EVENTS AT OTHER LOCATIONS AS WELL. Three thousand miles away, in Fremantle Harbor on the west coast of Australia, the crew of an American submarine prepared for their fourth war patrol. The submariners were hoping for some good luck. During the previous three sorties, the USS *Sturgeon* had fired torpedoes at several targets but had sunk only one merchantman. The problem was with the "fish." The torpedoes either ran too deep or simply failed to explode— shortcomings that were chronic throughout the fleet. However, the *Sturgeon's* fresh reload of twenty-four torpedoes held promise: they were fitted with new Mark-15 or -16 warheads, each packed with hundreds of pounds of high explosive called "torpex."

In addition to stowing the long torpedoes aboard, the *Sturgeon's* crew provisioned the boat with ninety-six thousand gallons of fuel oil, more than three thousand gallons of lubricating oil, ammunition for the topside machine guns and 3-inch deck gun, and an assortment of foodstuffs. Under the watchful eye of the supply officer, the crew filled the escape trunk in the forward torpedo room with potatoes, and hundreds of pounds of Australian beef went into the refrigerators. The cook even stowed enough fresh lettuce to last more than a month.

By noon, the 308-foot submarine was almost ready. The commanding officer, Lieutenant Commander William L. "Bull" Wright, was likely wondering if his professional career was riding on this patrol. A graduate of the U.S. Naval Academy, Class of 1925, he was under some pressure to make up for the mediocre results of the previous three patrols. Furthermore, his torpedo data computer officer was none other than Lieutenant Chester W. Nimitz Jr., the son of the Commander-in-Chief, Pacific Fleet (CINCPAC).

AT THAT VERY MOMENT, CINCPAC HIMSELF WAS DEEPLY INVOLVED IN THE defining moment of his own career. Seven thousand miles east of Fremantle, Admiral Chester W. Nimitz was in a command center at Pearl Harbor, where for the past several hours he had been tracking a major battle between three of his Pacific Fleet carriers and four big Japanese flattops. The decisive engagement that his counterpart, Admiral Yamamoto, had been seeking for months was still unfolding near a pair of tiny islands named Sand and Eastern, otherwise known as Midway. Because of the nineteen-hour time difference between Fremantle and

Midway, it was just 1700 hours on June 4 at Midway, and Yamamoto's dream of annihilating the Pacific Fleet was going up in smoke. Three of his prized carriers were already engulfed in flames, and the fourth was destined for a similar fate.

Twelve hours later, Admiral Nimitz was greatly pleased with the outcome of the battle. All four Japanese carriers had been sunk, and despite the loss of the *Yorktown*, it was obvious that he and his carrier commanders had won a great victory. Under the circumstances, he was probably unaware that his twenty-seven-year-old namesake had just departed Fremantle on a hazardous war patrol.

THE *STURGEON* GOT UNDERWAY AT 2230 ON JUNE 5. WITHIN AN HOUR SHE was in the teeth of a force five wind that churned the ocean, making heavy work for her four Hoover, Owens & Rentschler diesel engines. The weather grew even worse the following day, and by late afternoon the sea state became so rough that Bull Wright was forced to reduce speed to ten knots. Even so, a rogue wave washed over the bridge, sending tons of seawater down into the control room. An electrical flashover in the pump room knocked out all power, and for nearly an hour the sub lay dead in the water, her round hull rolling perversely. One engine was restarted shortly before 1900, allowing the sub to make headway at five knots, and by morning the remaining three diesels were back on line.

During the next several days, with the exception of training dives, the *Sturgeon* ran on the surface at fifteen knots. Because of a solid gray overcast and frequent rain showers, there was little risk of detection from the air, and she made rapid progress to the South China Sea. Anticipating plenty of targets, Wright began to hunt off the western coast of Luzon. He knew the Japanese were transporting men and supplies to their newly acquired territories in convoys of merchant ships, which then returned to the home islands with loads of raw materials.

Surprisingly, however, the first two weeks yielded nothing. The first convoy was not sighted until the night of June 24, when nine merchantmen escorted by a pair of destroyers approached from the south, possibly out of Manila. Taking advantage of the conditions—the night was moonless and the sea as smooth as glass—Wright raced north to get well ahead of the convoy. Once in position, he picked out the largest target. Eight of the cargo ships were fairly small, but the third vessel in line stood out clearly: a big transport estimated at seven thousand tons.

Wright ordered the crew to take the sub to periscope depth and set up his first shot in the early hours of June 25. He passed the order to rig for depth charging, and then ordered the outer bow tube doors opened. One remained stuck in the closed position, so he elected to fire a three-torpedo spread at the target, identified from the profile books as the *Toyohasi Maru* "or a very similar type."

The sky was beginning to lighten when the first torpedo sped from its tube at 0529; the second was launched six seconds later, and the third followed after another eight-second delay. Distance to the target was 3,600 yards, or roughly two miles. Immediately after the third torpedo was fired, one of the Japanese warships hoisted a signal flag, increased speed, and then turned toward the *Sturgeon*. The Japanese had detected the submarine, or more accurately, its periscope.

Wright took the *Sturgeon* deep and altered course. He could no longer observe the course of the torpedoes through the periscope, but several people in the control room had their stopwatches running. The torpedoes, which sped through the water at forty-six knots, would take more than two minutes to cover the calculated distance to the target—a long time for the anxious crew to wait. At two and a half minutes, an explosion was heard, seemingly a confirmed hit. "As these were 700# heads," Wright noted in the *Sturgeon*'s log, "I feel reasonably sure that the target was sunk."

Two minutes after the explosion, splashes were heard as depth charges from the warship hit the surface. Now it was the submariners' turn to sweat. Twenty-one detonations were felt, some of them strong enough to crack the glass in a few gauges, but otherwise the submarine sustained no damage. Sonar operators listened as the two destroyers searched in vain for thirty minutes. One of the warships then departed, evidently to shepherd the convoy, and two hours later the other destroyer gave up the hunt.

Wright kept the boat submerged for the rest of the day, heading westward on the electric motors until after dark. When the sub finally surfaced, the crew opened hatches to allow fresh air into the hull, and they stood down from the attack. The whole evolution—from stalking the convoy and firing the torpedoes to avoiding the angry escorts—had lasted eighteen hours. All in all, it had been a fairly typical day.

Wright decided to hunt next in the waters off the northern tip of Luzon, and patrolled west of Cape Bojeador. An old stone lighthouse, though no longer functional, made an excellent landmark. For several days in a row, the sub dived at dawn and hunted at periscope depth, and then surfaced at dusk to recharge the batteries and patrol throughout the night. The routine of silent hunting became all too familiar to both submarine and crew, who waited impatiently for another target to come along.

AT RABAUL, THE SIZE AND INTENSITY OF ALLIED BOMBING RAIDS HAD BEEN gradually gaining strength. Several missions specifically targeted the wharves and "military camp," an indication that the planners were unaware the former home of Lark Force was now a POW stockade. From the air it resembled an active military compound—which of course it had once been. Even when the camp was not identified as a target, it was dangerously close to the wharves and warehouses that were being hit with increasing frequency. By some miracle the bombs did not harm the POWs, but there were several close calls.

One day, as a large group of prisoners worked in a copra shed alongside the Toboi Wharf, an Allied plane roared over at low level and strafed the building. A few men were "slightly wounded and scorched" by incendiary bullets, but no one was seriously hurt. Stray bullets hit the POW stockade on other occasions, and during one bombing raid several small bombs landed in the compound. The only damage was caused by a piece of shrapnel that pierced the cookhouse roof and knocked the handle off a large stewpot containing the next morning's rice.

The Japanese were not blind to the hazards faced by the prisoners. Their own personnel also worked in the stockade, and the risk to all hands became greater as more prisoners were brought in. Colin Stirling and his party, having dodged the Japanese for more than four months, were finally captured near Sum Sum plantation on June 2. Their arrival at Rabaul added six more prisoners to an already overcrowded population. In all, some twelve hundred POWs and civilian internees were crammed into one corner of the camp, originally built to accommodate nine hundred men.

The work parties assigned to dig *benjo* holes eventually used up every available space, including the parade ground. Heavy rains flooded the shallow latrines, causing the entire camp to become "foul in the extreme," and it wasn't long before dysentery was added to the list of afflictions bothering the prisoners. "The weakened men were now suffering from recurring gastric malaria," wrote Hutchinson-Smith, "and tropical ulcers and wet beri-beri were becoming common as the Japanese became more vigilant in safeguarding [their] food stocks." The occurrence of beriberi among the prisoners was of particular concern. It indicated a serious deficiency of thiamine, thanks to the prison diet that consisted almost entirely of rice.

But the prisoners weren't the only ones suffering a food shortage. As early as May 16, the stockpiles reserved for the Japanese were running low. Army signaler Jiro Takamura observed, "There is no food left to requisition and there is nothing good to eat nowadays." His complaint raises a critical question: Why, when Simpson Harbor was crowded with cargo ships, were the Japanese running out of food?

The answer lies in the Imperial Japanese Navy's planning. With the Southern Offensive well underway, the great majority of merchantmen were dedicated to providing the arsenal necessary to defend the empire's rapidly expanding territory. Rabaul was a prime example. In the months following the invasion, the Japanese placed nearly one hundred 75mm antiaircraft guns around the caldera, as well as almost two dozen 120mm and 127mm dual-purpose guns. And that was only the heavy stuff. The navy installed about one hundred Type 96 25mm multi-barrel cannons, while the army added another 120 automatic cannons and heavy machine guns. Eventually, the Gazelle Peninsula was covered by almost 370 antiaircraft guns, most of which were arranged in a ring starting at the tip of Crater Peninsula and extending around the caldera all the way to Kokopo.

Even more impressive was the assortment of ground and coastal defenses. The Japanese divided the northern end of New Britain into areas of military responsibility, with the navy controlling the defense of the harbor and township while the army handled the outer regions of the Gazelle Peninsula. The navy alone placed thirty-eight heavy coastal defense rifles around Blanche Bay and the northern coast of Crater Peninsula—all but one with a bore of 120mm or larger—and the emplacements were augmented by at least fifty concrete pillboxes housing large-caliber machine guns. The army added dozens of 150mm howitzers, 75mm infantry guns, mortars, and antitank guns to their area of coastal defense, and also built a system of inland bunkers. The latter were armed with an astounding array of weapons: almost 240 heavy cannon and howitzers, approximately the same number of antitank guns, twenty-three heavy mortars, and nearly six thousand machine guns and grenade launchers. The defenses required hundreds of shiploads of weapons, spare parts, and ammunition.

In addition to the defensive weapons and other material being sent to Rabaul, troops were being shipped southward by the tens of thousands. Prior to the commencement of the Southern Offensive, the General Shipping Transport Headquarters had been placed under the control of the Southern Army. It is well worth noting that of the 1.75 million shipping tons allotted to the offensive, 1.45 million tons were designated for troop movement. The balance was set aside "for the transportation of supplies to rehabilitate the natural resources of the southern area." Simply put, the Japanese concentrated nearly all their shipping on the transportation of troops and weapons, and failed to provide enough ships to maintain an adequate food supply.

Another factor affecting the availability of food at Rabaul was its distance from Japan. The supply line exceeded three thousand miles, virtually all of it over water. At least eighty merchantmen were sunk fleet-wide during the first six months of the war, including a significant number by American submarines. Some of those losses had a direct impact on the shortages at Rabaul.

To alleviate the food problem, the Japanese decided to relocate the Australian POWs and civilians. Rumors began to circulate that they would be shipped to Japan, but most people discounted the talk as "so much empty camp chatter." In the wee hours of June 22, however, the prisoners were surprised by a sudden development.

David Hutchinson-Smith later related the details:

> At about 4:30 a.m. we were awakened by unusual activity on the part of the guards. There was shouting and stomping and we could hear the men and civilians moving about and talking. Many of us rose, but when we went to leave the hut we found light machine guns [trained] on the doorway at each end, and the Japanese made it unmistakably clear that we were to remain inside. We could see the men and civilians collecting their miserable

possessions and discussing the movement. Then they were formed into parties of about fifty men, the sick having to be supported or half-carried, and several transported on improvised stretchers or old doors.

The actual movement out of the compound did not commence until about 9 a.m. and it was in the interim that Stewart Nottage asked that [the officers] be permitted to go with the men, or that, if we had to stay, the men be allowed to remain with us. This request the authorities refused.

John May led prayers through the open side of our hut and read the Psalm for the day, which was singularly appropriate, and Vic Turner spoke encouragingly to the members of his flock. We shook hands with the men and a large number of acquaintances, and learned from them in whispers that they expected to go to Hainan.

The Bible passage read by John May from the officers' hut that morning was Psalm 107. Whether or not he followed a standard lectionary, the selection was not only fitting but an uncanny precursor of events to come. Verses 23 and 24 were the clinchers: "They that go down to the sea in ships, that do business in great waters; These see the works of the Lord, and his wonders in the deep."

While the commissioned officers remained inside their barrack, Warrant Officer McClellan got the prisoners into formation on the parade ground. The guards attempted a roll call and had the usual difficult time getting a valid count. The accuracy of their last nominal roll is somewhat questionable, but it is widely accepted that between 1,053 and 1,057 individuals stood in ranks on the dusty parade ground. Eight hundred and fifty were soldiers, all between the rank of warrant officer and private. Included were 706 members of Lark Force and 133 commandos from the 1st Independent Company, the remainder consisting of men from the New Guinea Volunteer Rifles. About 90 percent of the total number hailed from Victoria, with more than four hundred from the 2/22nd Battalion alone.

Among them, none enjoyed closer bonds than Arthur Gullidge, Bert Morgan, Jim Thurst, and the other surviving musicians. Sans instruments, they were bound in friendship by their passion for music and their faith. On a broader scale, the soldiers of the 2/22nd Battalion had been together for two years. There were at least twelve sets of brothers or cousins in the unit, but even beyond brotherhood, the Victorians were uncommonly close. Their commitment was absolute.

Two hundred-odd civilians were also gathered on the parade ground. A significant number were senior government representatives, including Harold Page, Harry Townsend, and "Nobby" Clark. One of the younger officials was Noel Mulvey, a surveyor with the public works department. He and Alice Bowman had decided to become engaged on the morning of January 4, just as the first wave of Japanese bombers approached Rabaul. The largest percentage of civilians consisted of local businessmen, some of whom had dedicated their livelihood to developing Rabaul. There were also sixteen missionaries in the crowd, most of them Methodists (including Laurie Linggood, Laurie McArthur, and John Poole), and thirty-one Norwegian sailors from the freighter *Herstein*.

Standing in the morning sun, the soldiers and civilians showed obvious signs of their unhealthy imprisonment. For at least three months, longer for some, they had grown weak from malnourishment while enduring unsanitary conditions—yet they still performed hours of manual labor each day. Their clothing hung in tatters from their skinny frames. Paradoxically, some men had swollen limbs because of beriberi, which caused painful edema.

At 0900, calling cheery farewells to the officers who had been ordered to stay indoors, the ragged-looking prisoners began to shuffle toward the gate. The long file headed slowly down Malaguna Road toward the waterfront, covered on both sides of the road by teams of machine gunners—an unnecessary precaution. Crowds of Asians, natives, and foreign laborers also gathered along the road, drawn by the spectacle of the white men carrying their own belongings.

TIED TO ONE OF THE WHARVES ALONG THE WATERFRONT WAS A LARGE SHIP with a rakish prow and clipper-shaped stern. Completed in 1926 for service between Japan and South America, the *Montevideo Maru* had the classic profile of a prewar transoceanic cargo liner. With a slender black hull almost 450 feet long and a large white superstructure amidships, it appeared to be a 10,000-tonner, though it actually displaced just 7,266 tons.

In its heyday with the Osaka Shosen Kaisha line, the *Montevideo Maru* could accommodate thirty-eight passengers in first class, more than six hundred in second class, and ninety-four in third or "special class," the domain of immigrants. But those days were long gone. In 1941 the Imperial Navy requisitioned the ship and assigned it to the Kure Naval District. After participating in the landings at Makassar during the Indonesian campaign in February 1942, it returned to Japan in early March and worked between the cities of Yokosuka, Kure, and Sasebo for two months. Leaving again for the Southwest Pacific, the *Montevideo Maru* stopped briefly at Java, and then sailed for Rabaul in early June with a load of troops and war material.

Now, after sixteen years on the high seas, the vessel showed a few wrinkles. Routine maintenance under naval control had become almost nonexistent, due mainly to the enormous workload imposed on the merchant fleet, and the ship was in need of cosmetic repairs at the very least. Not that its outward appearance mattered to the POWs: their journey was guaranteed to be unpleasant. They were not passengers, but human cargo.

The *Montevideo Maru* boasted five holds, though the Numbers 4 and 5 holds aft were partially occupied by large tanks of fuel oil which fed the twin Mitsubishi-Sulzer diesel engines. Additional space was taken up by the tunnels for the port and starboard propeller shafts. The three remaining holds—one amidships and two forward—were likely fitted with wooden 'tween decks to accommodate troops. The Imperial Army crammed soldiers by the thousands into its crudely equipped transports, and the troops were expected to endure days or even weeks of excessive heat and unsanitary conditions without complaining. They called it *chomansai*, extreme overload. For them, it was just another element of army life.

After struggling up the *Montevideo Maru*'s gangways, the prisoners were directed toward ladders that descended into the dark holds. There is no way to know with certainty which of the compartments they went into—perhaps all five—but logic suggests that they occupied the two forward holds at the very least. With slightly more than five hundred men in each, the conditions would be terribly cramped yet still considered luxurious by the standards of the Japanese army. A detachment of naval guards was assigned to provide security, a task that would be greatly simplified by confining the prisoners in two holds.

Among those who watched the POWs file aboard was Jiro Takamura. Unlike most of his countrymen, he had developed an appreciation for the Australians and was actually sorry to see them go. Although well aware of the "insufficient food" situation, he nonetheless enjoyed spending time with the POWs who worked in his shop. He was also proud of their accomplishments. "They repaired 5 cars, more than 20 telephones and about 10 radios," he wrote in his diary. "It is a wonder that only 6 men could do so much work in a little over a month's time. This is not all. Spiritually we have gained a lot from them. They never left a job unless it was completed."

Takamura observed that the hatches were battened down after the prisoners disappeared into the holds. He quietly honored them by remaining at the wharf until the Montevideo Maru departed. Later that evening he wrote: "Saw them off, and watched the ship until it disappeared over the horizon." Two days later he noted that the ship was bound for Hainan, an island off the south coast of China, thereby confirming what some of the prisoners had been told.

AFTER EIGHT FULL DAYS AT SEA AT AN AVERAGE SPEED OF ALMOST FIFTEEN knots, the Montevideo Maru was three thousand miles from Rabaul. The captain had elected to stay east of the Philippines rather than plowing straight across the Celebes Sea—which was both tricky to navigate and a popular hunting area for submarines—but the longer route had required extra time. Reaching the eastern entrance of the Babuyan Channel on the night of June 30, he put on extra speed for the five-hour dash through the chokepoint. Once clear of the channel, it was just two days to Hainan across the South China Sea.

Inside the holds, the prisoners knew almost nothing about their destination except its name. Awaiting them on Hainan Island was a camp for hard labor. The POWs there built roads under extremely harsh conditions—not as evil as the infamous "death railway" camps in Burma and Thailand, perhaps, but a dreadful place nonetheless. Considering the lack of medical attention and the starvation diet forced upon the POWs by the

Japanese at Hainan, the men aboard the *Montevideo Maru* faced long, grim years of hardship. The odds of surviving the entire war under such conditions were not favorable.

And yet the prisoners would have gratefully accepted those odds, if only to get out of the dark, slimy holds of the *Montevideo Maru*. Two more days inside that floating oven would be an eternity. The heat and humidity within the steel hull must have been unbearable, and it is highly probable that some of the sickest men had already perished during the first eight days of transit.

There was good reason why the *Montevideo Maru*, like all the other Japanese vessels employed as POW transports, was considered a "hellship." Throughout the war tens of thousands of POWs and slave laborers were shipped between Japan's territories aboard dozens of different ships, and in each case the conditions were utterly despicable. If the journey was supposed to be short, food and water were sometimes withheld. On longer trips, only small portions of moldy rice and containers of filthy water were passed down into the holds by the guards.

There were no sanitation facilities down below except a few buckets, the only toilets being topside. These were crude wooden *benjos*, suspended precariously over the side rails, and to use them the prisoners had to be strong enough to climb the ladders to the main deck. Even then, the facilities were only available during daylight hours, as the holds were locked at night for security. Not that it mattered to the men who were sick with dysentery or even simple diarrhea: too weak to move, they defecated where they lay, which in turn caused outbreaks of bacterial disease. On top of that was seasickness, a virtually endemic problem that only grew worse as the air within the enclosed holds became increasingly foul. After just one or two days of accumulating excrement, urine, and vomit in the holds, the stench was indescribable; after eight days inside the *Montevideo Maru*, the prisoners knew the definition of hell.

The ship carried no special markings that identified it as a POW transport, and was therefore indistinguishable from the legitimate targets being hunted by Allied aircraft and submarines. Therefore, no one should have been surprised that an American submarine lurked west of Luzon on the night of June 30, waiting for the next ship that passed through the Babuyan Channel in the moonlight.

AT 2216, A LOOKOUT ABOARD THE STURGEON SIGHTED A SHIP RUNNING alone with no lights. It first appeared to be on a northward course, but after Bull Wright observed it for a few minutes, he concluded that it was a cargo-passenger liner headed west, and fast. He ordered all four diesels on line, and the submarine surged forward at flank speed.

The *Sturgeon* was supposedly capable of making twenty-one knots on the surface, but it could barely keep up with the ship. "For an hour and a half we couldn't make a nickel," Wright later reported. "This fellow was really going, making at least 17 knots and probably a bit more, as he appeared to be zig-zagging."

Wright needed to get well ahead of the ship in order to set up a proper attack, but he could draw no closer to the speeding liner than eighteen thousand yards—approximately ten miles. Nevertheless he held on like a determined terrier, and shortly past midnight his persistence was rewarded. The ship abruptly slowed to twelve knots, allowing the *Sturgeon* to close the distance quickly. "After that," Wright noted, "it was easy."

An interception point was plotted along the ship's projected path. For the next hour and a half the *Sturgeon* raced ahead, and at 0146 on July 1, Wright took the sub down to periscope depth. Then, deciding to make his attack using the stern tubes, he turned *away* from the target. It was a simple matter of efficiency. One of the bow tube doors still did not function, and the torpedoes in the four aft tubes were fitted with the largest warheads currently available.

Watching through the periscope as the ship drew closer in the moonlight, Wright judged its heading to be "slightly left of west." This would bring it no nearer than five thousand yards to his current position, so he maneuvered the *Sturgeon* with the electric motors, narrowing the gap by a thousand yards. He then began relaying periscope information to Lieutenant "Chet" Nimitz, who stood before the torpedo data computer (TDC) console.

Four aiming points were calculated using a method known as "divergent shifting points of periscope aim from aft forward." As Wright called out data from the periscope, Nimitz twisted knobs on the TDC panel to set the target's estimated length, speed, and angle off the stern. A position keeper then tracked the target and predicted its location at the point of impact based on constant updates from the *Sturgeon's* navigational equipment. The assorted information was fed into the angle solver, which automatically determined the proper settings for each torpedo's internal gyroscope. The solutions were passed verbally to the men in the aft torpedo room, who dialed them manually into the weapons.

At 0225 the first torpedo was fired at a range of four thousand yards—almost two and a half miles. Three more torpedoes followed at eight-second intervals, and then Wright ordered a full-rudder turn to bring the bow tubes to bear. Lieutenant Nimitz didn't think the maneuvering was necessary. "We won't have to use any more," he said aloud. "One of those will get him."

At 0229, VIRTUALLY THE SAME TIME THAT THE INVASION OF RABAUL HAD begun exactly 158 days earlier, a warhead containing the equivalent of seven hundred pounds of TNT detonated against the *Montevideo Maru's* starboard hull. The blast ripped open the fourth and fifth holds, and moments later a secondary explosion occurred in the fuel oil tank. The first explosion was heard clearly throughout the submarine, and Wright confirmed the hit. Observing through the periscope, he saw the bright flash of an explosion approximately one hundred feet aft of the single stack. The ship's lights came on briefly, and then flickered out. From his brief glimpse of the illuminated vessel, Wright made an educated guess that it was the *Rio de Janeiro Maru* or a "very similar type . . . he was a big one."

Wright could also clearly see that the ship was listing to starboard and settling rapidly by the stern. Nimitz was correct: one torpedo had been enough.

ABOARD THE *MONTEVIDEO MARU*, THE CREW AND NAVAL GUARDS SCRAMBLED for their lives. Those not on duty had been jolted awake in the darkest hour of the night by explosions and alarms; now they groped along passageways in absolute darkness, searching for exits. The lights had come on for only a minute or two after the torpedo struck, and then oil from the ruptured tank spilled into the engine room, forcing the engineers to deliberately shut down all power.

Some of the crewmen made it to the lifeboat stations—there were three on each side of the superstructure and two more along each side of the aft deckhouse—but because the ship was listing so rapidly *and* going down by the stern, only the three lifeboats on the starboard side of the superstructure had a prayer of being launched. The sailors weren't quick enough. Within six minutes the ship's bow had risen high out of the water, and all three lifeboats capsized from their davits, with one sustaining major damage.

There is no evidence that any of the hatch covers were unfastened during the eleven minutes that the *Montevideo Maru* remained afloat. The Japanese were concerned only about saving their own lives. Dozens got safely into the water, but twenty crewmen and guards were either killed by the explosions or drowned. The surviving Japanese righted the capsized boats and climbed aboard. One boatload headed west; the other two remained more or less stationary until daylight, and then headed east toward Luzon.

For the prisoners down in the pitch-black holds, those last eleven minutes were measured quite differently. If any men were confined in the aft two holds, they did not suffer long. Those not killed outright by the exploding torpedo were knocked senseless by its concussive effects, and then quickly drowned as tons of seawater rushed in.

The truly unfortunate victims were those in the forward holds. Before the end came, they endured eleven minutes of mind-bending terror. No one could see what was happening; they could only feel the ship canting steeply, and their ears were assaulted by the screech of collapsing bulkheads and painful pressure changes as air was forced from flooded spaces. Some men probably attempted to reach the hatches, but as they groped upward they found no escape. The effects of adrenalin gave them strength only for a short time. Then, as their black world tilted ever more crazily, they slid aft and piled up against the lowest bulkhead. Under the crush of filthy bodies, those at the bottom quickly lost consciousness.

The panic that surely accompanied those final minutes can only be imagined. Sentimentalists would like to believe that some of the prisoners calmly faced their impending death, but the circumstances strongly suggest that a contagious, mass hysteria swept through the black holds. And who could blame the victims: in the middle of the night they were plunged into an unfathomable nightmare, each second filled with the tormenting sounds of water rushing in and the ship breaking apart. As the minutes wore on, the men who were still conscious would have instinctively tried to claw their way upward, their shouts and screams only adding to the freakish pandemonium.

The terror mercifully ended at 0240. With a final hiss of foul-smelling air, the bow of the *Montevideo Maru* slid beneath the waves.

Wright waited ten minutes before bringing the *Sturgeon* to the surface. He had no inkling of the tragedy that had just occurred, and thus made no attempt to maneuver the boat among the floating debris to search for survivors. Instead, satisfied with the knowledge that he had sunk a large enemy ship, he called for an eastward course toward Cape Bojeador.

With the exhaust from her diesel engines burbling softly, the *Sturgeon* moved off in the darkness to resume the hunt.

CHAPTER FIFTEEN

THE LONG WAIT

"Oh, the hunger and the cold . . ."

—Lorna Whyte Johnson,
Australian Army Nursing Service

The stockade on Malaguna Road seemed desolate after the exodus of more than a thousand men on June 22. Only sixty Australian officers and fewer than a dozen civilians remained. Some of the officers were ordered to clean up the vacant barracks. Although eerily quiet, the Fibro huts yielded many prizes: scraps of food, extra clothing, and even enough tobacco for a few hand-rolled cigarettes.

After they cleaned up the camp, the officers wired off a smaller compound consisting of four huts in the northeast corner of the stockade. Food was more plentiful, and instead of laboring outside the camp, the remaining POWs passed the time doing domestic chores.

Without permission, a few energetic officers built a platform for deck tennis between two of the huts. They hoped it might precipitate a change in fortunes, and the 2/22nd Battalion certainly had a strange history when it came to tennis courts. The first had been built at Trawool, but as soon as it was finished the battalion received orders to Bonegilla. The soldiers built a new court, and were transferred to Rabaul. Later, as POWs, they built yet another court, this time for Japanese officers at the naval headquarters building, and after it was finished the enlisted POWs and civilians were taken away. Some of the officers had become superstitious, and half-jokingly decided to tempt their own fate by building the deck tennis platform in the middle of the stockade. At first all it got them was "an ear-bashing" from Captain Mizusaki, who was irate that they built it without permission; but they had faith in their latest effort.

The days passed quickly as the officers continued working on the tennis platform and doing chores. Two more civilian internees arrived on July 2, bringing news about events on the outside. Robert Evenson, the plantation manger at Pondo, and his assistant, William Korn, had supposedly been "paroled" when Pondo was captured in early February. For a few months they had been allowed to continue overseeing the plantation, but recently the Japanese had taken over the lucrative operation and sent both men to Rabaul. They revealed the stirring news that hundreds of Australian soldiers had escaped from New Britain.

Other civilians were similarly helpful. Alfred Creswick, an engineer retained by the Japanese to maintain the cold-storage plant, known as the "Freezer," smuggled two dozen oxtails into the stockade on July 4. He hid the meat on a Japanese supply truck, and the prisoners working in the cookhouse found it. Stewart Nottage, out on a foraging party that same day, brought in a forequarter of beef. That evening the prisoners binged on stew and steaks, and there was more stew for breakfast the next morning. Nottage then began cooking the rest of the beef to keep it from spoiling, but at 0930 the officers received an unexpected order: "Pack up and assemble at the gate." The tennis court had worked its magic.

In the cookhouse, Nottage was among the first POWs to hear of a place called Zentsuji. Soon the whole camp was abuzz. The officers were being sent to Japan.

Fifteen miles away at Vunapope, a nearly identical scene had unfolded on July 4. An interpreter arrived from Rabaul in company with several naval officers and called for the Australians being held there. Eighteen women lined up in ranks: seven civilian nurses, six AANS sisters, four Methodist mission nurses, and a widowed plantation owner. They were introduced to Captain Mizusaki, who surprised them by saying, "Please, just call me Michael."

The Japanese went upstairs and inspected the women's dormitory, after which the interpreter announced: "You have been handed over to the Imperial Japanese Navy and these officers will visit you every month."

The following day, however, Mizusaki returned to Vunapope and ordered the nurses to pack their belongings. As word spread throughout the mission that the women were leaving, some of the nuns and other members of the staff came forward with a collection of towels, dresses, linens, and even several bottles of wine. Mizusaki, spying some rolls of mosquito netting in the growing pile of goods, told the women, "You will not need those. You are going to Paradise." His words sounded ominous, but no one had the courage to ask him what he meant.

The women were ordered to load their possessions on a truck, which took them to a familiar swimming beach near Rabaul. They boarded a Daihatsu landing craft and were taken to the middle of Simpson Harbor, where the 7,000-ton cargo ship *Naruto Maru* rode at anchor. A wooden gangway was suspended over the side near the stern, and a small boarding platform bobbed vigorously on the swells. Taking the lead, Kay Parker hopped on and said, "Come on girls, it's not as bad as it seems." The women followed her up the ladder to the aft cargo deck, where they were met by a nonplussed naval guard.

Though not expecting females, the armed guard recovered quickly from his confusion and pointed to a hatch over the aft hold. "Down there," he said in English, and one by one the women descended another ladder into the empty compartment. It was dark and grimy, but Parker put everyone at ease with her characteristic good humor: "Ladies, welcome to this spacious cabin which has been put at our disposal by the kind Japanese. Ventilation could be better, there is no water, there are no sea views, the beds will be rather uncomfortable and there is only just the remotest possibility that the lights will come on later. The galley is closed for the time being, as the cooks have gone ashore for a few beers!"

A FEW MILES AWAY AT THE MALAGUNA ROAD STOCKADE, SIXTY OFFICERS hastily threw together their belongings. Stewart Nottage collected the foodstuffs and utensils authorized by the Japanese, and at midday on July 5 the POWs boarded several trucks for the ride to the waterfront. In their excitement over leaving, they didn't realize the civilian internees were not coming with them. Al Creswick, Gordon Thomas, and ten others were outside the camp doing odd jobs, and there was no time to say farewell.

As with the women from Vunapope, the officers were ferried out to the *Naruto Maru*. They were met by several armed naval guards, one of whom barked commands at the POWs until they lined up in formation.

The pretentious Captain Mizusaki then climbed onto a hatch cover to make a speech. Holding a baton and posturing "like an orchestra conductor," he warned the officers to obey all regulations and watch after themselves, and then ordered them down into the hold.

Douglas B. Millican, a captain from the 1st Independent Company, started down the ladder first with David Hutchinson-Smith right behind him. They had descended partway when they heard shrieks from below. It was the nurses, whose joy at seeing the men alive bordered on hysteria. One by one the Australian officers descended into the hold and joined a growing melee, everyone shouting and hugging and shaking hands as they exchanged heartfelt greetings. The women looked basically the same as the men: thin, haggard, their clothing in "pretty bad shape," but no one seemed to care. They were simply happy to see each other after more than five months of separation.

The women, having heard through the grapevine about the sailing of the *Montevideo Maru*, were anxious for any news about the men who had gone aboard. The Methodist sisters were especially concerned about Linggood, McArthur, and Poole, and Alice Bowman wanted to know if her fiancé, Noel Mulvey, was with them. Kathleen Bignell, the plantation owner, learned that her twenty-two-year-old son had been taken aboard. Born at Tulagi and raised in the Solomons, Private Charles E. Bignell had enlisted in the 2/22nd Battalion a week after Pearl Harbor. In response to the women's many questions, the officers replied that they had seen the men walking out of the stockade on June 22, but there was nothing more to tell.

The aft hold of the *Naruto Maru* had no 'tween decks, and the compartment was crowded with seventy-eight men and women. The Australians sweltered in the below-deck heat for the remainder of the day and throughout the night. No one managed to get much sleep, mainly because numerous "*benjo*-runners" were active after eating too much stew the previous day. To give the women some privacy, the forward part of the hold was cordoned off by draping blankets over a cord stretched across the compartment.

In the morning the Australians discovered that their floating prison was still anchored in Simpson Harbor. Their nerves frayed each time an aircraft was heard overhead, but the *Naruto Maru* finally got underway on the afternoon of July 6. Unable to see what was happening, the last remnants of Lark Force were denied a parting glimpse of Rabaul as their ship began the long voyage to "Paradise."

A FEW DAYS AFTER THE *NARUTO MARU* SAILED, WORD REACHED RABAUL OF a terrible disaster. Jiro Takamura wrote the pertinent details in his diary on July 9: "Navy men say that the ship with the [POWs] which headed for Hainan Island was sunk by an enemy submarine on the way. Probably all of the [prisoners] have been killed. Their compartment was locked, so none could have been saved."

Gordon Thomas also learned about the sinking. "On July 11," he recalled, "we heard in Rabaul that 'Montevideo Maru' had been sunk, and all on board had perished. Such tragic news was unbelievable; but, unfortunately, it proved to be only too true." Gordon's information wasn't completely accurate: not everyone aboard had perished. Some of the Japanese crewmen and guards had reached the coast of Luzon, which is how the story came to light so soon after the sinking.

In addition to the prisoners, the *Montevideo Maru* carried an Imperial Navy crew of eighty-eight officers and men plus the embarked guard detachment of sixty-four ratings commanded by an ensign. According to the Osaka Shosen Kaisha line's official loss report, twenty Japanese personnel were drowned or missing after the torpedo attack. Therefore, more than 130 got into the lifeboats. Maritime historian Peter Cundall, one of the foremost Western authorities on Japanese ships and wartime losses, believes that two lifeboats headed east and reached Luzon; another went west and was found by a Japanese warship. The number of survivors per boat has never been determined.

For the two boatloads that reached Luzon, the hardships were just beginning. The survivors landed near the Cape Bojeador lighthouse on the evening of July 2, rested overnight, and then walked five miles the next day to the village of Bubon. They planned to set off in the morning for a Japanese army camp at Laoag, about twenty miles south, but at 0900 Filipino guerillas attacked them. "The party was absolutely defenseless," stated one official account, "and although clubs and rocks were used for what they were worth, the majority of the personnel were either dead or missing after the attack." Fifty-five members of the crew, including the ship's captain, were slain along with an unknown number of guards. The latter were unarmed, having lost their weapons when the *Montevideo Maru* sank.

One crewman eventually walked to Laoag, where an army patrol was organized to bring in the rest of the survivors. Three other crewmen walked in under their own power, and over the next few weeks an additional twenty-eight survivors were located, all described as "starved, fatigued and near death."

Reports by various agencies in Japan contained conflicting information about the number of survivors. Whatever actually happened, only a small number of crewmen lived to tell about it. Moreover, the Japanese maintained silence about the sinking until the end of the war, which is why only a few Australian POWs at Rabaul heard about the disaster. Three more years would pass before the rest of the Commonwealth learned the awful truth.

FOR THE AUSTRALIAN OFFICERS AND WOMEN ABOARD THE *NARUTO MARU*, those same years would seem extraordinarily long. Little did they realize that during their time in Japan, they would never have as much food as they did during the sea voyage.

For nine days they shared the hot, steel-walled hold of the *Naruto Maru*, the floor of which was strewn with old straw. Steel rings mounted along the bulkheads gave clues to the identity of the previous occupants: draft animals. At night, when the deck hatches were locked, the hold was stuffy and foul-smelling. During the day, the prisoners were occasionally allowed topside. Two oil stoves made from forty-four-gallon drums were available for cooking on the aft deck. With the supplies brought from Rabaul, the Australians ate well during the voyage. Their rations included rice, pumpkins, taro, bananas, coconuts, and pineapples, plus tins of bully beef, butter, peaches, and cheese. There was even food left over when they reached the port of Yokohama on July 14.

After disembarking in the industrial heartland of Japan, the women were taken to the Bund Hotel, an establishment that had catered to Western tourists before the war. Inside they met sixty-two-year-old Etta Jones, an American who had been confined to the hotel for more than a month. She and her husband, Foster Jones, had been captured on June 7 when the Japanese overran Attu Island in the Aleutians. Etta, a schoolteacher with the Bureau of Indian Affairs, was shipped to Japan, but Foster, a radio operator and weather observer, was dragged away and executed.

While the women settled in at the Bund Hotel, the officers were taken to the Yokohama Yacht Club. They were surprised to find a lavatory with real Western-style toilets, and with childlike joy some of the men repeatedly pulled the chains, flushing away just for the fun of it. In the upstairs sleeping quarters, fresh *tatami* mats covered the floors, and thick white Imperial Navy blankets were provided. "Damned good Aussie wool," exclaimed one officer after feeling the soft material.

The comforts proved to be temporary. After receiving a medical screening for dysentery and other diseases, all but seven officers were scheduled for immediate transfer to Zentsuji, a large POW camp on the island of Shikoku. The exceptions included Joe Scanlan, John Mollard, Geoff Lempriere, and Ted Best, who were held for additional questioning. They remained "in quarantine" at the yacht club while fifty-three others departed by train on July 18.

After a journey of thirty hours, which included a ferry trip across the Inland Sea, the majority of Lark Force officers arrived at Zentsuji. The camp already held more than two hundred Americans captured at Guam and Wake Island, along with a few dozen Australian, Dutch, British, and New Zealand prisoners from Singapore. Also present were RAAF pilots Bob Thompson and Paul Metzler, who had been captured six months earlier by the cruiser *Aoba*.

The newcomers were pleased to see that their predecessors were in relatively good condition. Indeed, they were among the most fortunate POWs in the empire, for the Imperial Army used the camp as a model for propaganda purposes. The International Red Cross (IRC) and other agencies were conned into believing that *all* Allied POWs were cared for as decently as those at Zentsuji.

Toward the end of August, Scanlan and three others arrived from Yokohama with the disturbing news that Mollard, Lempriere, and Best had been sent to Ofuna, a secret camp run by the Imperial Navy. Captives sent there were not recognized by the Japanese as POWs; instead they underwent prolonged interrogation, sometimes for months, which was based on a regimen of physical and mental intimidation. Interrogators used clever variations of the good cop/bad cop method to extract information, and the naval guards had carte blanche to abuse the prisoners at will. Between beatings, the captives were interrogated by well-dressed intelligence officers educated in American and English universities, whose job was to play the sympathetic role. Such methods were highly effective. Contrary to the popular notion that Allied prisoners bravely refused to divulge anything except their name, rank, and serial number, some gave useful information to the Japanese at Ofuna.

At Zentsugi, meanwhile, the general conditions remained favorable for several months. In late 1942, however, a new supply officer arrived and immediately cut the food rations. The POWs suspected that he was selling rice and other supplies on the black market.

The prisoners were also frustrated by a supposed goodwill gesture in early November 1942. Red Cross parcels were doled out at the rate of one small package per three prisoners, but most of the contents had either spoiled or were pilfered by the Japanese. Later, when the Red Cross delegate made an inspection visit to the camp, he was not sympathetic to the POWs. They doubted his allegiance, for according to their information, he not only had a Japanese wife but had lived in Japan longer than he had lived in his native Switzerland.

With the onset of cold weather, the expressions of disgust and frustration among the prisoners became more pronounced. The winter in 1942 was brutally cold. The air near the Inland Sea was constantly damp, and Zentsuji was blanketed with heavy snowfalls. The prisoners spent a lot of time dwelling on their discomforts, which only made matters worse.

Finally, a brief distraction occurred on January 15, 1943. Fifty enlisted men, mostly Americans, departed for other camps, and a few hours later 149 new prisoners arrived. All were American army or naval officers captured in the Philippines. As bad as things had been on New Britain, the new arrivals had been through ordeals the men from Lark Force could scarcely comprehend. Having first survived the infamous "Death March" up the Bataan Peninsula, the Americans had been put aboard a hellship that transported them to Japan. Not surprisingly, they arrived in horrible shape.

The Japanese refused to provide any help or medical care for the newcomers. It wasn't long, recalled Hutchinson-Smith, before problems developed within the POW barracks:

> The morale of the new prisoners generally was very low. Many of them were so far gone as to be able to make little or no attempt to help themselves. It was a losing battle for the helpers to keep the rooms clean; many of the men were genuine dysentery patients without any power to control themselves, but others soiled their quarters, bedding and clothes for no apparent reason other than that they were almost completely demoralized. Some were quite capable of washing and keeping themselves clean, but there were others whose long hair was matted with filth and whose bearded faces were stained with the dirt of months of neglect.

Within a matter of weeks, three of the American officers died. The Japanese turned out in dress uniform for the funerals and made a big show of paying respect to the dead, but their hypocrisy infuriated the POWs.

On February 16, the camp administrators announced that all officers and warrant officers except those in sick bay would take part in labor services. The healthiest individuals were put in the "agricultural squad," which grew vegetables and performed outdoor work that was deemed strenuous, at least for the stamina levels of half-starved men. The "gardening squad" cared for the prison grounds, and the "sanitation squad" had the thankless task of cleaning out the *benjos* and open-line drainage ditches.

Several more deaths occurred among the American officers during the spring of 1943, and that summer hundreds of new prisoners arrived, crowding the barracks. The Australians from New Britain and Singapore, numbering about ninety by this time, had become the old-timers at Zentsuji, though they barely took notice. The food rations were reduced again, and all of the prisoners grew thin. Hutchinson-Smith quipped, "there was hardly a respectable pair of buttocks in the whole camp."

In addition to weight loss, the POWs suffered muscle cramps caused by the lack of salt in their diet. Most could not sit with their legs crossed for more than a few minutes without feeling the prickly sensation of numbness. Blackouts and near-fainting spells were also common, especially during periods of exertion.

When several more American officers died during the last months of 1943, the camp seemed cloaked in gloom. Another cold winter set in, and the prisoners tried to distract themselves by performing variety shows and plays. The food situation did not improve, but news about the progress of the war, which generally sounded positive, helped to uplift the POWs.

Sometimes the Japanese themselves inadvertently brought good news. On June 10, 1944, the camp superintendent asked Joe Scanlan if he thought the Allies would attempt a landing in Europe. Scanlan, in the presence of several other prisoners, replied that such an invasion was "essential to victory against Germany." Amused, the Japanese officer asked Scanlan when such a landing might occur. The Australian replied that the weather conditions in June were ideal. At this the superintendent laughed. He then asked, "What would you say if I told you that British and American forces landed in Normandy four days ago?"

The officer went on to boast that the Americans would be thrown back into the English Channel, but the prisoners paid him no attention. The truth of the great offensive was out. "Needless to say," wrote Hutchinson-Smith, "everyone was elated at the news but wisely refrained from outbursts that would undoubtedly have provoked the Nips."

Greatly encouraged by the information, the prisoners managed to get through another brutal winter, and their optimism soared when American B-29 Superfortresses began striking the home islands in the spring of 1945. Although the POWs at Zentsuji did not experience the sort of close calls that had bothered them at Rabaul, they did feel the pinch of an increasingly acute food shortage. The ration of rice dropped to under three hundred grams per man per day, and even if more had been available, the cookhouse was constantly short of fuel for the coal-burning stoves.

Eventually, the Japanese were forced to close down the camp. On June 23, 1945, more than three hundred feeble Americans stumbled out of Zentsuji's main gate on their way to other camps. Two days later it was the Australians' turn to leave. Just prior to their departure, a young officer from the 2/19th Battalion succumbed to malnutrition. Captured at Singapore, Lieutenant Charles P. Furner was the only Australian to die at

Zentsuji. That it happened on the last day in camp was highly distressing to his countrymen.

From Zentsuji, the Australians traveled by train and ferry to a new camp in the mining region of Hokkaido, northernmost of the main islands. The first morning of their journey found them approaching the main railway station in Osaka. As their train rolled through the outskirts of the city, they were awed by scenes of utter devastation. For miles in every direction, virtually as far as the eye could see, the landscape was covered with mounds of debris and twisted wreckage.

Upon reaching the station the POWs were ordered off the train. Shortly thereafter, air raid sirens began to wail, and the Australians suddenly realized they were standing inside one of the few intact buildings in the center of Japan's second-largest city. It wouldn't be their first time in the line of fire, but this was no small-scale raid. More than one hundred B-29s of the Twentieth Air Force were coming from the Marianas to hit the Osaka arsenal on June 26; simultaneously, another seventy-one Superfortresses would hit secondary targets around the city. The POWs, able to hear the deep, throbbing hum of the approaching bombers, could not find any shelters to hide in. They did the next best thing, and sat on the concrete floor of the waiting room with their backs against the walls.

Antiaircraft guns began firing at approximately 0845. The POWs huddled nervously, mindful of the plaster ceiling high above the center of the waiting room. Soon the whoosh of falling bombs became audible, followed by the crump of explosions. The blasts came closer, some hitting so close to the building that the doors blew in. Clouds of dust billowed through the doorways and windows, showering the men with debris. In the middle of the attack, some of the POWS and guards got up and staggered to the *benjos*. But they were unusable, clogged with inches of accumulated filth because the city's water service had been destroyed.

Hutchinson-Smith tried in vain to appear indifferent as he sat against a wall. His expression caught the eye of James W. S. Chisholm, a captain with the 2/18th Battalion captured at Singapore. Getting on his feet, Chisholm sauntered across the room in the middle of the raid, stopped in front of Hutchinson-Smith, and said, "You're a bloody liar, and so am I!" It was just the tonic they both needed.

The occupants of the train station endured the explosions and billowing dust for more than an hour before the attack finally subsided. Later, when they climbed back aboard their train, they saw that a large, eight-story building near the station, previously undamaged except for broken windows, had been reduced to a heap of smoking rubble. Other nearby damage included a still-burning train. The POWs' extraordinary luck had held once again.

IF ANYTHING, THE FEMALE PRISONERS HAD ENDURED MORE HARDSHIP THAN the officers. Shortly after the men departed for Zentsuji prison in July 1942, the women were moved to the Yokohama Yacht Club. Quartered upstairs in the clubhouse, they found the food and living conditions quite tolerable. But when winter approached, the Australians discovered that they weren't accustomed to cold weather. Some of the older women, especially Mary Goss, had lived in the tropics for fifty years or more and felt chilled even when the weather was actually mild. Later, when the temperatures dropped below freezing, they experienced real misery.

The Japanese kept the captives occupied with menial tasks of the sort their own women were obliged to perform. Each prisoner was given bundles of silk thread and taught how to hand-knit tiny drawstring bags. They would hold miniature charms called *omamori*—wooden tablets inscribed with Shinto incantations for good luck—which soldiers carried in battle. The women also produced hand-made envelopes out of colorful paper, but later they started eating the glue when their food was severely rationed. When the Japanese discovered this, they put a stop to envelope production.

In the late summer of 1943, the women were moved temporarily to the police headquarters building of Kanagawa Prefecture. About two weeks later they returned to the yacht club and discovered that a pair of tough characters had taken over as supervisors. One man, known only as Komatsu, had an advanced case of tuberculosis; the other, nicknamed "Basher," was a sadistic individual on furlough from the army. The women endured a great deal of face-slapping and intimidation from both men until the following spring, by which time Komatsu had died and "Basher" had returned to active duty. The man who replaced them was much different. Fat and elderly, with a congenial disposition and a penchant for singing, he was nicknamed "Papa-san," an unavoidable cliché.

In July 1944, after two years in the relative comforts of the yacht club, the women were moved to the village of Totsuka, west of Yokohama. Taking their belongings—which by this time included some old futons and thin blankets—they moved into their new "home," a low, wooden structure built around three sides of a central courtyard. As the women spruced up the empty rooms, they realized with horror that they were in a former tuberculosis hospital. There was no indoor plumbing, only a well outside with a hand pump, and the *benjo* consisted of slits in the floor above a concrete pit.

The amount of labor they were forced to perform increased significantly. They had to haul coal and firewood, piled alongside the main road near the village, uphill to the compound. The women drew water for cooking and washing from the well in heavy pails, and then emptied them into a large barrel outside the cookhouse. The captives, who also had to operate the pump for the local villagers, often made more than one hundred trips a day to the well. During the harsh winter of 1944-45, said to be one of the coldest in the previous thirty years, the pump was frequently frozen until mid-afternoon. It would thaw for a few hours, during which the women had to pump all the water for the villagers and their own needs before the handle froze again.

The younger women performed most of the heavy labor. The hardships took their toll, recalled Alice Bowman. "We were so weak we could only stagger about and, with sunken eyes and general debilitation, we felt we had aged many years."

Eileen Callaghan, an army nurse, contracted tuberculosis and began to deteriorate rapidly. Her three roommates at Totsuka—Kay Parker, Mavis Cullen, and Lorna Whyte—did what little they could to comfort her. "Night after night in those cold winters we used to cuddle into Cal and she'd have these terrible TB sweats," remembered Whyte. "We'd all be wet and trying to dry out but we had nothing to change into. The futons . . . were wet with the perspiration and sodden with B.O. and dirt because we could never have baths. We could wash our face but it was too cold to wash any other part. All you had was a bucket of water but you had to break the ice and throw that over you if you wanted to bathe."

The women arrived at Totsuka too late in the growing season to raise a garden, and by winter they were truly starving. "We were getting so desperately hungry, we would do anything," Whyte added. "If you had to take a guard [his] tray, it didn't matter if he had TB or if he was coughing all over it—if it had a crumb of rice on it, you took it. When you had to go and collect it, you'd take whatever was left on that tray and eat it."

One day, while trying to find the source of a foul odor that lingered near the hospital, the women discovered a graveyard behind the building. It was a real oddity in Japan, where the dead are almost always cremated. In this case, villagers had put the corpses in shallow graves without coffins. The cemetery was supposedly off limits, but the women continued to explore and found a small shrine. It was apparent that visitors occasionally left gifts of food to honor the dead; subsequently, the women made sure the gifts didn't go to waste. On a regular basis they would creep through the fence at night—being careful to cover their tracks if there was fresh snow on the ground—and take whatever edible items had been left behind.

Snow still covered the ground when the women went to bed on the night of March 9, 1945. They fell asleep to the sound of fierce winds howling through the trees, but were awakened before dawn by the mournful wail of air raid sirens. To the northeast they could see the glow of fires stretching clear across the horizon. Tokyo was ablaze. The center of the city was only twenty-three miles from Totsuka, and some of the overcrowded neighborhoods were within fifteen miles, easily close enough for the women to see the results of Mission 40, one of the largest B-29 raids of World War II. A total of 279 Superfortresses hit Tokyo with incendiary bombs during the early morning hours of March 10. Multiple blazes, fanned by unusually strong winds, merged into massive, tornado-like firestorms that tore through neighborhoods crammed with flimsy wooden structures. A fourth of the city was destroyed and approximately eighty-four thousand people were killed. From the relative safety of Totsuka, Alice Bowman was enthralled by the sight of the burning city. "Flames were caught in the swirling winds and danced upward, turning into fireballs feverishly feeding upon themselves," she later wrote. "Explosions tortured the air and the shocking scene took on the spectacle of a volcano in violent eruption."

Throughout the spring, the captives were able to glean enough information from stray copies of the *Nippon Times* to realize that the end of the war was nigh. The food shortage continued, but one day the women were thrilled by the sight of several single-engine fighters with white stars on their "turned-up wings." The planes happened to be F4U Corsairs from American aircraft carriers, and soon they were appearing with regularity. On one occasion, the prisoners saw a fight in which Corsairs shot down Japanese planes.

When a representative of the Red Cross visited Totsuka for the first time in July, the women were stunned to learn that word of their shipment to Japan had never been forwarded to Australia. Somehow, they had been "misplaced." The visit by the Red Cross boosted their morale, yet the bombing raids continued, and the women constantly worried about the safety of other POW camps, several of which were much closer to the targeted areas.

In early August, the women listened with skepticism to stories about a "big bomb" that had supposedly killed seventy thousand people and destroyed the city of Hiroshima. Several days later they heard rumors about another huge bomb which had devastated Nagasaki. Still they weren't convinced, but a few days later they noticed a crowd of Japanese gathered in front of the camp administrator's house. Loudspeakers were attached to a radio, and many of the villagers "prostrated themselves" on the floor while listening to Emperor Hirohito, whose voice had never before been heard over the airwaves. It took the women only a short time to realize what was happening: Japan had capitulated. The war was over.

Later, having survived three years of misery, Lorna Whyte spoke for all of them when she made a vow to never feel hungry or cold again.

THE WAR'S END FOUND THE LARK FORCE OFFICERS SAFE AT THE Nishi-Ashibetsu camp in the coal mining region of Hokkaido. In addition to the Australians, the camp population included three British and fifty-two American officers, most of whom worked in a nearby mine. The news about the surrender did not reach their remote location until August 18, and they continued to labor in the mine for a few extra days. Shortly thereafter, food and medical supplies began to appear in great quantities, much of it dropped by low-flying B-29s. The containers were rigged with parachutes, but sometimes the 'chutes failed and the contents came crashing down with potentially deadly force.

After each drop, hordes of Japanese and Korean civilians descended from the hills and pilfered the supplies. Justifiably frustrated, the ex-POWs played tricks on them. On one occasion, when a Japanese man scavenged a tube of shaving cream, an Australian officer told him it was *joto meshi*— good food. The hungry civilian squeezed a large amount directly into his mouth, then rapidly departed, his face looking contorted and pale.

Although technically liberated, the ex-POWs had to wait at Ashibetsu while arrangements for transportation were sorted out. Delayed by nearly a month, they grew more annoyed with each passing day. Finally a convoy of trucks drove into camp on the morning of September 12. Out hopped an officer of the 1st Australian Prisoner of War Contact and Enquiry Unit. After introducing himself, Captain Francis J. Fenwick tried to field dozens of questions about current events in Melbourne and Sydney. When he finished, an American army doctor announced that it was his happy duty to start the ex-captives on their journey home. "Well . . . ," he said with a smile, "if you haven't anything else to do, let's go."

Transported to the Chitose airport, the officers slept that night on mattresses with pillows and sheets in a barrack formerly used by Imperial Navy flight students. The next day, several twin-engine transports flew the ex-prisoners to Atsugi airfield, about twelve miles west of Yokohama. After another overnight stay, the officers were flown to Clark Field in the Philippines via Okinawa. Some had to wait as long as two weeks at Manila for an RAAF flight to Australia, but by the end of September all sixty officers from Lark Force were home.

By then, most of the women from Totsuka were also home. The exceptions were two nurses: Eileen Callaghan had been placed aboard a hospital ship in Tokyo Bay because of tuberculosis, and Marjorie Anderson fell ill with malaria and was hospitalized at Okinawa. The others reached Darwin on September 12, then flew to Sydney the next day in an LB-30, the cargo variant of the B-24 Liberator heavy bomber.

Unaware that they were among the first captives to return to Australia, the women were overwhelmed by a tumultuous welcome at Mascot Airport. Emerging from the airplane, they had to shield their eyes from dozens of popping flashbulbs. Throngs of cheering spectators pressed forward, many of them elegantly dressed, which made the women suddenly felt dowdy in their ill-fitting uniforms.

No one cared how they looked. One of the happiest people there was Hilda Keary, the matron of army nurses. Back in 1941 she had scolded Kay Parker and the other AANS sisters at Rabaul for their "uniform revolt"; later she deeply regretted her behavior. Lorna Whyte Johnson recalled, "When we got back to Sydney after four years, she was at the airport with tears streaming down her face. She said that all through the war, she couldn't believe that she could have done such a terrible thing—telling us to put our stockings back on—and here we were, prisoners of war. This dear soul was standing there, just overwhelmed to see that we'd all returned."

LIKE MANY PEOPLE IN AUSTRALIA, THE REPATRIATED WOMEN WERE EAGER FOR news about the men who had been aboard the *Montevideo Maru*. Nothing had been heard for more than three years. Even after the officers returned in late September, the whereabouts of the ship's 1,050-plus prisoners remained a mystery.

At Rabaul, a formal surrender ceremony had been conducted aboard the British aircraft carrier HMS *Glory* on September 6, fully three weeks after the capitulation of Japan. Since then, the AIF had been holding thousands of Japanese in several makeshift camps pending investigations into war crimes. No one in Australia was aware yet that four civilians from Rabaul—Gordon Thomas, Al Creswick, George McKechnie, and Jim Ellis—had been found alive on New Britain. They were with dozens of Catholic internees who had been moved to the Ramale Valley after Vunapope was destroyed by bombing in 1944. At least eight other civilians, including Bob Evenson and Bill Korn, were never seen again.

Thomas was aware of the *Montevideo Maru*'s sinking, but his limited information did not reach Australia immediately. In fact, the ship's loss was not announced publicly until early October. Credit for the investigation and subsequent reporting goes mainly to Major Harold S. Williams of the Recovered Personnel Division. A former businessman, he spoke and read Japanese fluently and was sent to investigate the case of the missing POWs. Arriving in Japan on September 27, he visited the Prisoner of War Information Bureau in Tokyo the next day and pressed them for information. The bureau insisted that nothing was available, but the dauntless Williams began to uncover a paper trail that same day.

First, he discovered a maritime casualty notice dated July 20, 1942, in which the Imperial Navy reported the sinking of the *Montevideo Maru* to its owners, the Osaka Shosen Kaisha line. Another file revealed that the navy had forwarded details of the sinking, including "a complete nominal roll of the 848 PWs and 208 civilians who were on board and presumed lost," to the POW Information Bureau the following January. Williams also discovered that the Japanese had never sent the information to the International Red Cross; instead, the bureau had deliberately withheld the facts despite numerous inquiries by the IRC and other agencies. The Japanese tried to claim that they had "persistently informed all enquirers that all known information had been transmitted," but later the bureau's director, Lieutenant General Hiroshi Tamura, admitted that the details of the sinking were not forwarded. This omission was "due to an oversight," he stated, yet his confession trapped the bureau in a lie.

Williams reported his findings to the Recovered Personnel Division in Melbourne, and on October 5 the Minister for External Territories broke the news about the tragedy to the House of Representatives:

> Investigation in Japan . . . has confirmed the Government's fears that the majority of Australian prisoners of war and internees captured in Rabaul, and still missing, lost their lives at sea. It has now been ascertained that the Japanese Navy Department officially informed the Tokyo Prisoner of War Information Bureau on the 6th June, 1943, that the SS *Montevideo Maru* sailed from Rabaul on approximately the 22nd June, 1942, carrying 845 prisoners of war and 208 civilians, and that this ship, during its voyage, was torpedoed near Luzon with a total loss of the prisoners . . ."
>
> As there is a total of 1,053 persons involved, it is expected that some time will elapse before all names are available, but next of kin can be assured that names will be progressively released as they become available in Australia . . .
>
> These servicemen and civilians, who died in such a tragic manner, have undoubtedly given their lives in defense

of Australia just as surely as those who died face to face with the enemy. To their next of kin the Commonwealth Government extends its deepest sympathy.

With amazing efficiency, the army delivered telegrams to some bereaved families that same day. At first the messages were neatly typed, but soon the telegraph offices were overwhelmed. Most of the subsequent messages were scribbled by hand with nearly identical wording: "IT IS WITH DEEP REGRET THAT I HAVE TO INFORM YOU THAT _____ BECAME MISSING ON 1ST JULY 1942 AND IS FOR OFFICIAL PURPOSES PRESUMED TO BE DEAD AND DESIRE TO CONVEY TO YOU THE PROFOUND SYMPATHY OF THE MINISTER FOR THE ARMY."

The story hit the newspapers on October 6, after which a backlash of angry questions and finger-pointing quickly followed. Not surprisingly, the conduct of the Japanese POW Information Bureau led to accusations of cover-ups and conspiracies. Even worse, the general lack of information left many people asking questions that could never be answered.

The telegrams themselves, so bluntly worded, devastated the lives of literally thousands of wives, children, sweethearts, parents, and friends. And in most cases, that was all they received. There was no sense of closure, nothing to cling to except fleeting memories about the men who would never return.

In Skenes Creek, Florence Thurst had only a few keepsakes by which to remember James, her strong and quiet son. She had a tiny gold locket that contained two photos: one of Jim, the other of his younger brother Bruce. The latter had come home after fighting in the wretched jungles of the Markham Valley in New Guinea as a commando, but even his safe return did not salve Florence's broken heart. Before the war she had lost her husband in a bizarre accident, and now fate had taken her eldest son. To make matters worse, she never received so much as a penny of pension after he was declared dead. Jim had sent her a portion of his army pay every month, but never filled out the paperwork for an official allotment. Florence, who lived to be ninety, loathed Australia for the rest of her years.

Every family associated with the tragedy was deeply affected. Because no one knew exactly what had happened, the loved ones could only speculate. Inevitably they wondered about the last moments for the men trapped aboard the *Montevideo Maru*, and such dark thoughts are poisonous. To this day, family members are tormented by uncertainties and unanswerable questions. The emotional scars will remain as long as there are descendants still alive to mourn the victims.

Thankfully, the government did take permanent steps to honor the men from Lark Force who gave their lives. In 1945, the Army Graves Service dedicated an extensive war memorial at Bita Paka. Known today as the Rabaul Memorial, the cemetery features a broad expanse of lawn bordered by flowering shrubs, with headstones for the Allied servicemen buried there. A huge bronze plaque lists those whose bodies were never recovered, including the men aboard the *Montevideo Maru* and others who simply vanished in the jungles of New Britain.

Across Australia, certain individuals from Lark Force are perpetually remembered by their communities. In particular, a number of memorials have been erected over the years in Brunswick and Melbourne for the Salvation Army bandsmen. Arthur Gullidge, whose compositions are still played, is honored by the Australian military through the Gullidge Award, presented annually to the top apprentice at the Defence Force School of Music.

Perhaps the most poignant event to honor the lost lives occurred at the Australian War Memorial in Canberra on July 1, 2002. Standing alongside the Roll of Honor, where the names of more than one hundred thousand war dead appear on a series of bronze panels, historian Ian Hodges described the role of Lark Force and the events that led to the tragic sinking. His presentation concluded with the words "As we stand here today on the sixtieth anniversary of the loss of the *Montevideo Maru* and look at the names of those who perished on that ship—and not forgetting that the civilians who died are not listed here—we should remember that sixty years ago today Australia experienced its worst maritime disaster. Almost twice as many Australians lost their lives in one night as did in the ten years of the Vietnam War. They, and the families and friends who endured years of not knowing their fate, deserve to be remembered."

IT IS VITAL TO RECOGNIZE ALL OF THE MEN AND WOMEN OF LARK FORCE, if for no better reason than to learn from the mistakes that were made at several levels, and to avoid repeating such tragic circumstances in the future.

Confident that they would be relieved within a year, that "great band of boys" arrived on New Britain in 1941 with great enthusiasm. Instead, they were abandoned by their own government. And within six months of the fall of Rabaul, 75 percent of the garrison was dead. Almost two hundred died at the hands of the Japanese—either through outright murder or by callous treatment as POWs—while dozens of others died by agonizing degrees in the merciless wasteland of the jungle. But those unfortunate statistics pale in comparison to the loss of more than a thousand souls aboard the *Montevideo Maru*. The sinking continues to rank as the worst maritime disaster in Australian history, and the fact that the ship was disemboweled by an American torpedo is the cruelest twist of all.

When the *Montevideo Maru* slid beneath the waves in the middle of the night, the heart and soul of Lark Force went with it. Thus ended one of the most tragic events of the Pacific war—and one of Australia's darkest hours.

EPILOGUE

Thanks to the Roll of Honor and other memorials, the men who died aboard the *Montevideo Maru* will not soon be forgotten—but neither can they rest in peace. Too many controversies and suggestions of conspiracy surround the disaster. Some have been answered, but others refuse to go away. Each time a new question is raised, the families of the dead must endure another round of heartache and uncertainty.

The controversies are divided into three main categories. First, some people believe the *Montevideo Maru* never existed. The story of its sinking, they say, was manufactured by the Japanese in order to conceal the massacre of the missing POWs and internees. Second, there are suggestions that a few prisoners actually survived the sinking and were taken to Japan, where they later died. Lastly, the various documents related to the sinking contain some discrepancies.

As to the first theory, there is no solid evidence to support the speculation that more than a thousand POWs and internees were massacred or died somewhere other than aboard the *Montevideo Maru*. Certainly the Japanese committed horrendous atrocities, yet it is highly unlikely that they would eliminate so many individuals—all potential laborers—so early in the war. Captives represented a cheap work force and were transported by the shipload to distant shores. In his extensively researched book, *Death on the Hellships*, author Gregory Michno identified 134 different vessels which made a total of 156 voyages with an aggregate of more than 126,000 POWs. Not all of them made it to their intended destination. The *Montevideo Maru* was the first of at least fifteen such vessels sunk inadvertently by the Allies. The most tragic episode occurred in 1944, when the *Junyo Maru* was torpedoed with the loss of 6,520 POWs. Throughout the Pacific war, more than 21,000 prisoners lost their lives aboard the hellships.

Secondly, the *Montevideo Maru* was real—of that there is no doubt. The ship was built for the Osaka Shosen Kaisha line and sailed between Asia and South American cities in the late 1920s and 1930s, a time when thousands of agricultural workers left Japan because of a recession. Prewar photographs, brochures, and sailing schedules show ample confirmation of the handsome ship's existence.

Also, the evidence that the *Sturgeon* sank the *Montevideo Maru* is overwhelming. The official report by the Imperial Navy states that the ship was attacked at latitude 18.40N, longitude 119.31E, and the position recorded in the *Sturgeon's* war diary is 18.37N, 119.29E, a difference of only three miles. Prior to their fateful encounter, the two vessels had crossed thousands of miles of ocean over a combined total of thirty-three days, and they were more than two miles apart at the time of the torpedo attack. Not only does this account for most of the variation in latitude and longitude, it also reveals that the plotting accuracy by both crews was remarkable.

Furthermore, the *Sturgeon's* crew recorded the time of the attack as 0229 local on July 1, 1942, while the crew of the *Montevideo Maru* logged the event at 0326. The latter followed Japanese Standard Time, which was one hour ahead of local time, meaning the ships' clocks were actually within three minutes of each other.

Regarding the known discrepancies, one of the most significant is that the *Sturgeon's* crew heard a single explosion, while the Imperial Navy report claimed that two torpedoes hit the ship's starboard side. The accumulated evidence suggests strongly that the submariners were correct. During several previous attacks, Lieutenant Commander Wright and his crew noted that the torpedoes which missed the target would eventually explode, presumably because the warheads crushed under intense pressure as they sank into the depths. On July 1, three distinct explosions were heard several minutes after the torpedoes were fired at the *Montevideo Maru*, accounting for three misses. Also, in contrast to the *Sturgeon's* detailed logbook, the Japanese report was based on information pieced together from different survivors. Undoubtedly there were variations among the eyewitness statements. The crew probably heard two detonations, but the second can be attributed to the explosion of the fuel-oil tank. Half empty after eight days at sea, the compartment and its contents would have been highly volatile.

Two specific references to the ruptured tank appear in Japanese accounts. First, the Imperial Navy report stated that the ship's engine room was flooded by fuel oil, forcing the crew to shut down the engines. The second reference came to light decades after the sinking, when a Japanese merchant sailor revealed information about the *Montevideo Maru's* final minutes: "When I got up on deck," stated seaman Yoshiaki Yamaji, "the ship was leaning to starboard. People were jumping into the water. Thick oil was spreading across the sea. There were loud noises . . . metal wrenching, furniture crashing, people screaming. I have not been able to forget the death cries."

Yamaji was eighty-one years old when interviewed in 2003 for an investigative report by Australian television. If indeed a former crewmember, he is the only survivor to speak publicly about the disaster since the war.

Interestingly, while some of Yamaji's recollections seem authentic, others seem less credible. For starters, the basis for his appearance on television was his allegation that he observed many Australian POWs in the water that night. He claimed they were holding onto firewood, which by itself is logical: there would have been firewood stacked on the main deck for heating the cook-pots. Yamaji also claimed that he was "told by an official of the company" that the POWs had been picked up by a Japanese warship and were taken to the city of Kobe.

The account might have seemed plausible had Yamaji stopped there; however, he went on to reminisce about the POWs in a manner that was both maudlin and highly questionable. "They were singing songs," he said. "I was particularly impressed when they began singing *Auld Lang Syne* as a tribute to their dead colleagues. Watching that, I learned that Australians have big hearts."

In the minds of military experts, Yamaji damaged his credibility with that particular description, which sounds not only fanciful and sentimental but contradicts his earlier statement. It also defies logic. Men who go into the water from a ship with a ruptured fuel tank find themselves struggling in thick, slimy oil. No matter how calm the surface of the South China Sea might have been on that particular night, the water was churned by men trying to get away from the ship, lest it pull them under. Therefore, whether they were Australian or Japanese, the men in the water would have been choking and retching on caustic bunker fuel, not singing.

Of even greater significance, there is no evidence to corroborate Yamaji's claim that POWs were rescued and taken to Japan. Warships that were designated as escorts, unless attached to the Combined Fleet or particular Battle Forces, were assigned to specific defense zones. They would not have ventured outside their zone without good reason, the delivery of POW survivors to Japan not being one of them. Thus, any "rescued" POWs would have been delivered only as far as the nearest suitable base, then transferred to another ship for transportation to Japan. This would have required documentation between the various military and government bureaus involved, both at the transshipment point and eventually in Japan. Furthermore, numerous military and civilian eyewitnesses would have seen the POWs.

In the estimation of maritime expert Peter Cundall, the suggestion that the POWs were saved by a warship smacks of face-saving on Yamaji's part. "It implies to me that he was aware the POWs had been left behind, and perhaps was trying to assuage guilt by suggesting they might have been rescued," Cundall says. "The creation of special camps would have been necessary, again generating records and reports. Even allowing for the fact that many records were destroyed at war's end and others lost through bombing and maladministration, it seems inconceivable that no record exists of any survivors, unless you discard the conspiracy theories and return to the notion that there were no POW survivors."

Even if some Australians did manage to escape from the holds of the *Montevideo Maru* before it sank—a remote possibility at best—they were seventy miles from the nearest land. They had no lifeboat, and their physical condition was poor. All of the available evidence suggests that the POWs drowned that night, a position accepted officially by the Australian government.

Another debated issue concerns the actions of various Japanese agencies. According to the records discovered after the war by Major Williams, the Imperial Navy notified the Osaka Shosen Kaisha line of the sinking on July 20, 1942, but did not forward the particulars to the Prisoner of War Information Bureau for nearly six months. Some people believe the long delay is evidence of a cover-up, but the circumstances can be easily explained. Less than a month prior to the sinking of the *Montevideo Maru*, the Japanese lost four aircraft carriers and hundreds of veteran aviators at Midway, a blow from which the Imperial Navy never recovered. Furthermore, the heavy losses continued: in the merchant fleet alone more than 240 vessels were sunk by the end of 1942. No wonder the sinking of one particular ship went unreported for months.

The bigger question is why the POW Information Bureau failed to notify the International Red Cross about the tragedy. Once again, there are logical explanations, the principal reason being bureaucratic ineptitude. Simply put, the agency was notoriously inefficient. The Japanese were utterly unprepared for the tens of thousands of Allied prisoners captured during the first months of the Pacific war. One infamous result was the death march forced upon 72,000 American and Filipino captives from Bataan, mainly because the Japanese lacked motor transportation to move them almost a hundred miles to the nearest suitable prison. The POWs had to walk the first sixty miles to a railhead as well as the last ten miles to the prison, the former Camp O'Donnell. En route, approximately seven hundred Americans and five thousand Filipinos died, and hundreds more succumbed later to starvation and disease inside the camp.

As for the *Montevideo Maru*, the POW Information Bureau repeatedly ignored inquiries from the International Red Cross regarding the prisoners. After the war, Lieutenant General Tamura explained that his personnel were forced to spend all their time notifying the IRC and other agencies about "living war prisoners," the implication being that information regarding dead POWs was not forwarded as a matter of policy. Perhaps the bureau wanted to avoid the embarrassment of having to publicly acknowledge the loss of the *Montevideo Maru*. Another distinct possibility is that personnel within the agency were involved in the lucrative black market, selling rice and other supplies earmarked for POWs. The theft of supplies was rampant, and it's entirely conceivable that members of the bureau received kickbacks in exchange for falsely keeping 1,050-plus deceased prisoners on the books for three additional years.

In late 1945, after twice failing to meet the conditions set by Major Williams for a formal apology, Lieutenant General Tamura signed a memorandum that stated: "Information of the loss of 1,053 Prisoners of War and Civilian Internees has not been forwarded to the Australian Authorities. This is a sheer dereliction on the part of this Bureau to have failed to advise the Australian Government on the subject in question. This Bureau sincerely expresses its deep regret and hereby tenders profound apology."

If Tamura thought the apology would get him off the hook with the Australians, he was correct—but he did not go unpunished. The United States separately investigated his lack of cooperation with the Red Cross and sentenced him to eight years of hard labor.

IN THE FINAL ANALYSIS, TWO POINTS SEEM INARGUABLE: THE MONTEVIDEO MARU was torpedoed, and there were Australian prisoners aboard at the time. Both points, established through a variety of sources, are backed by multiple eyewitness accounts.

Ultimately, readers must decide for themselves what they believe regarding the disaster and the alleged conspiracies. Wherever the truth lies, the men who were lost must be allowed to rest in peace. Soon enough, their entire generation will exist only in memory.

NOTES

The following pages contain abbreviated citations to the various quotations and other references found in this book. A complete bibliography is provided separately. Most of the official documents, including reports issued by the Allied Translator and Interpreter Section (ATIS) and some Japanese records, were duplicated at the Australian War Memorial (AWM) in Canberra. Other important references, private diaries, and unpublished manuscripts were obtained from the Lark Force Association. Documents related to the USS *Sturgeon* were found at the U.S. National Archives and Records Administration, College Park, Maryland. The Japanese Monographs were copied at the Nimitz Library, U.S. Naval Academy, Annapolis, Maryland. The Albert F. Simpson Historical Research Center, Maxwell Air Force Base, Montgomery, Alabama, provided the U.S. Army Air Force materials. Microfilm of the 1942 *Osaka Mainichi Daily News* was loaned by the Georgia State University, Atlanta, Georgia. Published books and articles, copies of military bulletins, and other named sources cited are in the author's collection.

Chapter 1—Diggers

Background of Sgt. Gullidge and enlistment of Salvation Army bandsmen: Cox, pp. 1–14.

Description of 2/22nd Battalion and Trawool camp: C. Johnson, pp. 2–6.

Lt. Cdr. Carr's background: anonymous-by-request Lark Force member, correspondence with author; C. Johnson, p. 8.

"We were British": Harris, correspondence with author.

Background of Thurst family: Bruce Thurst, author's interview.

Battalion march from Trawool to Bonegilla: C. Johnson, p. 12–17; Cox., pp. 23–24.

"I'm chasing the bugle": quoted in C. Johnson, p. 22.

"The Salvationists who joined": quoted in Cox, p. 27.

"bivvy": from a letter by Gullidge, quoted in Cox, p. 37.

"wadies": ibid., p. 39.

AIF enlistment statistics: Hasluck, p. 613.

Background of Pvt. Kollmorgen: author's interview.

" 'pannikins' of tea": Melbourne Herald, February 14, 1941.

Details of Melbourne parade, including "Slope arms!": Melbourne Age, February 14, 1941.

"for God and the King": quoted in Cox, p. 43.

Chapter 2—Evil Spirits

Details of the caldera-forming eruption: Miller, author's interview.

Early exploration of New Britain: R. W. Johnson, p. 9; Stone, p. 2.

"a wretched, barbarous race in the extreme": Campbell, pp. 8–9.

Topography of Crater Peninsula: R. W. Johnson, p. 2.

Background of R. K. P. Moore and acquisition of German plantations: "Lost Lives."

Descriptions of pre-war Rabaul: Stone, pp. 9–11.

"paddled by natives": Pearson diary, p. 2.

"euphorically comfortable": R. W. Johnson, p. 14.

Details of 1937 eruption: R. W. Johnson, pp. 25–45; Stone, pp. 12–18.

Medical situation at Rabaul: AWM 54 (608/5/3).

"every man took his dose": Bloomfield, p. 3.

Army nurses and the "uniform revolt": L. Johnson, author's interview.

"*a train going over a big overhead bridge*": quoted in R. W. Johnson, p. 139.

"*To stand was to rock like a drunken man*": Pearson, p. 8.

Chapter 3—Hostages to Fortune

"*a slender chain of forward observation posts*": Wigmore, p. 394.

"*by ship, motor boat, canoe*": Feldt, p. 6.

Placement of coastal guns, and "*expert and most urgent advice*": AWM 113 (MH 1/121, Part 1).

Description of antiaircraft battery and training: Selby, pp. 7–8; Bloomfield, p. 6.

"*The nurses were not supposed to go out with the troops*": L. Johnson, author's interview.

Details of the "Bung," including "*sitting placidly by*": Pearson, p. 8.

Games and gambling, including "*which of two flies*": Pocket Guide to Australia, p. 29; Bloomfield, p. 3.

"*They were all outstanding young men*": L. Johnson, author's interview.

Personality of Pvt. Webster: Harry, "New Britain, 1941/42," p. 8.

"*could thump out a honky tonk*": Harry, correspondence with author.

Profile of Pvt. Harry: Harry, author's interview.

Popularity of battalion band: Cox, pp. 54–56.

Personalities of Turner and May, including "*only dire threats of punishment*": Selby, pp. 13–14.

Carr's difficulties, and profile of Scanlan: Harry, interview and correspondence with author.

Dispersion of 2/22nd companies: AWM 54 (607/8/2).

Lend-Lease agreement and details of harbor defenses: AWM 68 (3DRL 8052/108)

"*a very capable fellow*": Harry, author's interview.

"*the stink of bad eggs*": Figgis, author's interview.

"*collected the spray*": Hasluck, p. 543n.

"*madness had overtaken Japan*": ibid., p. 557.

"*was full of excited speculation*": Selby, p. 10.

Description of Frisbee Ridge: Bloomfield, p. 8.

"*In making this recommendation*": Cable 154, December 15, 1941.

"*Under the foregoing circumstances*": MP729/6 (16/401/493)

.Arrival of 24 Squadron, including *"no facilities existed"*: AWM 54 (81/4/194).

"There was a hushed atmosphere": H. Johnson, extracts from *Una Voce*, March 2002.

Internment of Japanese men: Aplin, p. 26.

Plans and details of Refuge Gully: Reeson, p. 144.

Propaganda, rumors, and news: Selby, pp. 16–17.

Scanlan's proclamations: Bloomfield, p. 15.

"You will fight on the beaches": quoted by Dawson, AWM 54 (607/9/3).

Chapter 4—Prelude to an Invasion

Imperial General Headquarters orders and war plans, including *"occupy Rabaul"*: Monograph No. 24, pp. 8–9; Monograph No. 45 pp. 39–46.

Organization of South Seas Detachment: AWM 54 (608/5/4).

Details of staff meeting at Truk and Imperial HQ objectives, including *"coordinately attack Rabaul"*: AWM 54 (423/4/162).

Japanese pre-invasion intelligence, landing site options: AWM 54 (608/5/4).

"It seemed impossible to believe": Selby, p. 15.

Details of early air attacks: AWM 54 (81/4/194).

Herstein situation, including *"continued to pester Canberra"*: Aplin, p. 26.

Japanese training methods and doctrine, including *"bodies and minds tempered hard as steel"*: Kawamoto.

"the heat began to increase": Miyake, *Osaka Mainichi*, February 10, 1942, p.3.

"very cramped and uncomfortable": AWM 3DRL/4005.

Description of *tsubo* system: Cundall, correspondence with author.

"On the day we crossed the Equator": Miyake.

"When we fight, we win": *Intelligence Bulletin*, Vol. II, No. 9, pp. 44–46.

"felt like a hunter": Fuchida, p. 54.

"The first indication" Bloomfield, p. 15.

Details of Wirraway combat: Gillison, p. 355.

"We sat at our guns": Bloomfield, p. 15.

"It was a bomber-fighter type": *Smith's Weekly*, May 9, 1942, p. 1.

Nakajima crew information: Wenger, correspondence with author.

Lerew's defiance, and *"We who are about to die"*: The Latin translation appears as "NOS MORITURI TE SALUTAMUS" in numerous published accounts, including the official RAAF history (Gillison, p. 358). However, a photograph of the actual message in the AWM collection reveals the wording as originally deciphered: "MORITURI VOS SALUTAMUS."

Chapter 5—Chaos

Trauma of Philip Coote: AWM 113 (MH 1/121, Part 1).

"a number of gray logs": Minty, p. 2.

"Keep swimming": ibid., p. 4.

Japanese attack on Kavieng and the *Induna Star*: Aplin, pp. 30–31.

"to be massacred": quoted by Carr, AWM 54 (607/8/2).

"The CO told me": AWM 54 (607/9/3).

"I hope you will have time to use it": quoted in Aplin, p. 38.

"as a last resource": AWM 54 (607/8/2).

Sgt. Gullidge hospitalized: Cox, p. 92.

"stood and watched helplessly": Bloomfield, p. 17.

"Rabaul took on the appearance": Bowman, p. 34.

Observing the Japanese fleet, Figgis's ship count: AWM 54 (607/7/1).

"The wires were pulled sharply": Selby, p. 36.

Disposition of rifle companies: AWM 54 (607/8/2).

"shouting instructions to the driver": Bloomfield, p. 18.

"fight with the army as guerillas" and Scanlan's response: AWM 54 (81/4/194).

"Send flying-boats": quoted in Gillison, p. 360.

Dialog between Scanlan and Dawson regarding food caches: AWM 54(607/9/3).

"a slaughter house": Collins, undated manuscript, p. 1.

"The battered bodies": Bowman, p. 26.

Conditions in Refuge Gully: Reeson, p. 139.

"When the Yanks get here": ibid., p. 121.

Arrival of the *Matafele*, and *"consent was not forthcoming"*: Aplin, p. 26.

"The action of certain civilians": AWM 54 (81/4/194).

Details of RAAF evacuation: ibid.; Stone, p. 78; C. Johnson, pp. 72–73.

Chapter 6—Vigorous Youth from Shikoku

Approach of invasion fleet, including *"As we gradually drew closer"*: Australia-Japan Research Project (hereafter, AJRP).

Pre-invasion environmental conditions: AJRP; AWM 54 (423/4/1162) and AWM 54 (423/4/158).

"good landmark for reckoning directions in the darkness": AWM 54 (608/5/4).

"with a weird beauty": AJRP.

General Horii's landing instructions: ibid.

2nd Company's search for coastal batteries: ibid.

Japanese landing at Vulcan, including *"We allowed most of them"*: Wigmore, p. 403.

Details of Cpl. Hamill's squad, including *"I didn't think we'd see them again"*: Pearson diary.

"I told them about the Jap task force": AWM 54 (607/9/3).

"An enemy bugler started to blow a call": Bloomfield, p. 20.

"a crescendo of wild, savage yells": Selby, p. 40.

2nd Battalion (IJA) at Nordup: AJRP.

A Company (AIF) at Vulcan: Wigmore, pp. 403–04.

Dawson's experience, including *"On turning the last curve"*: AWM 54 (608/5/4).

"doing a lot of yelling": quoted in C. Johnson, p. 61.

"the Japs very close": AWM 54(607/8/28).

"bursting round the truck": ibid.

"retreat to special anchorage positions" and *"to fire signal shots irresponsibly"*: AJRP.

"courageously continuing to land": ibid.

Chapter 7—Every Man for Himself

Scanlan's change of HQ: Wigmore, p. 406; Harry, "New Britain 1941/42," p. 6.

Components of AWA-3B radio: Feldt, p. 10.

"the deteriorating situation": Harry, "New Britain 1941/42," p. 6.

"To CDH, Port Moresby" and decoded message: Appel, in AWM 54 (607/8/28).

"hopelessly bogged": Harry, "New Britain 1941/42," p. 7.

"aerial protection for the ground units": AJRP.

"I was flat in the side cut": quoted by Harry, "New Britain 1941/42," p. 7.

Japanese rations (footnote): *Intelligence Bulletin Vol.I, No.1, Section III*, p. 78.

"He said we were overwhelmed": Pearson, AWM 60 (259).

"Vehicles could not travel on the roads": AWM 54 (607/7/1).

Death of Pvt. Ascott, etc.: Parsons, AWM 60 (259).

"about three pannikins of tea": Pearson diary.

Situation at Three Ways: Bloomfield, p. 22.

"wild and inaccurate" and *"Over the ridge"*: Selby, p. 41.

Communications between Appel, McInnes, and Mollard at Three Ways: AWM 54 (607/8/28).

"Owing to the difficult country": AWM 54 (607/8/2).

"The mountain air filled with smoke": AWM 54 (423/4/158).

"At intervals in the grass": ibid.

"McInnes gave the order": Selby, p. 42.

"completely helpless": Bloomfield, p. 22.

"I wondered": Selby, p. 42.

"Carr rushed off": correspondence with author, name withheld by request.

"At this stage": AWM 54(607/8/2).

"useless to prolong the action" and *"every man for himself"*: Wigmore, p. 408.

"for transmission to all companies": AWM 54 (607/8/2).

"Austin Creed rode up": Kolmorgen, author's interview.

"In view of doubt": AWM 54 (607/8/2).

"known to be attempting": ibid.

"The colonel's orders": Selby, p. 43.

"Were it not for the seriousness": Bloomfield, pp. 22–23.

Scanlan's invitation to Harry, including *"somewhat premature"*: Harry, "New Britain 1941/42," p. 7.

"We found there were only two": L. Johnson, author interview.

"The Japanese jumped off": ibid.

Intimidation of Lt. May: C. Johnson, pp. 130–131.

"We had little knowledge": Pacific Islands Year Book, 1950, p. 31.

Surrender of civilians at Refuge Gully: ibid.

Japanese proclamation: quoted in Reeson, p. 154; full text in Stone, p. 485.

"They were attacked from all quarters": AWM 54 (607/9/5).

"using all available cover": Wigmore, p. 410.

"*The Japs were firing*": AWM 54 (607/9/5).

"*some retreating Australians*": quoted in Stone, p. 66.

"*places on the road*": quoted in Wigmore, p. 411.

Catalog of captured weapons and equipment: AWM 54 (423/4/158).

Loss of *Kaga* pilot: Hata, et al, p. 376.

"*The Imperial Army*": AJRP.

Lyrics of *Nankai Dayori*: AWM 3DRL/4005.

Chapter 8—You Will Only Die

"*Great quantities of Japanese shipping*": Harry, "New Britain 1941/42," p. 8.

Night journey to Malabunga: AWM 54 (607/7/1); Harry, "New Britain 1941/42," p. 8.

"*a concerned group of missionaries*": ibid., p. 9.

"*a desert*" and "*At its best*": Feldt, p. 36.

"*The only plan*": Harry, p. 10.

Text of Horii's leaflet: AWM 54(607/8/2).

"*Travers called us together*": AWM 60 (259).

"*Our first thought*": AWM 60 (259).

South Seas Detachment's pursuit of Australians: AWM 54 (608/5/4).

"*The position appeared*": AWM 60 (259).

"*The butai could not advance*": AWM 54 (423/4/158).

"*Practically every man*" and details of malaria outbreak among the Japanese: AWM 54 (608/5/4).

"*an inspiring and energetic leader*": Wigmore, p. 657.

"*nowhere to be seen*"; "*As I lay awake*"; and other details of the antiaircraft gunners' trek: Bloomfield, pp. 26–30.

"*We discussed plans*": Selby, p. 47.

"*He gravely doubted*": ibid., p. 48.

"*My first view of it*": Pearson diary, p. 13.

"*hanging on like grim death*" and details of river crossing: Selby, p. 50.

"*Each day we felt ourselves growing weaker*": ibid., pp. 51–52.

"*Wherever we tried*": ibid., p. 53.

"*It was our first real meal*": ibid., p. 56.

Bloomfield's white flag discovery: Bloomfield, pp. 32–33.

"*It seemed unfair*": Selby, p. 58.

"*The plantation was plainly visible*": ibid., p. 64.

Chapter 9—Tol

Details of Pvt. Kennedy's capture: Wigmore, p. 406n.

"in the forests": AWM 54 (608/5/4).

Details of capture near Reid River: Lyons.

Captured officer's interrogation and execution: Stone, p. 90. The quoted account did not identify the officer by name, but Garrard is the most likely candidate based on the date of his death. All of the other officers captured at Tol were spared, at least initially.

Details of bayonet training: *Intelligence Bulletin Vol. II, No. 5, Section I*, pp. 56–57.

"An agonized scream": Lyons, p. 6.

"He put away his sword" and details of Pvt. Collins' escape: Lyons, p. 4; Wigmore, pp. 666–667.

"When my turn came": Lyons, p. 5.

"an evil and terrible omen": Selby, p. 67.

"An excited native": ibid.

Conversation between orderlies, including *"You might be sorry"*: Cook, p. 7.

"The bastards are here!" and other details of Cook's escape: Cook, pp. 7–8.

"waved the paper across the Aussie's face": ibid.

"not a trace of fear": Cook, quoted in Cox., p. 99.

Stabbing by bayonet: Cook, p. 9.

Text of Japanese messages posted at Waitavalo plantation: Selby, p. 75.

"One can imagine my joy": Cook, p. 11.

"sheer hard logic": Selby, p. 85.

"There was the Commandant": ibid., pp. 83–84.

Chapter 10—Escape: *The Lakatoi*

"I knew he was the appropriate man": Feldt, pp. 38–39.

Disagreements between McCarthy and Cameron: Wigmore, p. 659.

"There was no lack of courage": Feldt, p. 41.

Messages from Japanese officer Ogama: AWM 54 (607/8/2).

"The Japanese had covered the distance": Hutchinson-Smith manuscript, p. 2.

"[Joseph] Rokker was ingratiating": ibid., pp. 4–5.

"We weren't racing down the coast": Figgis, author's interview.

"It wasn't very nice": ibid.

"We lifted out several sheets of iron": Lyons, p. 5.

"as Irish as Paddy's pig": Feldt, p. 7.

"on all matters edible": Harry, "New Britain 1941/42," p. 13.

Translation of native words: Murphy, *The Book of Pidgin English*.

Dialogue between Carr and Dwyer: quoted by Harry, "New Britain 1941/42," p. 13.

"Mollard stressed": ibid., p. 14.

Encounter with native gang at Milim village: ibid., p. 16.

Harry's overland trek, including direct quotes: ibid., pp. 17–19.

Appel party's evacuation to Pondo, and list of men's ailments: AWM 54 (607/8/2).

"a collection of contradictions": Feldt, p. 39.

"It would have been hard": ibid., p. 40.

"I worked all night and day": Baker, quoted in C. Johnson, p. 121.

"All the rest were sick": Feldt, p. 46.

Account of McInnes' party: Aplin, pp. 243–65.

Chapter 11—Escape: *The Laurabada*

Dawson's early struggles: AWM 54 (607/9/3).

"a wonderfully eloquent gift": Selby, p. 111.

"Morale gradually deteriorated": AWM 54 (608/5/3).

"With one exception": ibid.

"From where I lay on the floor": Selby, pp. 150–51.

"There were some deaths": Palmer, AWM 54 (608/5/3).

"every stone and tree": Selby, p. 149.

Struggle of Hannah, Hart, and Taylor: Taylor diary, p. 14.

"had very kind faces" and details relating to Hart's broken leg: ibid., p. 15.

Hart's recovery (footnote), including *"spot on"*: Harry, correspondence with author.

"It was all a diversion": Harry, "New Britain 1941/42," p. 23.

"jerked them into line": ibid., p. 22.

"Send all men": Selby, p. 180.

"brittle sticks": Selby, p. 184.

"near to weeping": ibid., p 187.

"black torrents": ibid., p. 193.

"My last memory of New Britain": Bloomfield, p. 58

Figgis, Harry, and the "mystery tin": Figgis, author's interview.

Dawson's escape and trek on New Guinea: AWM 54 (607/9/3).
Death of Pvt. Dowse: Harry, correspondence with author.

Chapter 12—Outcry
"The Public Guardian": Smith's Weekly, May 16, 1942, p. 1.
Reunion of Perkins, Taylor, and Webster at Tol: Harry, correspondence
    with author.

Chapter 13—Inside the Fortress
"Japanese soldiers fanned out": Stone, p. 123.
"I was left to work on board the ship": AWM 3DRL/4005.
Construction of buildings and output of sawmills: United States Strategic
    Bombing Survey (Pacific), p. 15.
"On every vacant piece of land": Thomas, Pacific Islands Yearbook, 1950,
    p. 31.
"The days . . . were filled": ibid.
Arrival of Duranbah and experiences of POWs: Hutchinson-Smith,
    pp. 7–11.
Profiles of Japanese camp personnel: ibid., pp. 11–12.
Working parties, food, and cigarette racket: ibid., pp. 16–17.
"They work hard with little rest": AWM 55 (12/140).
"Beating, bashing, and bludgeoning": Hutchinson-Smith, p. 20.
"Matsui came out": ibid., p. 21.
"Sergeant Ozaki and others": AWM 55 (12/40).
"Colonel Scanlan was interrogated": ibid.
"We just ignored him": L. Johnson, author's interview.
"Drunken Japs": Bowman, p. 65.
"an appearance of sublime self-confidence": White, quoted in Stone, p. 259.
"Guide to Soldiers in the South Seas": copy by Hisaeda, AWM 3DRL/4005.
Showa swords and beheading: Cook, et al., pp. 40–43.
Torture and execution of Capt. Gray, including "in order to study":
    Bowman, p. 70.
"prisoners and coolies" and details of POW encampments: AWM 55
    (12/40).
Organization and names of brothels in Rabaul: AWM 54 (208/2/4).
"We had never dreamt": quoted in Park.

"*One morning after breakfast*": Bowman, p. 67.
"*The cathedral had already been desecrated*": ibid., p. 68.
Death of Pvt. French: Cox, p. 108.
Capt. Fraser and musicians, ibid., pp. 108–109.
"*The sake flowed freely*": Hutchinson-Smith, p. 36.
"*The Japanese never lost an opportunity*": quoted in Stone, p. 273.

Chapter 14—Cruel Fates
Details of first B-17 raid: Salaker, p. 145; Steinbinder diary.
"*3 enemy planes*": Hisaeda, AWM 3DRL/4005.
"*In March, giant planes appeared*": Bowman, p. 80.
Torture of female prisoners: Stone, p. 263.
"*little monkeys*": L. Johnson, author's interview.
Contents of POW letters home, and "*instead of a bomb*": Cox, pp. 111–112.
Attack on the *Komaki Maru*: GP-22-HI; Cundall, correspondence with author.
"*An enemy plane was shot down*": AWM 55 (12/140).
"*looked to be out of control*": Bowman, p. 81.
"*They must all be very happy*": quoted in *Intelligence Bulletin Vol. I, No. 6, Section II*, p. 19.
"*That night at muster*": Hutchinson-Smith, p. 19.
Details of *Tencho-setsu*: Osaka *Mainichi*, April 29, 1942, p. 1.
"*Still terribly meager*" and "*too busy to be bothered*": Hutchinson-Smith, p. 33.
Profile of Capt. Mizusaki: ibid.
"*making better progress than expected*": Japanese monograph No. 45.
"*A sleek Jap aircraft carrier*" and "*Day of the Armada*": Bowman, p. 82.
"*Japanese take Moresby*": ibid., p.83.
"*a battered and dirty replica*": ibid.
"*by radio telegraphy and fires*": B5563/2 (1911).
"*all sorts of silly reports*": statement of Capt. S. Arnoly, AIF, August 11, 1949.
Character traits of Alfred Harvey: Arnoly (see preceding note) described Harvey as "a bit queer." Also, C. O. Harry, in correspondence, referred to Harvey as an "odd bod."

"*dispose of them by shooting*" and details of Harvey family trial and
  execution: B5563 (CA 3055).
"*I remember hearing*": B5563/2 (2249).
Details of USS *Sturgeon's* fourth war patrol, including quotes by Lt. Cdr.
  Wright: SS187/A12-1, Serial 06, USS *Sturgeon* war diary.
"*slightly wounded and scorched*": Hutchinson-Smith, p. 19.
POW stockade conditions and health situation, including "*foul in the
  extreme*": ibid., p. 40.
"*There is no food left*": AWM 55 (12/140).
Fortifications and weapons: Naval Analysis Division, *United States Strategic
  Bombing Survey (Pacific)*, pp. 13–14.
"*for the transportation of supplies*" and statistics of Imperial Navy shipping:
  Japanese Monograph No. 24, p. 9.
"*so much empty camp chatter*" and details of prisoner exodus: Hutchinson-
  Smith, p. 42.
Specifications of *Montevideo Maru*: Cundall, correspondence with author.
Observations of Takamura: AWM 55 (12/140).
Montevideo Maru's voyage and conditions: Cundall, correspondence with
  author.
Details of torpedo attack and related quotes by Wright and Nimitz:
  SS187/A12-1, Serial 06.
Details of the sinking: Cundall, correspondence with author, which
  includes the full text of the loss report issued by the OSK line.

Chapter 15—The Long Wait
Deck tennis platform, and "*an ear bashing*": Hutchinson-Smith, p. 44.
Civilian help, foraging for food: ibid., p. 45.
"*Please, just call me Michael*" and other quotes attributed to Capt.
  Mizusaki: Bowman, p. 88.
"*Come on, girls*": ibid., p. 91.
"*Ladies, welcome*": ibid., p. 92.
"*like an orchestra conductor*": Hutchinson-Smith, p. 47.
"*pretty bad shape*": ibid.
"*Navy men say*": AWM 55 (12/140).
"*On July 11 we heard*": Thomas, *Pacific Islands Year Book, 1950*, p. 31.

Ship's crew discrepancies and survival accounts: AWM 54 (779/1/1); AWM 54 (779/1/26A).

"The party was absolutely defenseless": quoted in Stone, p. 275.

"starved, fatigued and near death": Extract from OSK report, via Cundall.

Details of Yokohama Yacht Club, and *"Damned good Aussie wool"*: Hutchinson-Smith, p. 54.

POW life in Japan: all quotes and details regarding the imprisonment of Lark Force officers are drawn from the Hutchinson-Smith manuscript unless otherwise noted.

Omamori charms: Tagaya, correspondence with author.

Personalities of Komatsu and "Basher": Bowman, pp. 140–142.

Conditions at Totsuka, including *"We were so weak"*: ibid., pp. 151–158.

"Night after night": Angell, "The Forgotten Prisoners of Rabaul."

"Flames were caught": Bowman, p. 187.

"turned-up wings": ibid., p. 183.

Rumors of "big bomb" and Emperor Hirohito's surrender address: ibid., p. 199.

"Well, if you haven't anything else to do": Hutchinson-Smith, p. 283.

"When we got back to Sydney": L. Johnson, author's interview.

Findings of Maj. H. S. Williams: AWM 54 (779/1/1).

Investigation in Japan: Hon. E. E. Ward, October 5, 1945.

"IT IS WITH DEEP REGRET": Sample telegram in C. Johnson, p. 148.

"As we stand here today": Hodges, Australian War Memorial presentation, July 1, 2002.

Epilogue

Hellship statistics: Michno, pp. 309–317.

Details of relative positions of *Montevideo Maru* and USS *Sturgeon*: OSK report via Cundall; SS187/A12-1, Serial 06.

"When I got up on deck" and other quotes from Seaman Yamaji: Australian Broadcasting Company, "Silence Broken" transcript.

"It implies to me": Cundall, correspondence with author.

"Information of the loss": quoted in AWM 54 (779/1/1).

BIBLIOGRAPHY

Books

Aplin, Douglas. *Rabaul 1942*. Melbourne: The 2/22nd Battalion AIF, Lark Force Association, 1980.

Bloomfield, David. *Rabaul Diary: Escaping Captivity in 1942*. Loftus, N.S.W.: Australian Military History Publications, 2001.

Bowman, Alice. *Not Now Tomorrow*. Bangalow, N.S.W.: Daisy Press, 1996.

Campbell, Ian. *A History of the Pacific Islands*. Los Angeles: University of California Press, 1989.

Cook, Haruka, and Theodore Cook. *Japan at War: An Oral History*. New York: The New Press, 1992.

Cox, Lindsay. *Brave and True: From Blue to Khaki—The Story of the 2/22nd Battalion Band*. Melbourne: Salvation Army Archives and Museum, 2003.

Craven, Wesley, and John Cate. *The Army Air Forces in World War II: Plans & Early Operations, January 1939 to August 1942*. Chicago: University of Chicago Press, 1948.

Ewing, Steve, and John Lundstrom. *Fateful Rendezvous: The Life of Butch O'Hare*. Annapolis, Md.: Naval Institute Press, 1997.

Feldt, Eric. *The Coastwatchers*. New York: Bantam, 1979.

Gillison, Douglas. *Royal Australian Air Force, 1939-1942 (Series 3, Vol. I, Australia in the War of 1939–1945)*. Canberra: Australian War Memorial, 1962.

Hasluck, Paul. *The Government and the People (Series 4, Vol. 1, Australia in the War of 1939-1945)*. Canberra: Australian War Memorial, 1952.

Hata, Ikuhiko, and Yasuho Izawa. *Japanese Naval Aces and Fighter Units in World War II*. Annapolis: Naval Institute Press, 1989.

Johnson, Carl. *Little Hell: The Story of the 2/22nd Battalion and Lark Force*. Blackburn, Vic.: History House, 2004.

Johnson, R.W. and N.A. Threlfall. *Volcano Town: The 1937-43 Rabaul Eruptions*. Bathurst, N.S.W.: Robert Brown & Associates, 1985.

Johnson, Stanley. *Queen of the Flattops*. New York: Dutton, 1942.

Lundstrom, John. *The First Team: Pacific Naval Air Combat from Pearl Harbor to Midway*. Annapolis: Naval Institute Press, 1984.

Manchester, William. *American Caesar: Douglas MacArthur 1880–1964*. Boston: Little, Brown, 1978.

Michno, Gregory F. *Death on the Hell Ships: Prisoners at Sea in the Pacific War*. Annapolis: Naval Institute Press, 2001.

Minty, A. E. *Black Cats*. Point Cook, Vic.: RAAF Museum, 2001.

Murphy, John. *The Book of Pidgin English*. Brisbane: W. R. Smith & Paterson, 1943.

Prados, John. *Combined Fleet Decoded*. New York: Random House, 1995.

Reeson, Margaret. *Whereabouts Unknown*. Sutherland, NSW: Albatross, 1993.

Salaker, Gene. *Fortress Against the Sun: The B-17 Flying Fortress in the Pacific*. Conshohocken, Pa.: Combined Publishing, 2001.

Selby, David. *Hell and High Fever*. Sydney: Currawong, 1956.

Special Services Division, Army Service Forces. *Pocket Guide to Australia*. Washington: War Department, 1943.

Stone, Peter. *Hostages to Freedom: The Fall of Rabaul*. Maryborough, Vic.: Australian Print Group, 1995.

Wigmore, Lionel. *The Japanese Thrust (Series 1, Vol. IV, Australia in the War of 1939–1945)*. Canberra: Australian War Memorial, 1957.

CD-ROMS
Dunn, Peter. *Australia @ War*. Runcorn, QLD, 2006.

Military Bulletins

Informational Bulletin No. 9. Care of Personnel in the Wet Tropics. Headquarters, Army Air Forces, January 25, 1944.

Intelligence Bulletin Vol. I, No. 1, Section III. Food. War Department, Military Intelligence Division, September 1942.

Intelligence Bulletin Vol. I, No. 5, Section III. The Individual Soldier. War Department. Military Intelligence Division, January 1943.

Intelligence Bulletin Vol. I, No. 6, Section II. Extracts From Diaries. War Department, Military Intelligence Division, February 1943.

Intelligence Bulletin Vol. I, No. 10, Section II. Notes on Boats and Ships in Amphibious Operations. War Department, Military Intelligence Division, June 1943.

Intelligence Bulletin Vol. II, No. 5, Section I. Enemy Bayonet Technique. War Department, Military Intelligence Division, January 1944.

Intelligence Bulletin Vol. II, No. 9, Section IX. Japanese Explanation of "Duty" and "Spirit." War Department, Military Intelligence Division, May 1944.

Intelligence Bulletin Vol. III, No. 5. The Imperial Rescript. War Department, Military Intelligence Division. January 1945.

Print Articles

Miyake, Toshio. "The Capture of Kawieng." *Osaka Mainichi & The Tokyo Nichi Nichi*, February 10, 1942, p. 3.

Thomas, Gordon. "In Rabaul, Under the Japs." *Pacific Islands Yearbook, 1950.* Sydney: Pacific Publications, 1950.

Thomson, J. P. "The Islands of the Pacific." *National Geographic*, December 1921, pp. 550–559.

World Wide Web Articles

Angell, Barbara. "Brave Women Pages: The Forgotten Prisoners of Rabaul." http://www.angellpro.com.au/rabaul.htm.

Australian Broadcasting Company. "Silence Broken on Australia's Worst Maritime Disaster." http://www.abc.net.au/7.30/content/2003/s961016.htm.

Australia-Japan Research Project. "Army Operations in the South Pacific Area: Papua Campaigns, 1942–1943. Chapter 1: Offensive Against Rabaul and Key Surrounding Areas. (Translation by Dr. Steven Bullard of *Senshi Sosho: Minami Taiheiyo Rikugun Sakusen, 1: Poto Moresubi–Gashima Shoko Sakusen [War History Series: South Pacific Area Army Operations, Vol. 1: Port Moresby-Guadalcanal First Campaigns]*. Tokyo: Asagumo Shinbunsha, 1968.) http://ajrp.awm.gov.au/ajrp/ajrp2.nsf.

Johnson, H. "The 2001 Christmas Luncheon Commemorating the 60th Anniversary Reunion of PNG Evacuees." Extract from *Una Voce*, March 2002. http://www.pngaa.net/Articles/articles_JohnsonH_Xmas_2001.htm.

Kawamoto, Minoru. "Some Moments In The Barracks Of A Japanese Army Recruit." http://www.star-games.com/exhibits/barracks.html.

"Lost Lives: The Second World War and the Peoples of New Guinea," www.jje.info/lostlives/people/moorerkp.html.

Miller, Rod. "The Montevideo Maru." http://www.montevideomaru.info/.

Park, Okryon. "Stories from the Comfort Women." http://www.koreatimes.co.kr/event/jeonshin/ (note: accessed in 2003/2004; now defunct).

Unpublished Manuscripts and Collections

Cook, William: Untitled. Narrative of the Tol massacre and escape from New Britain. 2/22nd Battalion, Lark Force Association, North Balwyn, N.S.W., undated.

Harry, C. O. "New Britain 1941/42." 2/22nd Battalion, Lark Force Association, North Balwyn, N.S.W., circa 2000.

Hutchinson-Smith, David. "Guests of the Emperor." AWM Private Collections, #MSS 1534, Australian War Memorial.

Lyons, Frank. Untitled. Excerpts from the 1944 Webb Commission's report on Japanese atrocities. 2/22nd Battalion, Lark Force Association, North Balwyn, N.S.W., circa 1980.

Pearson, Percy. "2/22nd Battalion Diary." 2/22nd Battalion, Lark Force Association, North Balwyn, N.S.W.

Steinbinder, John. Untitled. Personal diary from December 1941 to December 1942. Author's collection.

Taylor, Archibald. Untitled. Extracts from personal diary. 2/22nd Battalion, Lark Force Association, North Balwyn, N.S.W., undated.

Official Documents—Australian

AWM 54 (81/4/194): RAAF Operations report compiled by S/L W.D. Brookes, February 24, 1942.

AWM 54 (607/7/1): AIF report compiled by Maj. P.E. Figgis, circa 1942.

AWM 54 (607/8/2): AIF report by Lt. Col. H.H. Carr, Capt. D.F. Field, Capt. E.S. Appel, Lt. A.R. Tolmer & Lt. J.G. Donaldson, March 1942.

AWM 54 (607/9/3): AIF account of escape by Lt. B. Dawson, circa 1942.

AWM 54 (607/9/5): Rabaul account of escape by Sergeant D. F. Ferguson, circa 1942.

AWM 54 (608/5/3): AIF report and medical extract by Maj. E. C. Palmer, August 22, 1942.

AWM 54 (779/1/1): Report from Maj. H.S. Williams regarding the sinking of *Montevideo Maru*, material dated October 6, and November 6, 1945.

AWM 54 (779/1/26A): American and Japanese accounts of the sinking of *Montevideo Maru*.

AWM 60 (259): Untitled. Collected statements in response to Court of Inquiry.

AWM 68 (3DRL 8052/108): Minutes, War Cabinet meeting, Melbourne, October 15, 1941.

AWM 113 (MH 1/121, Part 1): Official inquiry into the Japanese landings at Rabaul, with attached summary by R.W. Robson, editor of "Pacific Islands Monthly."

B5563/2 (1911): Prisoner of War Information Bureau: Sworn Testimony of Shojiro Mizusaki, Tokyo, circa 1949 (National Archives of Australia).

B5563/2 (2249): Prisoner of War Information Bureau: Sworn Testimony of Minoru Yoshimura, Tokyo, circa 1949 (National Archives of Australia).

Cablegram 154, Prime Minister's Department to Australian Minister,

Washington, December 15, 1941 (National Archives of Australia).

MP729/6 (16/401/493): Cable 152, Chief of Naval Staff, Prime Minister's Department to Australian Minister (Naval Attache), Washington, D.C., December 12, 1941 (National Archives of Australia).

Minutes, Parliamentary Debates, Canberra, Vol. 185, October 5, 1945 (National Archives of Australia).

Official Documents—Japanese

AWM 3DRL/4005: Diary of Akiyoshi Hisaeda, March 10, 1941 to November 16, 1942.

AWM 54 (208/2/4): ATIS translations of miscellaneous captured documents.

AWM 54 (423/4/158): ATIS Enemy Publications, Detailed Battle Report No. 2 (Rabaul Occupation Operations), June 2, 1943.

AWM 54 (423/4/1162): "Military Intelligence Section, Full Translation of a Report on the Japanese Invasion of Rabaul," May 9, 1946.

AWM 54 (608/5/4): "Japanese South East Area Operations Record (South Seas Detachment Operations) Monograph No. 143 (Army)," circa 1946.

AWM 55 (12/140): ATIS Information Request Report No. 103, Japanese statements and diary excerpts relating to prisoners of war, May 4, 1944.

Official Documents—American

Department of the Army, Office of the Chief of Military History, *History of the Southern Army, Japanese Monograph No. 24*, Washington: U.S. Government Printing Office, 1946.

Department of the Army, Office of the Chief of Military History, *History of Imperial General Headquarters, Army Section, Japanese Monograph No. 45*, Washington: U.S. Government Printing Office, 1946.

GP-22-HI (Bomb): 22nd Bombardment Group History, February 1, 1940 to January 31, 1944, Albert F. Simpson Historical Research Center.

SS187/A12-1, Serial 06: War diary of fourth War Patrol, USS Sturgeon, NARA.

Naval Analysis Division. *United States Strategic Bombing Survey (Pacific):
The Allied Campaign Against Rabaul.* Washington: U.S. Government
Printing Office, 1946.

Correspondence Received by the Author
Cundall, Peter. November 1, 2003; December 17, 2004; May 16, 2005.
Figgis, Peter. August 3, 2003.
Harry, C. O. August 26, 2002.
Harris, Ted. January 5, 2005.
Michno, Gregory. May 14, 2005.
Murphy, John. June 7, 2004.
Wenger, Michael. November 11, 2003.

Author's Interviews
Figgis, Peter. August 9, 2001.
Harry, C. O. August 7, 2002.
Kollmorgen, Frederic. August 13, 2002.
Johnson, Lorna (Whyte). November 9, 2001.
Miller, C. Daniel. March 26, 2002.
Thurst, Bruce, May 10, 2005.

INDEX